T0306011

A HISTORY OF EUROPEAN ECONOMIC THOUGHT

A *History of European Economic Thought* grafts the history of economic thought onto Global History by showing how significant economic ideas have influenced the process of Europe's formation from the very beginning to the present day.

This work combines two classical stories that until today have followed parallel paths. On the one hand, there is the political history of Europe, which is often limited to a few fleeting references to the ideas of the great economists of the past. On the other hand, there is the history of economic thought, which examines Europe as a whole, as a distinct supranational community, only with reference to the institutions created after World War II.

The volume sheds light on the constitutive values of Europe, which also stem from a particular economic culture, and provides essential reading for students and scholars of the history of economic thought.

Antonio Magliulo is Full Professor of History of Economic Thought at the University of Florence, Italy.

A HISTORY OF EUROPEAN ECONOMIC THOUGHT

Antonio Magliulo

Routledge
Taylor & Francis Group

LONDON AND NEW YORK

Cover image: jpa1999

First published 2022
by Routledge
4 Park Square, Milton Park, Abingdon, Oxon OX14 4RN

and by Routledge
605 Third Avenue, New York, NY 10158

Routledge is an imprint of the Taylor & Francis Group, an informa business

© 2022 Antonio Magliulo

British Library Cataloguing-in-Publication Data
A catalogue record for this book is available from the British Library

Library of Congress Cataloging-in-Publication Data
Names: Magliulo, Antonio, 1962– author.
Title: A history of European economic thought / Antonio Magliulo.
Description: Abingdon, Oxon ; New York, NY : Routledge, 2022. |
Includes bibliographical references and index.
Identifiers: LCCN 2021056635 (print) | LCCN 2021056636 (ebook)
Subjects: LCSH: Economics–Sociological aspects–History. |
Europe–Economic conditions.
Classification: LCC HM548 .M342 2022 (print) |
LCC HM548 (ebook) | DDC 330.94–dc23/eng/20211222
LC record available at https://lccn.loc.gov/2021056635
LC ebook record available at https://lccn.loc.gov/2021056636

ISBN: 978-1-032-03767-7 (hbk)
ISBN: 978-1-032-03765-3 (pbk)
ISBN: 978-1-003-18888-9 (ebk)

DOI: 10.4324/9781003188889

Typeset in Bembo
by Newgen Publishing UK

To my masters

CONTENTS

Towards a Global and Comparative History of Economic Thought   x

1 Medieval Economic Thought and the Birth of Europe   1
   Introduction 1
   The Long Conception of Europe Until 1250 2
   Scholastic and Byzantine Economic Thought 9
   The Birth of Europe in 1453 14
   In Short 16

2 Mercantilism and Physiocracy in the Making of a Europe of
   Absolute Monarchies (1517–1776)   19
   Introduction 19
   The Disintegration of Christian Europe 19
   Mercantilism and Despotic Absolutism in Westphalian Europe 24
   Physiocracy and Enlightened Absolutism in the European Republic of Letters 29
   In Short 34

3 Classical Political Economy and a Europe of Liberal
   Nation-States (1776–1870)   36
   Introduction 36
   Revolution in Europe and Resurgent Nationalism 37
   Classical Political Economy and Nascent Liberalism 40
   A Europe of Liberal Nation-States 55
   In Short 59

4 Neoclassical Economics *vs.* Etatism and a Europe of Empires
(1871–1918) 62
Introduction 62
The Decline of Liberal Europe 63
Neoclassical Economics and Etatism 64
A Europe of Empires at War 74
In Short 75

5 Neoliberalism(s) and Corporatism: A Europe of Sovereign
Nations and Its Failure (1919–1943) 78
Introduction 78
The Paris Order and the Divergent Critique of Keynes and Mises 79
Business Cycles and the Great Depression: Hayek vs. Keynes and
Röpke's Synthesis 84
Europe Towards the War Between Neoliberalism, Keynesianism
and Corporatism 95
In Short 102

6 The Invention of Functionalism and the "Separated Unification"
of Europe (1944–1973) 105
Introduction 105
The Two Europes in the Yalta and Bretton Woods Order 106
The Rise of Keynesianism and Marxism and the Invention of
Functionalism 111
The Marshall Plan and the Separated Unification of Europe 126
In Short 132

7 Decline of Etatism, Rebirth of Neoliberalism and United
Europe (1974–2007) 136
Introduction 136
The Crisis of Keynesianism and the Collapse of Marxism 136
The Rebirth of Neoliberalism 138
The Enlargement of the EEC and the Establishment of the
EU and EMU 139
In Short 146

8 Crisis of Neoliberalism, the Greatest Recession and Unfinished
Europe (2008–) 148
Introduction 148
The Great Recession of 2008 and the Last Obstacle to European
Unity 149

The Economic Trilemma Becomes a Political Trilemma 152
*The Crisis of Neoliberalism, the Pandemic Shock and the
    Recovery Plan 153*
In Short 158

Conclusion   160

Bibliography   *168*
Index   *179*

TOWARDS A GLOBAL AND COMPARATIVE HISTORY OF ECONOMIC THOUGHT

One of the greatest challenges of our time is to manage the cultural diversity of numerous peoples. In only a few decades, we have suddenly gone from a world of independent nations to a world of interdependent transnational communities, still divided into nations but with increasingly porous borders, which narrow to embrace small local communities and widen to encompass the entire world. We live in a melting-pot society where people with different stories, languages and cultures meet and clash every day.

The rise of this melting-pot society has led to a rediscovery of the comparative method in the social sciences. Classical disciplines flourish once again: comparative economics, comparative law, comparative politics, comparative philosophy and comparative sociology. Scholars compare economic, political, juridical and cultural systems in order to identify the main divisive and unifying factors that make coexistence among various people and countries peaceful or conflictive.

The comparative method has obviously been rediscovered by historians as well. World or Global or Comparative History is an emerging area that investigates the processes of transnational and intercultural interactions that occur among human groups on the planet. This is not a new universal story. The subject of inquiry is not the entire world but the phenomena (economic, political, social and cultural) that transcend national boundaries, giving rise to new forms of human coexistence: for example, the forms of cultural *métissage* that arise from migration flows or the formation of transnational communities such as Islamic or Jewish ones. World History uses (though not necessarily) the comparative method: for example, it does not need it when it studies the general characteristics of the *Umma*, the Muslim community, but does use it in order to highlight the identity changes occurring in the Islamic communities of various Western countries.[1]

In 1950, Oscar Halecki, in his *The Limits and Divisions of European History*, proposed to study Europe "as a whole", as a clear and distinct supranational community, rather than the sum of several nations. In his preface to the book, Christopher Dawson observed that, in the immense literature on European history, paradoxically, few works might be considered genuine writings of European history in Halecki's sense: "It seems paradoxical to say that European history has always been a neglected subject", he writes,

> but if we accept Professor Halecki's definition of European history as "the history of all European nations considered as a whole, as a community clearly distinct from any other", we shall find that of the vast number of books nominally concerned with European history very few indeed satisfy the definition.
>
> *Dawson 1950: vii*

In recent decades, a huge body of literature has flourished around the topic of European history and identity. Nowadays, several histories have dealt with Europe as a whole from various perspectives: political thought, philosophy, religion, economics, culture and so forth.[2] However, we still lack an outright History of European Economic Thought.

This book is a first attempt to explore Europe as a transnational community from a history of economic thought perspective. Thus, I would like to outline the methodological approach I have adopted by briefly examining (a) how historians of economic thought have looked at Europe thus far; (b) why we need a new look at Europe; and (c) what story I have tried to tell you.

The history of economic thought is the discipline that investigates the evolution of economic knowledge over time and its influence on society. It first studies the making of political economy that, beginning with the Greek philosophers, achieved an epistemological independence only in 1776 with Adam Smith's *Wealth of Nations*. From the outset, economic knowledge does not confine itself to learned intellectual circles but overflows into civil society. Economists and their followers write articles for newspapers and deliver speeches in academies, clubs and parliaments. In this way, they become producers of economic culture understood as a simplified representation of economy, of its own fundamental problems and possible solutions. Economic culture is a vision, a way of thinking and a popular mindset of the economic world. When David Ricardo spoke in the English Parliament, he did not expose his classical theory of international trade but he applied it to argue the necessity of abolishing the Corn Laws. Ricardo's writings influenced Richard Cobden's thinking and inspired the actions of the Anti-Corn Law League, which finally led to the abolition of the Corn Laws in 1846.

The history of economic thought is a three-dimensional tale based on the relationships between theories, cultures and economic policies.[3]

Such a complex subject has required a division of labour. Over time, without any explicit theoretical explanation, a vertical and horizontal division of labour research occurred *de facto*. History, to use an image, was cut vertically into the three above-mentioned constitutive dimensions. We had, and still have, mainly histories of economic analysis, culture and economic policy. In this context, the primacy went to the first story. The same label of *history of economics*, very popular in the Anglo-Saxon world, evokes a particular emphasis on the analytical dimension. The greatest effort has been devoted to the reconstruction of the *mainstream*, that is, the principal path followed by economists to elaborate, through a selective process of hypotheses and models, the body of theories that nowadays shapes normal economic science (in Kuhn's sense). Perhaps the champion of this approach remains the late Mark Blaug (2001: 157), who considered economics the last chapter in an ongoing history of economics. He writes: "History of economic thought is not a specialization within economics. It *is* economics – sliced vertically against the horizontal axis of time". Other historians have preferred to retain the memory of *untaken roads*, rather than the mainstream, considering economics a pluralistic discipline comprising alternative paradigms and models. The main practitioners of this approach are probably the supporters of a heterodox economics.[4]

Together with this vertical division, we find a horizontal division of labour research. There have been, and still are, historians who have tried to connect, rather than separate, the three constitutive dimensions of economic discourse. This effort was manifested mainly in the context of the historiography on national styles and traditions in which we find a storytelling focused on a close relationship among theories, cultures and economic policies.[5] In the history of Italian economic thought, for example, several studies describe how economists' thinking has generated a widespread economic culture that inspired strategic choices of economic policy.

Simplifying and schematising, we can state that in the last decades we have mainly had a *universal* history of economic theories and a *national* history of economic cultures and policies. The first field includes only the great economists of the past, those who have provided a lasting contribution to the advancement of economic knowledge, regardless of their origin or nationality. It is useful to remember, in order not to repeat them, the errors of the past, to recall the theoretical achievements laboriously accomplished over time and to preserve the alternative paradigms to the dominant one. The second field is also a history of national economic cultures and policies and helps us explain the cultural identity of local and national communities.

The latter approach has *de facto* been used also to analyse Europe. Historians of economic thought have considered Europe as the sum of several national stories. The literature contains numerous works on national styles and traditions: Italian, French, German and Spanish, among others. Moreover, historians have tried to identify some cultural ties among nations dealing with several processes of the international spread of economic ideas. A huge literature flourished around the ideas of Smith, Ricardo, Keynes and others "across nations" all over the world. The aim was to assess the level of theoretical advancement or backwardness as well as the cultural identity of individual nations.[6]

Historians of economic thought have explored Europe as something more than a sum of nations, namely as an institution, only with reference to the theories and policies of economic integration that arose following World War II.[7] However, something has changed recently.

Vincent Barnett (2014) edited *The Routledge Handbook of the History of Global Economic Thought*, a book structured into five great regions – Europe, the Americas, the Middle East, Africa and Asia-Pacific – and which provides the first, penetrating, global overview of the history of economic thought. Barnett has still adopted a nation-centred approach; Europe is presented as a collection of eleven national stories: England, Scotland, Ireland, Italy, Greece, Spain, Portugal, Germany, Sweden, Russia and Ukraine. However, Europe cannot merely be the sum of 27 or more nation-states, just as Global History cannot be the sum of the over two hundred states in the world.

Cardoso and Psalidopoulos (2016) edited *The German Historical School and European Economic Thought*, which examines how the ideas of the Historical School spread and were interpreted in various European countries between 1850 and 1930. Here too, editors have adopted a nation-centred approach and consider only some countries, and yet, the process of the international spread of economic ideas is now carried out within European boundaries.

In short, historians of economic thought have thus far examined Europe both as an institution and as a collection of nation-states, developing an individualising comparison aimed at emphasising the national character of the countries that comprise it.

We need a new perspective on Europe simply because Europe is much more than the sum of single nations and was born much earlier than the common institutions.

This was quite clear in the past. Leading historians, such as Halecki, Dawson, Bloch, Febvre, Duroselle and Le Goff, have imagined Europe "as a whole", as an "organic complex" of nations (in Latin, *complexus* means "what is kept together"), as a "community clearly distinct from any other".

This is much clearer nowadays in a global society inhabited by individuals with multiple and intertwined identities. In 1782, a somewhat disappointed Rousseau wrote: "Today, no matter what people may say, there are no longer any Frenchmen, Germans, Spaniards, or even Englishmen; there are only Europeans". Today, we could repeat – albeit with less disappointment – there are no longer only Italians, French, Brazilians and so on, but also Europeans, Americans, Africans, Arabs, Asians. Transnational communities live inside and outside national boundaries.

A nation-centred approach is still necessary but no longer sufficient. Culture shapes our identities, and it is more and more a transnational phenomenon: culture as mind-set, as a way of thinking about interpersonal and international relationships, one's own and other people's interests, the role of markets and governments, and so on.

Culture has become the privileged field of research of several disciplines. Experts in cross-cultural management, for example, are studying the behaviour of consumers belonging to different countries or the organisation of transnational companies with workers coming from multiple cultures, and development economists are comparing the performance of a variety of capitalisms marked by distant values.[8]

Historians of economic thought can make a considerable contribution to the history of transnational communities, extending the three-dimensional approach applied with success to national contexts. As they are interested in studying the relationships among economic theories, cultures and policies, they could explore and compare economic paradigms, cultural models, and the policy choices of great transnational communities such as Africa, America, Arabia, Asia and Europe.[9]

In particular, we need a history of European economic thought that investigates the evolution of economic knowledge over time and its influence on European society seen as a distinct supranational community and that provides a comprehensive comparison that might highlight what people and nations have in common and how they differ.

In 1993, five European publishers decided to publish simultaneously and in different translations a series entitled *The Making of Europe*. The direction was entrusted to Jacques Le Goff, who chose as incipit these words: "Europe is in the process of constructing itself. The hope that it holds out is great. This will only be realized if Europe is mindful of its history".[10]

Europe deserves to be built, Le Goff maintained, but we have realised that it can also be destroyed. In fact, it is easier to demolish it than to complete its establishment.

Studying history allows one to transform unsettled and open questions in the present into questions posed to the past. As for Europe, the many questions dramatically active in the present are striking: Why is Europe not able to make the last mile in terms of political unity? Is it preferable and necessary to return to a model of intergovernmental cooperation that restores lost sovereignty to nation-states, or is it desirable and possible to build a model of European democracy? Is there a European economic culture? What unites and what divides the "several Europes" that re-emerged after the fall of the Berlin Wall?

These questions have prompted me to ask myself how economic culture, which has sprung from the systematic reflection of economists, has influenced the birth and development of Europe. Mine is not a history of theories of European economic integration, which already exists and retains all its value intact. Ricardo and Keynes, for example, have written nothing on the subject, yet their ideas have exerted a powerful influence on the making of modern Europe, and this must be taken into account.

When we observe the past, more or less consciously, we adopt a certain vision of history. There are three great visions of the past.

The first is the materialistic vision, systematised by Marx, according to which men act, changing history, to defend the material interests of the social class to which they belong. Ideas or ideologies are just a veil, placed on the surface or superstructure of society, to cover and ennoble the real struggle that takes place in the underlying social structure between opposing class interests.

The second is the idealistic vision in which Keynes also seems to recognise himself. Men delude themselves into believing they are acting to defend concrete material interests. In effect, they operate under the influence of powerful ideas developed by some economist or political philosopher of the past.

The last is a compound "realistic" vision, which dates back to St. Augustine and which, in various ways, includes thinkers such as Acton, Weber and Hayek.

According to Weber, it is wrong to oppose interests and ideas. People act to defend interests, but their perception of their own and others' interests stems from a worldview created by ideas. Weber (1915 [1946]: 280) writes:

> Not ideas, but material and ideal interests, directly govern men's conduct. Yet very frequently the "world images" that have been created by "ideas" have, like switchmen, determined the tracks along which action has been pushed by the dynamic of interest.

According to Hayek, it is wrong to oppose experience and reason. Men act to satisfy felt material and spiritual needs, starting from an inherited tradition, that is, from a set of tacit and explicit norms that regulate human conduct. Tradition stands between instinct and reason. The success or failure of a social order depends on the ability to satisfy perceived human needs. Reason, by judging experience, helps to change it. Hayek (1982: 17–18) writes:

> The cultural heritage into which man is born consists of a complex of practices or rules of conduct which have prevailed because they made a group of men successful but which were not adopted because it was known that they would bring about desired effects. Man acted before he thought and did not understand before he acted.

Lastly, for Acton (1907), men seek the satisfaction of a priority need: that of being free. History is the time that God gives man to achieve true or full freedom.

I espouse this third perspective. I believe that men act in the incessant search for a satisfaction filled with constitutive demands for happiness, freedom, justice and beauty. Every experience is assessed in relation to those needs. Reason, by judging the experience, discovers its value or weakness and pushes men to continue or change their ways, always in searching for what meets their heart's needs. Economic ideas are simply a dimension of human reason, and the history of economic thought guards the attempts to validate or refute the various economic experiences that have taken place over time.

This book was born as an attempt, perhaps reckless – indeed certainly reckless given the absence of a reference literature – to graft the history of economic thought onto World or Global History by showing how significant economic ideas have influenced the process of Europe's formation.

The research aims to join together two classical stories that until today have followed parallel paths: on the one hand, the political history of Europe, which is often limited to a few fleeting references to the ideas of the great economists of the past, and on the other hand, the history of economic thought, which looks at Europe as a whole, as a distinct supranational community, only with reference to the institutions created after World War II.

The West-Centre-East tri-partitioned Europe has been the main approach chosen by scholars to investigate the political history of the Old Continent.[11] We will adopt a similar approach. The European journey, from its origins to the present day, has been reconstructed through eight great stages, each marked by conventional and symbolic dates. These stages serve a useful orientation function, as does the biblical expression "already and not yet", to describe the European evolution: in effect, Europe is an open and ongoing process and even today is "already and not yet" a genuine supranational community.

The eight stages in which this volume is structured are the following:

1. Medieval Economic Thought and the Birth of Europe;
2. Mercantilism and Physiocracy in the Making of a Europe of Absolute Monarchies (1517–1776);
3. Classical Political Economy and a Europe of Liberal Nation-States (1776–1870);
4. Neoclassical Economics *vs.* Etatism and a Europe of Empires (1871–1918);
5. Neoliberalism(s) and Corporatism: A Europe of Sovereign Nations and Its Failure (1919–1943);
6. The Invention of Functionalism and the "Separated Unification" of Europe (1944–1973);
7. Decline of Etatism, Rebirth of Neoliberalism and United Europe (1974–2007); and
8. Crisis of Neoliberalism, the Greatest Recession and Unfinished Europe (2008–).

This volume, therefore, is a first if rudimentary path in the history of European economic thought. The reader should certainly not expect an exhaustive compendium of political history or of the history of economic thought. One will find some events merely mentioned, while others are dealt with in more detail. But the reader is asked not to forget the book's overriding purpose: To open a new path by linking the history of economic thought to global history – although I may have only succeeded in pointing a way forward in hopes that others, better equipped, will be able to tread this new path.[12] I am also aware that different histories of European economic thought can be written, and thus, I have entitled my volume *A* History of European Economic Thought, with the "A" in italics. My hope is that this book will generate a renewed and common interest in a global and comparative history of economic thought, starting with Europe.[13]

This work stems from a book published in Italian in 2019. Its manuscript was read and commented on by some colleagues who gave me valuable suggestions. The published book was then reviewed in various journals. Both the initial suggestions and the subsequent reviews were particularly useful for me in preparing the present English edition. In particular, I would like to thank Piero Barucci, Gabriella Gioli, Piero Roggi, Giampaolo Conte and Omar Ottonelli, as well as the reviewers Pier Luigi Belvisi, Flavio Felice, Fabio Masini, Alberto Mingardi, Maurizio Serio and Stefano Solari. Special thanks to Fabio Masini, who read and commented on the English manuscript, and to Michel Pharand, who helped me refine the English text. The usual disclaimer applies.

Notes

1 Among the founding fathers of world history is William McNeill (1963), a Toynbee pupil, who wrote his masterpiece, *The Rise of the West*, in 1963. In 1982, the World History Association was established, in 1990 the first issue of the *Journal of World History* was published, and in 2000, the *American Historical Review* introduced the section "Comparative/World"; see Di Fiore and Meriggi (2011), Subrahmanyam (2014), Conrad (2016) and Stanziani (2018). I consider particularly important the comparative history of political thought written by Antony Black (2003, 2008, 2009a, 2009b, 2011a, 2011b).
2 See, in particular, Black (2003) and Zamagni (2017).
3 On a three-dimensional approach to the history of economic thought, see Barucci (2005). On the concept of economic culture, see Phelps (2006) and Gregg (2013).
4 On the methodological debate, see Backhouse (1994, 2001), Blaug (2001), Kurz (2006), Palma (2008) and Coats (2014).
5 On national styles and traditions, it is sufficient to mention the series "Routledge History of Economic Thought": www.routledge.com/books/series/SE0124/.
6 On the international spread of economic ideas, see Hall (1989), Mizuta and Sugiyama (1993), Pasinetti and Schefold (1999), Lai (2000), Augello and Guidi (2001) and Asso (2001).
7 It is sufficient to mention one of the latest books devoted to the topic: Dyson and Maes (2016).
8 On cross-cultural management, see Hofstede, Hofstede and Minkov (2010). On the relationships between culture and development, see North (1990), Harrison and Huntington (2000), Sen (2004), McCloskey (2010, 2016) and Mokyr (2016). On the varieties of capitalism, see Hall and Soskice (2001).
9 See, for example, Baeck (1994), Popescu (1997), Montecinos and Markoff (2009), Ermis (2013), Islahi (2014).
10 The five publishers are C.H. Beck Verlag, München (German); Basil Blackwell, Oxford (English); Editorial Crítica (Grijalbo Commercial, S.A.), Barcelona (Catalan and Spanish); Gius. Laterza & Figli, Roma-Bari (Italian); and Editions du Seuil, Paris (French).
11 See Halecki (1950), Szűcs (1996), Arnason and Doyle (2010), Livezeanu and Klimó (2017).
12 Also for this reason, the bibliographical references given in the text include only the essential ones. For a general overview of European history, see Febvre (1944–45 [1999]), Halecki (1950), Chabod (1964), Hay (1968), Curcio (1978), Duroselle (1964, 1990), Davies (1996), Szűcs (1996), Mikkeli (1998), Pagden (2002), Rossi (2007), Arnason and Doyle (2010). For an overview of the history of economic thought, see Landreth and Colander (1994), Backhouse (2002), Screpanti and Zamagni (2005), Roncaglia (2005), Kurz (2016).

13 A first step in this direction has been the special issue of the journal *History of Economic Thought and Policy* that I edited in 2019 (Magliulo 2019), with essays by Horvath (2019), Marinova and Nenovsky (2019), Penchev and Özgur (2019), Stassinopoulos (2019), Avtonomov (2019) and Campagnolo (2019), followed by a book on Central Europe written by Horvath (2020). A pioneering contribution to the history of European economic thought is the volume edited by Roggi (1994).

1

MEDIEVAL ECONOMIC THOUGHT AND THE BIRTH OF EUROPE

Introduction

"Europe arose when the Roman Empire crumbled" (quoted by Le Goff 2007: 2). This provocative statement, taken from a review written by Marc Bloch in 1935, opens an enlightening debate on the relevant issue of the birth of Europe, one that remains ongoing among historians of various disciplines.

The vast majority of leading historians have maintained that Europe is a cultural union of peoples born during Medieval Christendom. Some have asserted that this unity occurred in the High Middle Ages with the rise of Charlemagne's empire. According to Febvre (1944–1945 [1999]: 82, my translation from Italian), "Carolingian Europe is the heart, it is the yeast that made European dough ferment. It is around Carolingian Europe that our Europe was built". In Dawson's (1956: 202) view, several elements comprising European identity merged at that time:

> Western Europe first achieved cultural unity in the Carolingian period. The rise of the Carolingian Empire marks the end of the dualism of culture that had characterised the age of the invasions and the full acceptance by the Western barbarians of the ideal of unity for which the Roman Empire and the Catholic Church alike stood. And thus in the new culture all the elements that constitute European civilisation were already represented – the political tradition of the Roman Empire, the religious tradition of the Catholic Church, the intellectual tradition of classical learning and the national traditions of the barbarian peoples.

Other leading scholars have asserted that cultural unity emerged only in the Late Middle Ages. According to Halecki (1950: 17), "Europe is the community of all nations which … accepted and developed the heritage of Greco-Roman

DOI: 10.4324/9781003188889-1

civilization, transformed and elevated by Christianity". This occurred in the first five centuries of the second millennium and also involved East-Central regions. Europe was not a Western invention:

> One of the main defects of ... the basic distinction between Western and Eastern Europe, lies in the impression obviously created that all of what is geographically "Eastern" is alien, or even opposed, to "Western" – that is, truly European – civilization. As a matter of fact, a closer study of the various historical regions of Europe confirms quite another impression, which first seemed paradoxical: it appears that some countries which are situated in the eastern, or at least the east-central, part of Europe have particularly close ties, cultural and even political, with the Latin West of the continent.
>
> *Halecki 1950: 138*

Le Goff deems the Carolingian world an "aborted Europe" (this is the title of chapter 2 of his *The Birth of Europe*) because "Charlemagne's vision was a 'nationalist' one. The empire that he founded was first and foremost Frankish and was inspired by a truly patriotic spirit" (Le Goff 2007: 29). According to Le Goff (2007: 198), Europe was born in the Late Middle Ages when the entire society was embedded in religion, and there were no threats "either from the emergence of nations or from the religious dissent".

In this chapter, I will try to sketch the influence of medieval economic ideas on the birth of Europe.[1] The chapter is divided into three parts. In the first, I outline the long conception of Europe from the very beginning to 1250 (a symbolic year). In the second, I summarise, in light of the valuable literature on the topic, some of the teachings of medieval economic thought. In the last part, I illustrate the prevailing forces that led to the "birth of Europe" in the symbolic year 1453. In the concluding section, I sketch the influence of significant medieval economic ideas on the making of Europe in the late Middle Ages by discussing the main theses provided by leading historians.

The Long Conception of Europe Until 1250

In the course he delivered in the 1944–1945 academic year, Lucien Febvre (1944–1945 [1999]: 30) stated, "Greece invented Europe" (my translation from Italian).

At the very outset, Europe was a mere mythological figure: the daughter of Agenor, king of Phoenicia (now Lebanon). The Greeks adapted a Semitic word that for Phoenician sailors meant "West". For them, Europeans were thus the inhabitants of the Western end of the Asian continent (Le Goff 2007: 8–9). Later on, "Europe" came to indicate a continent as well. Herodotus, in his *Histories*, divided the world into three continents: Asia, Libya (or Africa) and Europe. Lastly, and above all, Europe became a cultural identity: a land inhabited by free men. Freedom, for the Greeks, was the hallmark of Europeans: it was, on the one hand, what made them similar and, on the other, what made them feel different from Asians, which were seen as subjects of despotic regimes. Some years ago, Federico Chabod posed a historical question à propos cultural identity:

> when did men living on European soil begin to think of themselves and with them their own land, as something essentially different, in terms of customs, feelings, thoughts, from men living in other lands beyond the Mediterranean, on the African coast, for example, or beyond the Aegean and the Black Sea on Asian soil? When, that is, did the name Europe begin to designate not only a geographical complex but also a historical complex; not only a specific physical factor, but also a specific moral, political, religious, artistic factor of the life of humanity?

Chabod (1964: 21, 23, my translation from Italian) replied,

> Between the age of the Persian wars and the age of Alexander the Great, for the first time, the sense of a Europe opposed to Asia was formed, in terms of customs and, above all, political organization; a Europe that represents the spirit of "freedom" as opposed to Asian "despotism".

According to Chabod, freedom was therefore the identity of Europe, an identity strengthened by comparison to Asian despotism. But what was freedom for the Greeks?

Even today it is difficult to formulate a clear and shared idea of freedom. However, following the studies initiated by Isaiah Berlin (1958 [1969]), we can say that true or full freedom is the possibility, guaranteed to any person, to "act" and "want". A person is free to act when, in her actions, she is not prevented by others, and is free to want when, in her decision, she is not forced by others. The first is also called "negative" freedom and is substantiated by the defence of civil rights against unjustified coercions and interferences by people and authorities. The second is also called "positive" freedom and is embodied in the recognition of political rights of participation in collective deliberations. True or full freedom is both negative and positive, that is, as Bobbio (1978 [2009]) points out, without one the other falls (*simul stabunt vel simul cadent*), because without civil rights, such as freedom of opinion and of the press, popular participation in political power is a deception, while, at the same time, without popular participation in political power, civil rights can hardly endure.

From Benjamin Constant to Quentin Skinner, an intensive debate arose around the real meaning of the two freedoms in the ancient and modern eras.

In a very broad sense, we can state that in ancient Greece, "positive" freedom prevailed over "negative" freedom: only the citizens of the *polis* were free, but the right of citizenship was reserved for the select few, and it was a partial and contradictory freedom at that. In the Athens of Pericles, during the fifth century BCE, no more than 40–50 thousand people participated in the *polis*: slaves, women and foreigners were excluded. Free men took care of the *res publica* and did not work;

work was considered a disvalue reserved for slaves. The inhabitants of the *polis* could take any decision regarding the life of the city. The positive freedom to want could violate the negative freedom to act. According to Benjamin Constant (1819 [2011]: 6): "Among the Spartans, Therpandrus could not add a string to his lyre without causing offense to the ephors. In the most domestic of relations the public authority again intervened. The young Lacedaemonian could not visit his new bride freely". And Lord Acton (1907: 12) remarked,

> On a memorable occasion the assembled Athenians declared it monstrous that they should be prevented from doing whatever they chose. No force that existed could restrain them; and they resolved that no duty should restrain them, and they would be bound by no laws that were not of their own making. In this way, the emancipated people of Athens became a tyrant.

Greece was "already and not yet" Europe. It was "already" Europe because it introduced and experienced an ideal of freedom and citizenship. The Greeks felt free because they were subject to the law and not to the will of a capricious despot. The freedom they recognised was the positive one of participating in collective deliberations. But it was "not yet" Europe because the positive freedom was reserved for the few, with the exclusion of women and workers (as well as foreigners), and it was a freedom of "want" that compressed – to the point of abuse and arbitrariness – the individual negative freedom of "act". Perhaps it is no coincidence that Alexander the Great's (Hellenistic) empire developed in the East, only partially touching the lands of today's Europe.

"Greece invented Europe", said Febvre, who concludes "But the Greek world was not a European world".

In 146 BCE, the Roman Republic destroyed Corinth, beginning the conquest and then the transformation of Greece into a Roman province.

The Roman *civitas* was more inclusive and a rights guarantor compared to the Greek *polis*. Anyone could become a Roman citizen, even the inhabitants of the provinces, as long as they respected the law, and no citizen could be convicted without first being tried by a Roman court.

The Roman *libertas* was wider than the Greek *eleutheria*: it was at once more positive (extension of political rights) and more negative (extension of civil rights). But it was still the freedom of the ancients: manual labour was in fact reserved only for slaves and positive freedom prevailed over negative freedom. Constant (1819 [2011]: 6) wrote: "In Rome, the censors cast a searching eye over family life. The laws regulated customs, and as customs touch on everything; there was hardly anything that the laws did not regulate".[2]

The cultural and political revolution began with Christianity, and in particular with the words spoken by Jesus during His last visit to the temple: "Render unto Caesar the things that are Caesar's, and unto God the things that are God's". They conveyed a new view both of freedom and community and of authority (*auctoritas*) and power (*potestas*). "Render unto God the things that are God's", meaning that every person is worthy of being free simply because she/he is the daughter/son and image of God (*Imago Dei*) and as such a citizen of a new civil community (*communitas*) that breaks down the narrow juridical boundaries of both *polis* and *civitas*. "Render unto Caesar the things that are Caesar's", meaning that authority is sacred and must be exercised, without violating God's space, to promote the good of all individuals.

Saint Paul was perhaps the best interpreter and witness of the Christian revolution. In his *Letter to the Galatians*, he enunciated a new principle of freedom and equality: "There is neither Jew nor Greek, there is neither slave nor free person, there is not male and female; for you are all one in Christ Jesus". In his *Letter to Philemon*, written between 58 and 60 CE, he affirmed a new idea of authority in asking Philemon, a rich pagan converted to Christianity, to forgive and welcome his own slave, Onesimus, as a brother in faith. Paul did not condemn the institution of slavery (Caesar's authority) but *de facto* abolished it by introducing a greater principle of brotherhood (the authority of God). Moreover, he pronounced the famous sentence "*nulla potestas nisi a Deo*" ("there is no authority except from God") that has been interpreted (and can be intended) either as "all authorities come from God" or, on the contrary, as "since authority comes from God, the ruler cannot abuse it".

In the third century, the territorial expansion of Rome ceased and a structural economic crisis began. The main cause of the crisis was a reduction in the workforce both internally (due to demographic decline) and, above all, externally, as a result of the reduced influx of slaves. The first effect was a growing insecurity (with barbarians at the gates) and a flight from the cities to the rustic *villae*. The economy contracted and fragmented into rural, closed, self-sufficient units with too little money in circulation.

Rome responded to the crisis with the extension of the right of citizenship, the division of the Empire into two parts (*pars Occidentis* and *pars Orientis*) ruled by two Caesars and the recognition, in 313, of the freedom of religion for Christians and for everyone else.

In 476, the barbarian Odoacer deposed the last Augustus of the *pars Occidentis*, Romulus Augustus, recognising the Augustus of the *pars Orientis* as sole Emperor. Thus began a new phase in Roman history, with a single Emperor ruling the two parts of the Empire, a phase in which the cultural influence of Christianity in Europe was enormous in both East and West, but differently so.

In the West, the Catholic Church of Rome defended its autonomy from the Empire, recovered and saved the classical philosophical tradition, ennobled work and converted the barbarians to Christianity and European civilisation.

Already in the seventh century, the Pope shrugged off the protection of the *basileus* – the Emperor of Constantinople – by ceasing to ask him for confirmation of his election. In the Benedictine abbeys, amanuensis monks preserved the works of the Greek and Roman classics for future generations. In these same abbeys, the revolutionary rule of the *ora et labora* was preached and experienced. Manual labour, from disvalue reserved for slaves as atonement for some punishment of the gods, became the active collaboration of man with the creative labour of God. The distinction fell, theoretically and practically, between the noble art of *otium* and the plebeian activity of *negotium*. The barbarians, attracted by the "European" lifestyle, were converted to Christianity and Romanity. Instead of the political conquest of a people or its cultural surrender, a new form of *métissage* took place.

In the East, the process of Christianisation assumed another form. Church and Empire identified themselves, and each sought the protection of the other. Constantine was venerated by the Greek Orthodox Church, but not by the Catholic Church, as a patron saint. In the East, the Orthodox Church became the guardian of a cultural tradition that did not experience the contamination of the barbarian invasion and that inspired a model of Caesaropapism that, with Justinian (483–565), became a regime of economic and political absolutism. Although historians have recently shed new light on Byzantine society, the classical assessment by George Ostrogorsky (1968: 31) remains valid:

> antagonism between the *imperium* and the *sacerdotium* was not characteristic of Byzantium, where there was on the whole a close and intimate relationship between State and Church, a fundamental interdependence of the Orthodox Empire and the Orthodox Church which together formed a single political and ecclesiastical entity.

Bloch said that Europe arose when the Roman Empire crumbled. In 710, the Empire was still alive, formally united and substantially divided into two parts. The Empire created a "Mediterranean Union", instead of a "European Union", which included, on the African coast, Petra and Palmyra, and excluded, North of the Rhine, Hungary, Bohemia and Germany. The Mediterranean was a *mare nostrum* while the *limes* was still on the Rhine.

The Islamic invasion that broke Mediterranean unity began in 711. The Arabs, unlike the barbarians, were not attracted by Roman civilisation and had no wish to integrate themselves.

For the Roman Empire, the centuries between 711 and 1250 (two symbolic dates) were marked by a double process of progressive centralisation of power (economic, political and religious) to the East and progressive disarticulation of power (always economic, political and religious) to the West. In the East, authority was consolidated, and in the West, freedom emerged. At the same time, the Mediterranean became a barrier and the *limes* shifted to the North of the Rhine.

In the West, the struggle between the Papacy and the Empire, between the Empire and the Communes, between the Church and the merchants can essentially be seen as a struggle for the affirmation of greater freedom: religious, political and economic.

"Charlemagne, without Muhammad, would be inconceivable", said Henri Pirenne. On Christmas night of 800, when the Pope crowned Charlemagne Emperor of the Romans, there was already a legitimate Emperor residing in

Constantinople. However, he was too distant, geographically and politically, from Rome, and the Pope felt the need for a closer defender.

Charlemagne (742–814) changed the borders of Europe with the entry of Germany and the exit of Spain, England, part of the Balkans, and the South of Italy. Above all, he established a new trifunctional social and economic order based on the distinction between those who pray (*oratores*), those who fight (*bellatores*) and those who work (*laboratores*). Thus, the labour revolution begun by the Benedictine monks in the fifth century obtained its first political recognition.

While Pope Leo III had crowned Emperor Charlemagne, Otto I of Saxony (912–973) temporarily succeeded in overturning the situation by affirming the primacy of the Empire over the Papacy. With the so-called Ottonian Privilege, he affirmed the twofold right (privilege) of the Emperor to approve, or disapprove, the appointment of Pontiffs and to forbid them crowning Emperors who were not of Germanic lineage. Thus was born, *de facto* – because the name will be assumed only later – the "Holy Roman Empire of the Germanic Nation" that would live, for a long time only formally, until 1806, when Napoleon Bonaparte decreed its death. That is how the Catholic Roman Empire became mainly Germanic. The Church reacted. At the Lateran Council of 1059, Pope Nicholas II decreed that Rome would no longer tolerate any imperial interference in electing Popes and that henceforth the election of the Pontiff would be an exclusive prerogative of a college of cardinals gathered in a conclave. The "investiture controversy" between the Church and the Empire began in 1075, when Pope Gregory VII promulgated the *Dictatus papae*, in which, among other things, the principle that the Pope "is allowed to depose Emperors" was reaffirmed, and closed in 1122 with the Concordat of Worms, which sanctioned a substantial autonomy for the Catholic Church.

The beginning of the process of separation between sacred power and political power – as shown by Harold J. Berman – marked the first in a series of revolutions that positively upset Europe. That process represented, in itself, beyond the immediate political consequences, an affirmation of a principle of *libertas ecclesiae* comprising an idea of full freedom.

The struggle between Church and Empire was followed by the battle between the Empire and the Municipalities to acquire the royal rights of taxation (*regalia iura*). In April 1167, the Municipalities of Northern Italy formed the first Lombard League, which defeated the Emperor Frederick Barbarossa (1122–1190). After a long period of truce, the new Emperor, Frederick II (1194–1250), tried to re-establish the Imperial hegemony. In March 1226, the second Lombard League was formed and, supported by the Pope, succeeded in stopping the Emperor's attempt. The League was dissolved in 1250, at the death of the Emperor, after having conquered a segment of communal autonomy, namely, of political freedom.

Finally, in Western Europe, a battle for economic freedom was underway. The Church had valued, while practicing it, manual labour, and *laboratores* had become part of the feudal trifunctional order. However, other relevant non-manual occupations had not yet received full legitimation from the Church and therefore from society. Paradoxically, there were two opposing claims: that of merchants and bankers – the protagonists of the emerging market economy – who demanded the (economic) freedom to be able to provide society with useful services in order to increase their personal well-being, and that of the mendicant friars, who demanded the freedom (including economic freedom) to renounce manual activities in order to live voluntarily in poverty by dedicating themselves to preaching and teaching.

In the meantime, in Eastern Europe, the Roman Empire was becoming increasingly Byzantine. A distinctive trait of the Byzantine Empire was its political and economic absolutism. The power was in the hands of a bureaucratic elite that, through a pervasive network of corporations, controlled the entire society. In the twelfth century, there was a rapprochement between Rome and Constantinople both in their common aversion to Frederick Barbarossa and in an appreciation of the Western lifestyle by the Byzantine *basileus* Manuel I Komnenos (1143–1180). This rapprochement, however, was dramatically interrupted in 1204 by the plundering of Constantinople by the Crusaders and the proclamation of the "Latin Empire of Constantinople" supported by Venetians. It was a deeper "schism" than that of 1054, which had truly separated Catholics and Orthodox. Despite its economic and political absolutism, Byzantine society was less static than was once believed. Orthodox monasticism spread a new culture of labour favouring the overcoming of the myth of autarky in which mercantile profit was acceptable, guilds were considered a community of workers (*koinotes* is the same word used for "village") and, next to the State, an exchange economy flourished, with economic agents demanding both freedom and justice. According to Angeliki E. Laiou (2002: 1129),

> it is the development of the monastic communities of Mount Athos that provides the clearest proof of the fact that the ideology of self-sufficiency was inadequate to encompass Byzantine realities. The early documents of Mount Athos, including the *typikon* issued by St. Athanasios (in 973–975), are indeed replete with ideas of self-sufficiency, which include agricultural activity and exclude any trading for profit. Within seventy years, the monks were selling their own surplus and that of others, fully participating in the economy of exchange.

Moreover, as Angeliki E. Laiou and Cécile Morrison (2007: 89) observe,

> Byzantium had a mixed economy, characterized by the coexistence of state regulation and a market-based economy … The role of the state in the economic process underwent significant changes in the course of the eleventh and twelfth centuries. Market forces seek to gain the upper hand. Justice in exchange survived as an ideal.

In short, in 1250, the Roman-Byzantine Empire was "already and not yet" Europe. It was "already" Europe because the great identity values that united and distinguished the peoples of Europe had already emerged: a larger positive and negative freedom (*libertas*), the value and dignity of labour (*opus*), and the social function of communities (*communitas*) beyond the right of citizenships. It was "not yet" Europe because these values were blurred and conflictual: people were still fighting for a larger freedom (starting from the *libertas ecclesiae*), non-manual workers – merchants and bankers – were not fully accepted, and the guilds – a new type of community acting both in East and West – did not yet enjoy true autonomy.

Scholastic and Byzantine Economic Thought

In 1250, the year Frederick II died, Thomas Aquinas was ordained a priest and two years later began teaching at the University of Paris.

We usually think of medieval economic thought as the reflection developed by scholastics around some great economic issues. In fact, the parallel reflection developed by Byzantine scholars belongs to the same stage in the evolution of economic thought, and both traditions are crucial in assessing the influence of economic culture in the birth of Europe.

Scholastic and Byzantine economic thought shared one great subject to investigate: the role of justice in regulating the economic activity of individuals and authorities. Behind this was the implicit (and intricate) relationship between individual freedom and public power and therefore between own good and common good – even if in the Byzantine tradition we do not find the latter expression.

From the parallel reflection of Scholastic and Byzantine economic thought, the constitutive values of Europe – *libertas, opus, communitas* – emerged clarified and reinforced.

At the core of Scholasticism, we find Thomas Aquinas (1225–1274), according to whom man is a political and social animal destined to live in communities in order to satisfy essential needs that would otherwise go unfulfilled. One's ultimate end is happiness or beatitude. However, there are two types of happiness. The first, conforming to human nature, can be achieved by cultivating the moral virtues (prudence, justice, fortitude and temperance) that orient one towards good. The second, which transcends human nature, is to take part in the divine nature by becoming a friend of God. It is possible to achieve the Highest Good only by accepting, as a gift from heaven, the theological virtues that lead to God: faith, hope and charity (Aquinas, 1270 [1947], *Summa Theologica, ST*, I–II, q. 62).

Charity is the supreme virtue that shapes all the others ("charity is the mother and root of all the virtues, inasmuch as it is the form of them all", *ST*, I–II, q. 62, a. 3). It is one's "love of friendship" for God that enables one, on the one hand, to receive the divine gift of wisdom necessary to justly assess human relationships and, on the other, to love one's neighbour as oneself, thus contributing to the common good of the communities in which one takes part. To love one's neighbour means, first of all, "rendering to each one his due"; that is, to be just (*ST*, I–II, q. 66, a. 6; *ST*, II–II, q. 25, a. 1).

Aquinas distinguishes three types of justice regulating interpersonal relationships. The first concerns mutual dealings between persons (commutative justice), the second the duties of the community (the whole) towards the individuals or parts (distributive justice) and the last the duties of individuals towards the community (legal justice). Aquinas considers the first two "species" of a "particular" virtue, namely the moral virtue of justice, and the last one a "general virtue" orienting the actions of all men and institutions towards the common good. This means that it is the duty of each actor to contribute, intentionally and directly, to the community's good (*ST*, I–II, q. 90, a. 2; *ST*, II–II, q. 61). In the *Summa Theologica*, he writes,

> as charity may be called a general virtue in so far as it directs the acts of all the virtues to the Divine good, so too is legal justice, in so far as it directs the acts of all the virtues to the common good.
>
> *ST, II–II, q. 58, a. 6*

In *De regimine principum ad regem Cypri*, he states that the only way to distinguish between good and bad government is to assess the purpose pursued by the ruler. A good government pursues the common good:

> If, therefore, a multitude of free men is ordered by the ruler towards the common good of the multitude, that rulership will be right and just, as is suitable to free men. If, on the other hand, a rulership aims, not at the common good of the multitude, but at the private good of the ruler, it will be an unjust and perverted rulership.
>
> *Aquinas 1267ca [1949], book 1, ch. 2*

Justice is therefore the foundation of common good coming from charity.

Scholastics, as part of an impressive theological reflection, carry out an economic analysis of commutative and distributive justice and therefore try to determine the just price of goods, including money, and labour. Two traditions of thought emerge: Dominican and Franciscan. It suffices here to emphasise the central and common point of both analyses.

In Dominican scholasticism (starting with Aquinas), an objective approach prevails: the just price is basically the average total cost of production determined, *de facto*, by a *communis aestimatio* internal to the guilds of arts and crafts into which the medieval economy was organised. The same approach was applied to assess the just price of money. In the beginning, lending at interest was condemned on the basis of the evangelical prohibition *Mutuum date, nihil inde sperantes* (lend hoping nothing thereby). The usurer (banker) sold time, which belonged to God, earning money without working and incurring a cost of production. Gradually, credit activity was legitimised on the basis of the just price theory. One argued that the lender, temporarily depriving himself of the availability of a sum of money, assumed a triple cost of production resulting from the risk that (a) the borrower would not be able to return the capital received (*periculum sortis*), (b) the borrower could return it late (*damnun emergens*) and (c) the lender could lose an alternative opportunity for profit (*lucrum cessans*). The lender was therefore entitled to demand compensation commensurate with the production cost of the lending activity.

In Franciscan scholasticism, a more subjective approach prevails. In particular, Peter Olivi (1248–1298) and St. Bernardine of Siena (1380–1444) focus on intrinsic motivations. In their writings, interest becomes the just price of capital, while usury goes back to the unfair price of money. One obtains interest – and this is not usury – when a person lends, with firm decision (*firmo proposito*), a sum of money, which thus becomes capital, destined to finance not the consumption of subsistence but a productive activity that generates profit (which contains "a seed of profit"). The just price tends to be identified with the price of a free market, that is, determined by a *communis aestimatio fori*. The market is conceived as a network of social relationships based on mutual trust and credibility, relationships strengthened or weakened depending on whether the belief that the counterpart is acting to increase or subtract the commonwealth prevails: "*per lo ben comune si die esercitare la mercanzia*" (for the common good you must exercise the merchandise), cried St. Bernardine of Siena in a sermon of 1425.[3]

Thus, Dominicans and Franciscans elaborated an economic theory of justice following, for the former, an objective approach based on the cost of production and, for the latter, a subjective approach based on the market price. But they pursue the same goal: to demonstrate that justice is necessary for the common good and that common good is a duty of justice for all: even in economic choices, it is a question of conceiving the own good or interest in relation to the common good or interest.[4]

The desire to contribute to the common good also inspires a rethinking of the value of labour. At the beginning of their experience, Franciscans considered manual labour an autonomous identity choice, sharing the fate of ordinary people. Later on, they decided to live on alms in order to completely devote themselves to teaching and itinerant preaching in a condition of absolute poverty. Franciscans were accused by the secular clergy of carrying out improper pastoral tasks and above all of living without work by exploiting the work of ordinary people. The question dealt with the nature and utility of the work. In the feudal trifunctional social order – as well as in the traditional social teaching of the Church – only the manual labour performed by *laboratores* was considered and legitimised.

The best defence of the Franciscans' choice was proposed by Bonaventure of Bagnoregio (1217–1274), Minister General of the Order, in his *De perfectione evangelica* (*On Evangelical Perfection*), published in 1256. There, inspired by the trifunctional order, he stated that for the order both of the Church and the Republic three kinds of work (*triplex genus operis*) are required: artificial or manual work (*opus manuale sive corporale*) to prepare food, clothing, housing and tools; civil work (*opus civile*) proper to the leaders who govern, to the soldiers who defend, to the merchants who trade, and to the familiars who serve; and spiritual work (*spiritual opus*) consisting of preaching, dispensing sacraments and so on.

Bonaventure uses the same term (*opus*, meaning work) to indicate different human activities. Manual labour (*labor*) is simply a particular kind of work (*opus*), but all human labour, not only manual, entails fatigue (stemming from original sin). Therefore, labour is work and all work entails fatigue (or *labor*).

Bonaventure was thus able to send a powerful message to both Church and society. To the first, that poverty and *spiritual opus* are the friars' two fundamental values; to the second, that all human work is a means of cooperating with God and useful for the common good of humanity.[5]

In the end, the desire to guarantee the common good inspired a rethinking of the role of public authorities in civil society. The reflection was once again triggered by scholastics. Aquinas, as we mentioned, considered monarchy the best way to govern a society where men coexist. He considered primarily three types of communities – family, city and kingdom – and did not carry out an in-depth analysis of guilds. Authority was conceived as descending directly from God, whereas the "plenitude of power" (*plenitudo potestatis*) belonged only to the Pope, who then transferred part of it to the Emperor.

Marsilius of Padua (1275/1280–1342/1343) completed his masterpiece *Defensor Pacis* (*The Defender of Peace*) in 1342 during the clash between Pope John XXII and Louis the Bavarian over the issue of *plenitudo potestatis*. According to Marsilius, sovereignty belonged to the people (*sibi princeps*), who exercised it through its most important part (*valentior pars*), that is, the members of the guilds of arts and crafts. The Church should have been considered only a part of society, and the plenitude of power should have belonged to the State, a Corporative State.

In addition, Marsilius also sent a powerful message to both Church and society: in order to ensure peace, and therefore, the common good, spiritual and political power must be divided and the State governed by people organised into guilds.[6]

Perhaps the best manifesto of Scholastic political and economic thought is the well-known *Allegory of Good and Bad Government* painted by Ambrogio Lorenzetti between February 1338 and May 1339 in the Sala dei Nove (Salon of Nine) of Siena's Palazzo Pubblico. The painting shows the features of good government (central fresco of the Sala), its positive effects on city and country (right side) and the negative effects of bad government (opposite side). In the central fresco, we can see, on the left, divine wisdom inspiring justice, which leads a unified people towards the common good symbolised by the Commune of Siena, and on the right, the theological virtues, with the predominant position of charity, inspiring the common good, whose first fruit is peace.

The real meaning of the *Allegory* is the radical alternative between "own" and "common" good. It is the search for common good oriented by virtues – above all by charity and justice – that leads to good government and its effects (prosperity, peace and harmony), and it is the search for own good that causes bad government and its effects (misery, violence and fear), as we can read in the fresco at left: "Because each seeks only his own good, in this city, Justice is subjected to Tyranny". The *Allegory* indicated an ideal towards which to strive in a real context: the Siena of old, torn apart by struggles for power and by the plague (which killed Lorenzetti).

We can glimpse the East's cultural path even if further studies would be needed to assess the contribution of Byzantine economic thought to the clarification and reinforcement of the constitutive values of Europe.

The main sources of the Byzantine tradition were the classical Greeks, beginning with Aristotle, the edicts of Roman emperors and the Roman law, systematised by Justinian, the Greek Fathers of the Church and notably Saint Basil of Caesarea. The result was, for centuries, an idea and ideal of justice feasible in a self-sufficient economy.[7]

In the fourteenth century, following the end of the Nicene Empire (1204–1261) and the recapturing of Constantinople, the myth of autarky declined and new thinkers also discussed economic issues. One should mention Nicholas Kabasilas (1322–1392), a mystic and theological writer, who condemned lending at interest, contesting the civil laws that allowed it for laymen; Constantine Harmenopoulos (1320–ca. 1385), an eminent jurist; "the less eminent but nevertheless very influential Matthew Vlastares, who produced a compendium of civil and ecclesiastical law, presented the civil laws that permitted lending at interest" (Laiou and Morrison 2007: 229); and George Gemistos Plethon (1355/1360–1452/1454), who depicted an ideal state based on agriculture.

During this period, an interesting mutual exchange of ideas occurred. In 1354, the first translations of Aquinas into Greek appeared, thus contributing to the discussion of *dignitas hominis*, while Plethon was a leading pioneer of the revival of Greek culture in Western Europe and the 1438–1439 Council of Ferrara and Florence relaunched Plato's ideas.[8]

Justice remained at the centre of economic life and culture. Byzantines, in particular, were interested in determining just price and just profit, and the commitment was entrusted to the State rather than economic theories. As Laiou (2002: 1132) observed,

> The concepts of just value, just price, and just profit are intimately interconnected. In Byzantium, it was primarily the state that gave specific content to these concepts that appear in rather too general and inchoate a form in the writings of churchmen. Once again, we have little theoretical or systematic discussion of the just value or the just price or the just profit. The information comes from legislative codes or novels or regulatory texts (primarily the *Book of the Eparch*) and is, perhaps not unexpectedly, fragmented.

Just profit was calculated on the basis of a margin that could be reached through negotiation: "Already in the early ninth century", write Morrison and Laiou (2007: 62), "the patriarch Nikephoros of Constantinople had stated that the profit of the merchant was 'just' if it did not exceed 10 per cent".

Just price was determined in a similar fashion: it was not legislated but established through codes and customs. The market price could not be less than half the just price. Otherwise, the seller would have suffered unjust damage. Thus, the market price was regulated on the basis of the notion of *laesio enormis* ("enormous damage"): "In such a case", writes Laiou (2002: 1133),

> the contract is annulled, unless the seller agrees to pay the full (just) price. This legal limitation on free negotiation and exchange was reinforced by the

Christian and patristic idea that negotiation necessarily involves lying, and is therefore morally wrong, as well as the more general idea that cupidity and greed are sinful for Christians.

Gradually, due to the decline of the Empire and the emergence of market forces, the just price became the market price, and the State, rather than determining the just price, guaranteed the enforcement of "just" contracts. As Morrison and Laiou (2007: 163) state,

> In context, this must be taken to mean that the just price is the market price. Thus the Byzantine state, formerly conceived as the "judge" who guarantees just exchange, becomes the legal authority that safeguards the sanctity of private contracts.

It is interesting to note that Byzantines focused on commutative and distributive justice without any explicit reference to legal justice (in Aquinas's sense). Moreover, they were interested in protecting, on the one hand, the seller, with the notion of *laesio enormis* and, on the other hand, the buyer, with the notion of maximum profit. During the fourteenth century, Byzantine thinking on justice shifted from State to market and therefore reinforced the role of merchants and guilds.

In short, during the Late Middle Ages, both Scholastic and Byzantine thinkers analysed the importance of justice for a market economy focusing on the relationships between individual freedom and public authorities. Overall, the constitutive values of Europe – *libertas, opus, communitas* – were clarified and reinforced.

The Birth of Europe in 1453

In 1250, when Frederick II died and Thomas Aquinas was ordained a priest, Europe was not yet born. It was "already" there, *in fieri*, but it was "not yet" visible. On the scene and quite visible were the traditional actors: the two Empires (the Byzantine in the East and the Germanic in the West), the two Churches (Catholic and Orthodox), the myriad municipalities and guilds, and the emerging merchants and bankers. Each was in search of its own freedom: political, religious and economic.

In the decades following 1250, unifying and disruptive forces were activated. The plague, famine, guild selfishness, the decline of Church and Empire pushed individuals to seek "their own good" while abandoning any perspective of the common good. At the same time, the unifying forces of European peoples intervened.[9]

In external relations between republics and monarchies, a greater economic integration was made possible by a series of trade agreements as well as the development of a network of markets that, connecting European villages and cities, fuelled the second great European revolution, namely the commercial revolution. The greatest agreement of all was the Hanseatic League, a trade alliance among more than 100 northern European cities to manage maritime traffic together. The development of markets, on the other hand, established a sort of territorial division of labour that increased the awareness of having common constraints and material interests.[10]

In internal relations, a series of institutions tended to unite, or at least not to separate, labour and capital. Limited partnerships were developing in industry and commerce, allowing capitalists to finance and participate in the business risk of entrepreneurs without the necessary share capital. In agriculture, the emphyteusis contract was spreading, which gave the holder the same rights as the owner on the condition that he paid a periodic rent and improved the fund. In the cities, arts and crafts guilds flourished. The Republic of Florence (1251–1559) was emblematic of this experience. In 1252, the Republic minted the florin, which immediately became the reference currency in European trade. The work ethic, in Florence as well as in other large commercial cities, favoured the spread of exchange letters and accounting records, making economic activity more rational and therefore more efficient. The Italian guilds, unlike the Byzantine ones, were more free and open: admission conditions were not burdensome, jobs could also be carried out beyond them, and the municipalities basically respected their autonomy.[11]

Politics also brought European peoples together more. Imperial bonds loosened and municipalities and nation-states emerged. In the Byzantine Empire, a weak State abandoned the economy. In the Roman-Germanic Empire, following the death of Frederick II, a chaotic period began. In 1273, the crown passed to the Habsburgs, who, instead of pursuing Germanic interests, embarked on an "apostolic" policy aimed at establishing a multinational and multi-ethnic Empire in central-eastern Europe. In 1452, Frederick III (1440–1493) went to Rome to assume the imperial crown which, for centuries, remained the prerogative of the Habsburg House. Not surprisingly, the title of "Apostolic Majesty" belonged to the Roman-Germanic Emperor. In central-western Europe, on the other hand, cohesive nation-states consolidated. In the Hundred Years' War (1337–1453), fought between France and England, perhaps for the first time a feeling of nationality emerged. The nobles, instead of referring only to villages and cities, began to mention English and French individuals. In the cities, originating in the guilds, a form of political democracy flourished. In Florence, only the members of corporations enjoyed the political rights of an active and passive electorate. In the municipalities, a more advanced democracy was established than in the past. Le Goff (2011: 91, my translation) writes, "Unlike the feudal contract that binds an inferior to a superior, the oath that binds the members of the primitive urban community is egalitarian". And Robert S. Lopez (1962 [2004]: 301, my translation from Italian), in a book significantly titled *The Birth of Europe*, noted,

> If we compare them to any other form of government prior to the great American and French revolutions, the communes strike us as the states that offered to the maximum number of citizens the opportunity to participate in one way or another in the management of public affairs. In comparison with the monarchical governments of their age, they even deserve to be celebrated as examples of progressive democracy.

Late Medieval democracy was a system of multiple sovereignties: following Bull's analysis (1977), it could be defined as "a society without a state".

Lastly, religion also united European persons and peoples more closely. At the beginning of the millennium, in 1054 and 1204, the Eastern schism between Catholics and Orthodox was consummated, and there followed, between 1378 and 1417, the Western schism with the transfer of the Holy See to Avignon. In the first decades of the fifteenth century, Christianity underwent a reconciliation. The Council of Constance (1414–1418) put an end to the Western schism by returning the Pope to Rome, and significantly the participants were divided by nations. The Council of Ferrara-Florence, which ended on 6 July 1439, overcame the Eastern schism. The newfound union was also designed to save Byzantium from the growing Turkish threat. However, it didn't have the desired effect; indeed, it ended by breaking up the internal forces of the Empire.

In 1453, the Turks conquered Constantinople. The Roman Empire died and Europe was born. Centuries before becoming a set of institutions, Europe was born as a "commonwealth of Christian nations", united and different. Unity was not ensured by the power of a great empire, which no longer existed, or by the hegemonic strength of one or a few large national states, which did not yet exist. It was, from the very beginning, a "unity in diversity" because the West was occupied by emerging nation-states like England and France, the Centre by the multinational Habsburg Empire and the East by former byzantine countries now conquered by the Ottoman Empire. Europe, contrary to Roman cities, was born first alongside an East–West axis (one could say a *Decumanus Maximus*) and later, in 1517, with the Protestant Reform, alongside a North–South axis (a *Cardo Maximus*). Unity was established around common values, such as economic and political freedom, industriousness and community, and in confrontation with the different cultural identities of extra-European people. Those shared values largely inspired common institutions: a market economy and a municipal democracy. The diversity emerged alongside the twofold East–West and North–South axis. Europe was Christendom: Europeans were Christians, and Christians were found only in Europe.

In 1458, Enea Silvio Piccolomini, a few months before ascending to the papal throne as Pius II, published a treatise entitled *De Europa*. Greeks, for the first time, had used the noun "Europe". Piccolomini definitively introduced the adjective "Europeans". He wrote: "*Europeos, aut qui nomine Cristiano censentur*" (Baldi 2003: 620). Europe, for Piccolomini, was Christendom, which, after the fall of Constantinople, also included the Byzantine East. Having become Pope, Piccolomini committed himself, without success, to organizing a Crusade to free the former Byzantine regions from the Turks. He believed that was a part of Europe to be liberated.[12]

In Short

In the first section, we outlined the long conception of Europe from the very beginning (Ancient Greece) to 1250 (a symbolic year). The surviving Roman-Byzantine

Empire was "already and not yet" Europe: more "not yet" than "already", considering the partial and clashing rise of its founding cultural values.

In the second section, we saw how medieval economic thought, focusing on the role of economic justice, achieved a new view of individual freedom, human labour and intermediate communities.

In the last section, we highlighted the prevailing forces that in 1453 (another symbolic date) gave birth to Europe as a "commonwealth of Christian nations" united by shared cultural values which have largely inspired common institutions.

It seems to me that medieval economic thought – both Scholastic and Byzantine – contributed to the birth of Europe by clarifying and spreading its founding values: *libertas*, *opus* and *communitas*. The cultural identity of Europe is not only freedom but also work and community. All of them have their roots in an idea (and ideal) of common good based on justice. The fundamental image of man as a social and political actor cooperating with God in building the world led to an increase in negative and positive *libertas*, labour as *opus* comprising merchants and friars and society as a *communitas communitatum*, including guilds. In the Scholastic West, the emphasis was on personal freedom, while in the Byzantine East it was on public authorities. Both were fighting from freedom, risking what Nikolai Berdjaev called Caesaropapism and Popecaesarism.

Of course, it is always difficult to determine how much ideas, ideologies or economic cultures influence people's choices and change social processes. Yet to some extent, more or less perceptible and documentable, they always have an influence. Medieval economic thought, with the university teachings of the great theologians and jurists, with the vulgar sermons of the mendicant friars, with the penances and advice of confessors scattered everywhere, certainly helped to change the mentality of the time.

I believe that the leading historians mentioned above are correct: Europe was born as Christendom. I agree with Halecki and Le Goff when they state that the Carolingian Empire did not establish a real European cultural unity, and I believe that Europe's symbolic date of birth is 1453, when actual unity was based on shared cultural values rather than on the power of ancient Empires or on new hegemonic nations. Medieval economic thought, as I have tried to show, gave a significant boost to the emergence of those cultural values.

Of course, further research is needed to thoroughly investigate the issues explored in this chapter. But Marc Bloch was right: Europe was born when the Roman Empire died, in 1453.

Notes

1 On classical and high medieval Europe, see Pirenne (1937), Halecki (1963), Cardini and Montesano (2006), Prodi (2009), Price and Thonemann (2010), Wickham (2010) and Jordan (2002). For an overview of medieval economic thought, see De Roover (1955), Langholm (1998) and Wood (2012). For a parallel overview of medieval political thought, see Canning (2003, 2011).

2 For an overview of Greek and Roman political thought, see Balot (2009).
3 See Todeschini (2004), Bruni and Zamagni (2004, 2016).
4 On Scholastic commutative and distributive justice, see De Roover (1958), Monsalve (2014), Chaplygina and Lapidus (2016) and Santori (2020).
5 On the issue of *labor* and *opus*, see Maranesi (2015).
6 On Marsilius, see Maiolo (2007), Black (2003, ch. 7), Di Bello (2009).
7 See Laiou (2002), Laiou and Morrison (2007), Makrides (2019).
8 See Plested (2012) and Demetracopoulos (2012).
9 For an overview of Europe from 1250 to 1453, see Le Goff (1990, 2007, 2012). On the late Byzantine Empire, see Ostrogorsky (1968, ch. VIII), Treadgold (1997, part VI), Laiou and Morrison (2007, chs. 5–6).
10 On the Hanseatic League, see Pirenne (1937, ch. 5); on the role of markets in promoting European integration, see Geremek (1996, ch. III).
11 On the flourishing of guilds in the aftermath of 1250, see Black (2003, chs. 5–8) and Rosser (2015). On the controversial role of the guilds in the late Byzantine Empire, see Maniatis (2001).
12 An English edition of Piccolomini's book appeared in 2013, translated by R. Brawn and introduced and annotated by N. Bisaha. They have translated (and completed) the Latin sentence with the following English words: "Europeans and the islanders who are counted as Christian during the reign of Emperor Fredrick III" (Piccolomini 1458 [2013]: 51). On the relevance of Piccolomini's book to European history, see also Hay (1968: 83–87).

2

MERCANTILISM AND PHYSIOCRACY IN THE MAKING OF A EUROPE OF ABSOLUTE MONARCHIES (1517–1776)

Introduction

"*L'état, c'est moi*". This pronouncement, attributed to Louis XIV, symbolises the change of epoch that took place between the sixteenth and eighteenth centuries, and more precisely – in keeping with symbolic dates – between 1517, the year of the Protestant Reformation that led to the European wars of religion, and 1776, the year of Turgot's last attempt to save the *ancien régime*. Those centuries marked the transition from a Europe of Christian nations to a Europe of absolute monarchies or, in other words, from a "society without a State" to a "society of absolute States".

How did this happen? What factors caused such a profound transformation of Europe?

Historians have tried to capture and connect the main forces at work: economic, political, social, cultural and religious.

In this chapter, we will try to discover what influence the main streams of economic thought of the time – mercantilism and physiocracy – exerted on the transformation of Europe.[1]

We shall examine first of all the disintegration of Christian Europe, second, mercantilism and despotic absolutism in Westphalian Europe, and third, physiocracy and enlightened absolutism in Europe's *République des lettres*.

The Disintegration of Christian Europe

There were several factors that led to the change and disintegration of Christian Europe.

First, economic and political factors. The great famine of 1315, the bubonic plague of 1347, and the devastating Hundred Years' War (1337–1453) fought between the French and the English severely tested the ideal of the common

DOI: 10.4324/9781003188889-2

good theorised by the scholastics, depicted by Ambrogio Lorenzetti on the walls of Siena's *Palazzo Pubblico* and partially experimented in many European cities and the countryside. Amidst the crisis, a contrasting feeling of economic and political individualism emerged: the temptation to save oneself, to go it alone, to think only of one's own interests.

Second, geopolitical factors. The fall of Constantinople in 1453 and the discovery of America in 1492 triggered powerful centrifugal forces, shifting the trade route from the Mediterranean to the Atlantic.

Lastly, and above all, cultural factors. Christianity, with the contribution of medieval economic thought, had tried to unite *fides et ratio*. Now, a process of disarticulation of a unitary mentality was beginning, particularly in Western Europe. Faith and reason split. The Catholic Church was unable to maintain the unity between faith and reason challenged by the parallel phenomenon of the decline of faith and by the emergence of an international market that led merchants to trade far away from their usual habitat, where it was easier to violate the economic ethics taught by the Church. Fanfani (1935: 177) wrote:

> Having left his city, exposed to risks of every kind, free from such ties as the laws of his country or the opinions of his acquaintances, surrounded by intriguing people who saw in him only someone to be cheated, he [the merchant] had to defend himself against the cheaters by cheating, against competitors by sharpening his wits to find new methods of competition, and against adverse circumstances by learning to overcome them. Although he may have been a God-fearing man, if it was urgent for him to take back to the warehouse at least the equivalent of what he had brought away, he was obliged to throw overboard something of his pre-capitalistic ideas, even if in paradisal conditions they might have appealed to him.

At the same time, Humanism, rehabilitating the classical tradition, affirmed a principle of *sola ratione*, while Protestantism, in the attempt to cleanse the Church of the sins of simony, affirmed a principle of *sola fide*.

The Protestant Reform generated a true anthropological revolution also affecting the European founding values.

In the Catholic's anthropology, as we have seen, man can attain the Supreme Good by embracing the God-given virtues. He is free to choose or reject the good. *Caritas*, which is the supreme virtue, impels each person to conceive of her own good in relation to the good of others and, possibly, of all: one's own good is a common good. Justice flows from *Caritas* because loving others means, first of all, "rendering to each one his/her due". Justice orients relations between individuals (commutative justice), between the community and the individuals or between the whole and the parts (distributive justice), and between the individual and the community or between the parts and the whole (legal justice). Legal justice, in particular, is a general virtue that commits each subject (person, community or institution) to seek, directly and intentionally, the common good of society. Consequently, each person, as an image and son of God, is sacred, the *de facto* holder of a series of rights that no one can violate (negative liberty) and is called to participate in the good of the community, not only to defend his own rights, but also to protect and extend those of others (positive liberty), precisely because his own good is a common good. Furthermore, each person, because he or she is the image and child of God, is called on to participate in the construction of the heavenly city, and all human work, manual and intellectual, becomes worthy and useful work. Finally, society, instead of being a mere sum of individuals or cities, is transformed into a community of communities, each one autonomous and dependent on the others. Europe was born as a union of Christian peoples united not by a political power (Empire or nation-states) but by shared cultural values.

In the anthropology of the Orthodox Church, we find the same dynamic, and in particular the centrality of justice, which orients social life, but with a relevant specificity. The freedom of man, son of God, is essentially expressed in his reliance on the authority of his father, represented by the basileus. In the Orthodox Central-Eastern Europe, a social and political model of Caesaropapism is affirmed, which legitimises and realises a stronger State control over society. If in Western Europe, a progressive separation between the Church's *auctoritas* and Empire's *potestas* emerges, in Central-Eastern Europe a transfer of the *auctoritas* of the Church to the *potestas* of the Emperor occurs: not a *potestas directa in temporalibus* of the Church (as in some moments in the West), but of the Empire. The result was an alteration or differenti-ation of the constitutive values of Europe. *Libertas*, *opus* and *communitas* were under more direct control of the political authority: individuals enjoyed less negative and positive freedom, manual labour was still considered inferior to the extent that servitude survived, and communities (from monasteries to guilds) were subject to imperial directives.

Protestantism conceives a negative anthropology, according to which man is incapable of choosing the good. Luther, in controversy with Erasmus, contrasts the traditional free will with the truly revolutionary idea of the servant will: man is unable, because of his corrupt nature, to freely choose the good. It is God who, in his infinite freedom, chooses some men, the predestined, healing their corrupt human nature with his own grace. The predestined are in a direct relationship with God and interpret his Word without any need for the mediation of the Church. They realise that they have been chosen by God according to the success they achieve in life, and it is in order to comply with God's will that they engage inten-sively in work and economic activity. Luther and Calvin introduced an inter-mun-dane ethic as an alternative to the traditional extra-mundane ethic (Catholic or Orthodox), which exalted a moderate use of wealth and an austere lifestyle. On the other hand, Protestant man sees success and wealth as a sign of divine predilection, considers work as a mission or task (*beruf*) to which God calls the chosen ones and, in order to respond to the divine call, is urged to use the resources at his disposal, starting with time and savings, in a rational manner. There is no longer a sacred community that helps to save individuals. Only God saves them, while the State, the secular authority in Luther's terminology, performs the function of repressing, with force if necessary, the perfidy of the wicked or the non-elected. The State is only a necessary evil.

Protestantism profoundly changes the constitutive values of Europe. There exist only individuals and State, while churches take on a national character (starting with the German church). One's own good is no longer necessarily a common good and individual freedom is disconnected from participation in community life: *libertas* becomes more individualistic, *opus* more inter-mundane and *communitas* less sacral and more subject to temporal power. To mark the differences, one could say that individualism, economicism and nationalism become the main features of Protestant Europe.

The Protestant Reformation and the subsequent Catholic Counter-Reformation opened up another corridor of identity in the European citadel: the East–West axis was joined by a North–South axis which, over time, gave rise to two distinct models of capitalism, which have been called "Nordic" and "Meridian". In the former, a negative anthropology prevails, typically Protestant, which considers man incapable of acting for the good of others and therefore "dangerously" committed to building social works. That man can only be saved by God and economic success is precisely the sign of divine predilection. The result is a model of dichotomous capitalism that tends to separate the individual and the State, giving the former maximum freedom of action and the latter a range of action that extends to include caring for the weakest and most disinherited, with a free market in the middle that performs the function of transforming the many private interests into the common good; this model, with reference to the Nordic countries of Europe, has been called "statist individualism".[2] In "southern" capitalism, on the other hand, a realistic anthropology prevails, typical of the Catholic tradition, which considers man as a being endowed with vices and virtues, capable of doing both evil and social good. The result is a type of coordinated capitalism that entrusts the achievement of the common good to the deliberate cooperation of individuals and institutions. This is a model that, with the evolution of southern Europe in mind, we could define as a "welfare society", with a State that recognises the public function of social works promoted by voluntary associations.[3]

In 1519, when the Habsburg Charles V became Holy Roman Emperor, it seemed that the ideal of a universal and not just European monarchy could be realised. Charles had also tried, unsuccessfully, to reconcile Lutherans and Catholics. Kissinger (2014: 14) writes: "A single, pious ruler now governed territories approximately equivalent to today's Austria, Germany, northern Italy, the Czech Republic, Slovakia, Hungary, eastern France, Belgium, the Netherlands, Spain and much of the Americas". The universalist attempt failed, in 1556 Charles abdicated and the process of disintegration resumed.

There were many factors for change, but one prevailed over the others: religion, from being a factor of unity, became a cause of war. From 1524 until the peace treaties of Westphalia in 1648, Europe was the scene of bloody religious wars.

The bloodiest of these wars, known in history as the Thirty Years' War, pitted Catholics against Protestants from 1618 to 1648. Begun as a religious war, it turned into a Franco–Habsburg political conflict for the control of Central Europe. The Catholic France of Cardinal Richelieu, instead of siding with the Catholic Habsburg Empire, defender of the common Catholic Church, supported the coalition of Protestant princes. France feared the hegemony of the Habsburg Empire and preferred, for reasons of national security, a Central Europe fragmented into myriad small states. The French decision showed, perhaps for the first time in an obvious way, that national interest had now conquered the European scene, displacing any residual universalist ideal.[4]

The Treaties of Westphalia outlined a new European order based on three main principles:

a. *Rex imperator in regno suo est*: sovereigns are not subject to any higher political authority;
b. *Cuius regio eius religio*: the sovereign establishes the religion of his kingdom;
c. *Balance of power*: in Europe, a system of alliances between independent states is created to prevent the hegemony of a single country.

Kissinger (2014: 26) writes:

> The Peace of Westphalia became a turning point in the history of nations because the elements it introduced were as uncomplicated as they were sweeping. The state, not the empire, dynasty, or religious confession, was affirmed as the building block of European order. The concept of state sovereignty was established. The right of each signatory to choose its own domestic structure and religious orientation free from intervention was affirmed, while novel clauses ensured that minority sects could practise their faith in peace and be free from the prospect of forced conversion.

If the medieval ideal was unity, albeit in diversity, between Church and Empire (it was the Holy Roman Empire), the "Westphalian concept – Kissinger (2014: 27) continues – took multiplicity as its starting point and drew a variety of multiple societies, each accepted as a reality, into a common search for order".

The solution to the problem of (religious) war becomes Absolutism, that is, the balance between absolute monarchies.

The new European order established in Westphalia once again raised the eternal question of the legitimacy of power: with what authority (legitimacy) can European sovereigns exercise absolute power over their subjects? Until then, the most accepted and persuasive answer had been that of Paul: *non est potestas nisi a Deo* ("there is no authority except from God"). That sentence could be interpreted in the sense that every constituted power is legitimate and must thus be respected ("render unto Caesar …") or, on the contrary, in the sense that, precisely because power descends from God, it must be used for the common good of the people and only thus becomes legitimate. The first interpretation seemed to prevail among the followers of Luther, while the second spread among the followers of Aquinas, who considered legitimate a government oriented to the common good regardless of the republican (elective) or monarchical (hereditary) form adopted.

In 1651, only three years after the signing of the Treaties of Westphalia, Thomas Hobbes offered a modern solution to the problem of the legitimacy of power by fully justifying the new European order.

Hobbes, as is well known, elaborates a theory of the social contract by distinguishing between state of nature and civil society. In the former, men, free from every constraint, fight to acquire goods and power: each is a ravenous wolf for the other (*homo homini lupus*). The state of nature is therefore a situation of perpetual warfare. The civil society arises to put an end to perpetual war by establishing peace. It arises when men, who are the sole repositories of authority, that is, of the legitimacy of power, transfer to an artificial entity, the State-Leviathan, the absolute power to control social life. With Hobbes (and before him with Luther), the mediation of the Church disappears. What in Luther was the direct relationship between individuals and God, with Hobbes becomes the direct relationship between individuals and State. Authority is in every man who, not by chance, Hobbes defines as *auctor*. It is individuals who, in order to live in peace, transfer to the sovereign the absolute power to govern society. With Hobbes, the Middle Ages ended and modernity began: the medieval Good Government bound to the pursuit of the common good was replaced by the absolute State, and society understood as a "community of communities" was replaced by a vision of society comprising only individuals.

At the time of the rise of absolute monarchies, the contribution to the elaboration of a doctrine of Absolutism came not only from political thinkers.[5] Mercantilism was a current of economic thought that partook of the dual movement of the disintegration of Christian Europe and the formation of a Europe of absolute monarchies.

Mercantilism and Despotic Absolutism in Westphalian Europe

Heckscher (1935 [1994], vol. 1: 19) defined mercantilism as "a phase in the history of economic policy".

Mercantilists were not professional economists, nor did they recognise themselves in a leader or in a common methodological approach: they lacked a clear distinction between political economy, the discipline which studies the functioning of economic systems, and economic policy, the discipline which studies the government of the economy.

Mercantilists were businessmen and merchants who, from their professional experience, developed a vision of the functioning of real economies from which they drew a set of economic policy recommendations to offer their sovereigns so that they in turn could effect appropriate measures to increase the wealth of their kingdoms.

In the background, one can detect the major historical events of the time: the decline of the medieval ethic of the common good and the rise of the Protestant

(Calvinist) ethic of individual economic success as a sign of divine benevolence and the moral legitimacy of borrowing money; the decline of the communes and the rise of nation-states; the economic development of capitalism thanks to long-distance trade.

The leading mercantilists were Gerard de Malynes (1568–1641), Thomas Mun (1571–1641) and Edward Misselden (1608–1654). From their experience as merchants, it emerged that wealth is formed in exchange. The only surplus they saw was the profit made by selling goods at a higher price than they bought them: it was a "profit upon alienation". The merchant was, therefore, the creator of wealth. But a distinction had to be made between internal and international trade. The underlying assumption was that the profits of one correspond to the losses of others. Some got rich at the expense of others, as Michel de Montaigne (1580 [1910], vol. 1, ch. 22) noted in 1580: "The profit of one man is the loss of another … no profit whatever can possibly be made but at the expense of another". This crucial assumption led to two related conclusions: domestic trade redistributes wealth among the country's residents but does not increase the wealth of the country itself, while international trade redistributes wealth among countries: it increases the wealth of one country by taking it away from others. In both cases, trade is a zero-sum game: the gains of some are matched by the losses of others. World wealth is like a freshly baked cake: it is fixed, it cannot be increased, it can only be distributed differently, and international trade is the only way for sovereigns to appropriate a larger share of the (given) world's wealth.

In 1776, Adam Smith accused mercantilists of making the gross mistake of confusing wealth with money (precious metals). Later on, more thoughtful and documented studies showed that mercantilists were clear about the distinction. They wanted to favour an accumulation of precious metals (gold and silver) in the sovereign's coffers simply because they believed that with those metals it was possible to buy, in any time and place, all the useful and necessary goods to ensure material well-being. The problem they set out to solve was to show the ruler of a country without gold and silver mines the most effective economic policy for accumulating precious metals. And they came to a shared conclusion. A country without mines can only accumulate precious metals by promoting a favourable balance of trade, that is, as Thomas Mun notes, to sell to foreigners more than one buys from them.

We now know the balance of payments as the accounting document in which the foreign exchange inflows and outflows between a country and the rest of the world are recorded, resulting (essentially) from the balance of exports and imports (current account), from capital transfers (capital account) and from direct and portfolio investments (financial account). For a long time, a simple distinction was made between the trade balance (the balance between exports and imports) and capital movements (related to the buying and selling of securities). Mercantilists were the first scholars of the trade balance.

The shared economic policy target was to achieve, increase or maintain a trade surplus in order to benefit from a continuous inflow of foreign capital. The debate raged on about which instruments were considered most effective in achieving the desired objective. In a first phase, called bullionism, some authors, for instance Malynes, advocated a strong regulation of foreign trade, including a ban on exporting gold. In a second and more advanced phase, known as mercantilism in the strict sense, the debate was whether to favour a bilateral or multilateral trading system. In particular, a dispute developed between Misselden and Mun, Director of the East India Company. The former argued that a country should only favour trade relations with countries willing to import more than they exported. The aim should be to achieve a surplus in the individual trade balances. Mun argued that it was necessary to look at the final balance of trade: Britain, for example, imported from India many of the raw materials it needed to produce manufactured goods for export. So it would have been an unforgivable mistake to look at partial balances and move to a system of bilateral trade. The best strategy for increasing a nation's wealth was to develop, as Britain did, a multilateral trading system to achieve a global trade surplus. Having clarified this first fundamental aspect, it was then a question of defining an organic economic policy. The mercantilists' proposal was inspired by a dirigiste vision of the economy. In particular, they believed that a number of convergent economic policy actions were needed to achieve the goal of a trade surplus: stimulate exports, by refunding duties, granting export premiums, concluding trade treaties, colonial conquests; discourage imports, by imposing duties and quotas; increase the competitiveness of the country, with the construction of new infrastructures (to enlarge the internal market), an increase in population (to keep wages down) and the public control of corporations (to avoid price increases and imbalances in production).

Based on an analysis of the balance of trade, the mercantilists formulated an initial version of the quantitative theory of money, later formalised by Fisher with the exchange equation $MV = PQ$, where M indicates the quantity of money in circulation, V its speed of circulation, P the general price level and Q the volume of transactions. Today, quantitative theory is used by monetarists to claim that inflation is always and everywhere a monetary phenomenon. That is, if we consider V and Q constant, an increase in M (the quantity of money in circulation) is necessarily followed by an increase in P (the general price level). Mercantilists, on the other hand, look at another causal chain that can be established between M and Q: an increase in M, resulting from a trade surplus, can lead to a reduction in the interest rate, an increase in Q and thus in output and employment. The message, which Keynes later liked, was that money can stimulate trade and not necessarily cause inflation.

In short, the mercantilists had a common guiding idea: to increase the wealth of nations, one must have a dirigiste government pursuing the goal of a favourable trade balance.

France became a model of political and economic absolutism for Europe.

"*L'état, c'est moi*", said Louis XIV (1638–1715). The king is the incarnation of the law: *rex lex*: a Sun King, from whom everything radiates. Through him, God exercises his authority over the people and those admitted to the court become the king's family members. An omnipotent and omnipresent State organised into districts controlled by Intendants appointed by the king and a State that is also an entrepreneur.

Jean-Baptiste Colbert (1619–1683), the greatest political interpreter of mercantilism, was appointed Controller General of Finance by Louis XIV in 1665. Trade, according to Colbert, is the source of finance, and finance is the vital nerve of war. In 1653, in a memoir presented to Mazarin, Prime Minister of the Kingdom of France, Colbert set out his guiding ideas on economic policy:

> All industries, even luxury industries, must be resurrected or created from nothing; a protective system of customs duties must be established; producers and merchants must be organised into guilds; maritime transport of French products must be returned to France; and colonies must be developed.
>
> *Luzzatto 1934: 476–477, my translation from Italian*

The realised programme did not differ greatly from the one announced: increase in the number of arts and crafts guilds (in Paris alone they rose from 60 to 114); creation of luxury royal manufactories (tapestries, porcelain, etc.); enlargement of the internal market with the construction of roads and navigation canals (the Canal du Midi); abolition of internal customs; imposition of export duties on key raw materials, including wheat (to keep wages down and to safeguard against famine); imposition of import duties on manufactured goods to protect national industry; and the establishment, in 1664, of two privileged companies to trade with the East and West Indies. Clearly, this amounts to a mercantilist policy.

Another model of an absolute State, for Europe, was England. In this case, it was a model of economic but not political absolutism. With the Glorious Revolution of 1688, England chose to defend the sovereignty of Parliament to contain the power of the Crown. Nevertheless, economic absolutism was not inferior to French absolutism. A complex system of economic regulation developed between the sixteenth and eighteenth centuries. In 1563, the Statute of Artificers came into force and was repealed in earnest only in 1813–1814. The English mercantile system provided for the control of production through an extensive network of guilds, a model of public assistance to the poor that severely limited the mobility of labour, and a state monopoly on foreign trade. The medieval guilds, which tended to be free and open, were thus replaced by a rigid productive organisation controlled by the State. Einaudi (1949 [1975]: 123, my translation from Italian) writes:

> The picture changes, when from the free life of the medieval commune we pass, through slow variations, to the regulated and crystallised life of the great monarchies of the seventeenth and eighteenth centuries, and of the minor political aggregations that formed alongside the kingdoms of France, England, Spain and the Germanic empire. Governments, to police and dominate, sought to regulate what were once free trade associations.

Public assistance to the poor was regulated by the Act for the Relief of the Poor of 1601. The Act, subsequently amended, made it compulsory for the poor to be resident and an authority was entrusted with the task of assisting them to specially funded parishes. Territorial assistance severely limits labour mobility. Lastly, relations between the English motherland and the colonies were regulated through the monopoly granted to the East India Company (1601) and the Navigation Acts approved between 1651 and 1699. In particular, relations between England and the American colonies were regulated according to mercantilist principles, with colonies producing raw materials and semi-finished products for the English market and buying finished products from the mother country (Bergamini 2003: 21–22).

Absolutism spread across Europe in a variety of patterns. In general, we can say that it reinforced the original characteristics of the Three (horizontal) Europes while maintaining (vertical) North-South dualism. In Western Europe (England, France and Spain), nation-states were consolidated that increasingly accepted the separation between temporal and spiritual power, governed populations of substantial ethnic and linguistic homogeneity and experienced an agricultural, and partly industrial, revolution that loosened the old feudal bonds. On the opposite side is Eastern Europe (the regions between Germany and Russia), partly occupied by the Ottoman Empire, with Caesaropapist monarchies governing heterogeneous and coexisting ethnic-linguistic groups that impose a new form of servitude on a predominantly agricultural population. In between emerges an enigmatic Central Europe (Austria, Germany and northern Italy) whose political and cultural borders largely coincide with those of the Habsburg Empire.[6]

Mercantilism favoured the separation of ethics and economics and the subordination of economics to politics: The State was assigned the primary task of strengthening its own power, internal and external, instead of promoting the good of the communitas. It also spread a conflicting view of national economic interests based on a particular theory of domestic and international trade. Lastly, it consolidated a dirigiste conception of public intervention in the economy. Mercantilists took an international view of economic problems, deepened the economic role of the State in defending the national interest, and studied the relations between balance of payments, money supply, prices and production. But they also revealed explicit limitations: they lacked a clear distinction between political economy and economic policy (between science and art), considered trade a zero-sum game without realising the common advantages generated by a more intense international division of labour, and believed it was possible to maintain or increase a balance of payments surplus while ignoring market adjustment mechanisms.

With the Order of Westphalia, Europe was transformed from a community of Christian nations into a geographical and political space occupied by national and multinational states governed by despotic monarchs who considered themselves the source of law (*rex lex*) and who, through their own intendants, directed the economy towards the objectives of State power. Mercantilism contributes to this transformation.

Physiocracy and Enlightened Absolutism in the European Republic of Letters

The mid-eighteenth century saw the beginning of the decline of despotic absolutism in both France and England. Absolutism entered a crisis because it disappointed the population's expectations of prosperity and freedom and also because, at the same time, it raised the bitter criticism of influential intellectuals. Economists contributed to explaining the reasons for this disappointing experience.

In England, old cities like York, where the Statute of Apprentices was in force, declined, and new cities flourished where economic freedom was in force. Einaudi (1949 [1975]: 128, my translation from Italian) writes:

> Manchester, Birmingham, Leeds, etc. sprang up in the clearing of the countryside or from small villages and became large and powerful, to the detriment of the old privileged cities. ... These remained, with their privileges, attached to the theory of the fixed quantum of work and demand and gradually became economically depressed. The new industrial towns prospered and boomed in a climate of freedom, as evidenced by the fall in prices and by the fact that new goods or those manufactured by methods other than those prescribed by the old statutes create new demand and new work.

In France, Colbert's mercantilist policy heavily damaged agriculture, the truly primary sector of the national economy. Twenty-two million of France's twenty-six million inhabitants lived in the countryside and 25% of iron production was destined for building ploughs; that is, agriculture also drove industry. Yet Colbert's policy damaged the agricultural sector in an attempt to artificially create an industrial sector (Luzzatto 1934: 483). Due to the constraints on the export of cereals, domestic supply increased and agricultural prices fell, while at the same time the privileges granted to industry kept the prices of manufactured goods high. The resulting fall in relative prices between agricultural and industrial products reduced the purchasing power of farmers. At the same time, taxes and duties on the peasants increased (tithes, gabelles, bounties and *corvées*) to finance the astronomical increase in court and war expenses (the Seven Years' War against England between 1756 and 1763).

Economists began to criticise mercantilism. Richard Cantillon (1680–1734) challenged the direct relationship, established in the primitive equation of trade, between money (M) and production or volume of transactions (Q), pointing out that the quantity of money, by entering into circulation in different sectors and markets, altered relative prices and thus the allocation of resources, even before changing the general level of prices. David Hume (1711–1776), on the other hand, contested the assumption, fundamental to the mercantilists, that it was possible to maintain a trade surplus without taking into account the adjustment processes that spontaneously took place in the market in the presence of trade surpluses or deficits. In particular, the inflow of precious metals led to an increase in the money supply and a consequent rise in domestic prices, which, on the one hand, stimulated imports and, on the other, penalised exports, thus restoring a substantial balance of trade.

Political philosophers began to devise a new social contract to escape the conflictual state of nature. Hobbes's Absolutism was flanked by a variegated current of liberals and democrats that included Locke, Montesquieu and Rousseau. If Hobbes feared the excessive freedom of action of individuals and, in order to ensure peace, had justified the concentration of power in the hands of the sovereign, the new "contractualists" feared the concentration of power in the hands of the sovereign and wanted to limit the State's freedom of action. They outlined two main solutions: Montesquieu theorised the division of power (executive, legislative and judicial), while Locke and Rousseau envisaged a rule of law, anchoring the government's actions in the recognition of natural rights such as life, liberty and property (Locke) or those established by people's delegates (Rousseau). The new political philosophers envisage a new social contract that assigns human law, rather than divine will, as the basis for the legitimacy of power. Everyone is bound to observe the law, both king and subjects. Montesquieu (1689–1755) wrote: "Freedom is the right to do anything that the law allows. If one citizen were able to do something that the law prohibited, then he would no longer be free, for others would have the same right ..." (quoted by Schulze 1996: 74). The king no longer embodies the State but is its first servant. He exercises power and is legitimised to exercise it, only insofar as he pursues the interest of the people. Rousseau (1712–1778) overturns Hobbes: "man is born free and everywhere he is in chains" (because of despotic absolutism). Montesquieu favoured a constitutional, enlightened monarchy based on the division of powers, while Rousseau wanted a democratic state that expressed the general will of the citizens: the former envisioned a "society of communities", the latter a "society of individuals".

Physiocracy stands at this historical crossroads and, fuelling itself at the source of both absolutism and liberalism, outlines a model of enlightened absolutism anchored in a particular "rule of law".

Physiocracy is a current of economic thought that flourished in the mid-eighteenth century, in part to save France from the financial disaster of the Seven Years' War. The proposed solution is based on economic growth rather than restraint in public spending. Growth, for the physiocrats, depends on the knowledge and application of the laws of the natural order. Physiocracy is a term invented by Dupont de Nemours in 1767 simply to denote the "domination of nature". The school's greatest exponent and acknowledged leader was François Quesnay (1694–1774), who was born in Méré, near Paris, and became Louis XV's first physician. The physiocrats were the first to be called "economists" (*les économistes*).

Physiocrats observed the enormous progress made in the agricultural sector, despite Colbert's adverse policy. In Picardy, in the north of France, the process of land enclosure had accelerated rapidly, capitalist methods of farm management had been introduced, and the new figure of the *fermier*, a true agricultural entrepreneur, had emerged. Mercantilists, as we know, had considered overall wealth to be a fixed quantity that could only be distributed differently between nations through international trade. Physiocrats were attracted by a deeper question: where does wealth, understood as net product, that is, the surplus between the inputs used in production and the output obtained, arise?

The answer can be found in Quesnay's main work, the *Tableau économique*, first published in 1758, and in a final version of 1766. It is structured around three interlinked guiding ideas:

First, the net product (*le produit net*) is only generated in agriculture. Only in this sector does a surplus occur between the resources employed (inputs) and the production obtained (output). For physiocrats, producing means increasing the availability of raw materials that can be used directly to satisfy human needs or transformed, through appropriate production processes, into goods that satisfy other human needs. To produce means to directly harvest and eat the fruit from a tree or to harvest grain from a field to start a process of bread production and distribution. Without grain, you cannot make bread, just as without timber, coal, linen, cotton, etc., you cannot make the many manufactured goods that improve our well-being. Thus, the source of wealth is agriculture alone.

Second, society is divided into classes. One is the productive class, comprising all those who work in the agricultural sector (from tenant farmers to labourers). They are the only productive workers precisely because, by working in the agricultural sector, they generate a net product. They are productive of wealth in terms of a net product. Another is the sterile class, which includes artisans, traders and manufacturers who process but do not create the raw material produced by the agricultural sector. The last class comprises landowners who hold and look after the precious commodity of nature.

Third, the economic exchange serves to reproduce the favourable conditions for the start of a new production cycle but does not, as the mercantilists believed, generate wealth. By means of a long numerical example, Quesnay shows how the net product, which is formed at the end of a production cycle, is received by landowners in the form of an annuity and then re-introduced into the economic system through a series of purchases and payments. For physiocrats, high rent is the basic premise of economic development. Indeed, by means of high rent, landowners will be able to make the land investments necessary to increase the productivity of their land and pay a single tax with which to finance all government public expenditures.

Physiocrats' economic policy proposal follows from the *Tableau* analysis. The aim is to promote the development of agriculture, on the one hand, by increasing the income needed to finance new land investments and, on the other hand, by reducing the tax burden on the productive class involved in land cultivation. To achieve the first result, it is necessary to increase the purchasing power of agricultural income by changing the relative prices between agricultural and manufactured products. In particular, it is necessary to increase the price of wheat (a *bon prix* is needed, say the physiocrats) by eliminating the export restrictions proposed by Colbert to keep quantity high and internal prices low and, at the same time, to reduce the price of manufactured goods by eliminating the privileges and monopolies, also proposed by Colbert, in favour of industrial producers. The second result, possible only after achieving the first, requires the introduction of a single income tax that would lighten the tax burden on the productive class by simplifying the production process. As we can see, the physiocrats' economic policy proposal is based on the free trade of goods and the simplification of the tax system. Vincent de Gournay summed it up in the liberal motto *"laissez faire, laissez passer"*.

Physiocrats had a broad vision of the economic role of the government that went beyond the contingent situation in pre-revolutionary France. They believed that there was a natural economic order, with agriculture at its centre. The economist was tasked with discovering and describing the laws of the natural order, while the sovereign, enlightened by his knowledge of that order, had the even more important task of enforcing the natural laws by adapting the positive order of the State to the natural order described by the economists. In this sense, with physiocracy, politics bends and subordinates itself to economics. De Nemours states that there is a natural and essential order that includes the fundamental laws of all societies. In contrast to Montesquieu, the theorist of the division of powers, Quesnay believed that the natural order could only be achieved by a strong State, such as the Chinese state. For this reason, he became known as the "Confucius of Europe".

On 20 July 1774, Anne Robert Jacques Turgot, one of the leading exponents of the physiocratic school, was appointed Controller General of Finance. Over the next two years, until 12 May 1776, he issued a series of edicts aimed at reducing court expenses, introducing the free movement of grain, applying a single tax on income and abolishing arts and crafts guilds: all clearly physiocratic reforms. His resignation in May 1776 marked a last robust attempt to save the *ancien régime*. In 1781 the banker Jacques Necker, who had become Director General of Finance at Louis XVI's court, published the State budget showing the enormous expenses of the court, and in 1782 proposed a radical fiscal reform.

Enlightened Absolutism, steeped in physiocratic ideas, conquered the courts of half of Europe, especially Central and Eastern Europe. The most famous names are those of Frederick II of Prussia, Maria Theresa and Joseph II of Habsburg, Catherine II of Russia, and Francis I and Peter Leopold of Lorraine. In 1775, Peter Leopold introduced free trade in cereals in Tuscany. In the 1780s, Joseph II abolished serfdom, abolished the *corvées*, abolished tax privileges for nobles and clergy, recognised freedom of worship and introduced social legislation in favour of the poorer classes.

Europe feels like, and is, a cultural community. Rousseau (1761 [1993]: 140–142) writes:

> all the powers of Europe form among themselves a sort of system in which they are united by the same religion, by the same law of the people, by customs, by letters, by commerce and by a sort of equilibrium which is the

necessary effect of all this ... Add to this the particular situation of Europe, more uniformly populated, more uniformly fertile, better united in all its parts; the continuous intermingling of interests which the ties of blood and the affairs of commerce, of the arts, of the colonies have produced among the sovereigns ... The inconstant mood of the inhabitants, which leads them to travel incessantly ... the invention of printing and the general taste for letters, which has produced a commonality of studies and knowledge ... All these causes put together make Europe not only, like Asia and Africa, an ideal collectivity of peoples who have only a name in common, but a real society with a religion, customs, habits and even laws, from which none of the peoples who compose it can depart without immediately causing serious damage.

Europe seems destined to become the new homeland. Rousseau himself noted this, with some disappointment, in 1782: "There are no longer, today, French, German, Spanish or English people. There are only Europeans" (Febvre 1944–45 [1999]: 206, my translation from Italian). For Voltaire, it is Europe as a *république des lettres*. Cultured men felt at home in Paris, Florence, St Petersburg and other cultural capitals: "Europe was a country of choice", writes Febvre (1944–1945 [1999]: 223, my translation from Italian),

> for men of high society, who had every pleasure in cultivating themselves without concern for material contingencies, and who formed, with all the men of high society of all the European countries, a kind of great society constituted beyond frontiers, beyond countries, superior to countries.

Later, in 1796, Burke wrote that "no European could be completely exiled in any part of Europe" (Chabod 1964: 19, my translation from Italian).

European identity, once again, is strengthened in confrontation with other identities, particularly the Asian one. In his *Lettres persanes* (1721), Montesquieu describes Europe's special characteristics, in particular its respect for women and passion for work, while François Quesnay, in *Despotisme de la Chine* (1767), extols the Asian model of enlightened despotism. But Europe also wanted to preserve the balance of power established in Westphalia. "The first half of the eighteenth century", writes Kissinger (2014: 35), "was dominated by the quest to contain France; the second was shaped by Prussia's effort to find a place for itself among the major powers" – a place won thanks to the tenacity of Frederick the Great, who ascended the throne in 1740. "England", Kissinger (1995: 70) further observes,

> was the one European country whose raison d'état did not require it to expand in Europe. Perceiving its national interest to be in the preservation of the European balance, it was the one country which sought no more for itself on the Continent than preventing the domination of Europe by a single power.

On the eve of the French Revolution, Europe presented itself as a republic of letters governed by enlightened rulers who seemed to have absorbed the lessons of physiocracy.

The main merit of physiocracy is to have raised (and set up) the problem of the origin of wealth, which mercantilists had relegated to the premises of economic reasoning, considering existing wealth as a given. The primary limitation is that of having pointed only to agriculture, to a gift of nature, as the origin of wealth itself.

In Short

Christian Europe disintegrated between 1517 and 1648. Although the causes were numerous, one prevailed over the others: religion, once a unifying factor, became the cause of wars. In 1648, the Westphalian treaties were signed. The absolute State was born in order to put an end to the wars of religion and to guarantee peace. The new order rested on two pillars: the absolute internal sovereignty of States and their balance of power in external relations.

Between the mid-seventeenth and mid-eighteenth centuries, a Europe of despotic monarchies developed, paying homage to the king as the embodiment of law and the State. Mercantilism contributed to the formation of a Europe of despotic monarchies by elaborating and spreading the doctrine of the State as "controller" of the economy. Despotic absolutism fell under the severe blows of a failed experience – that of French agriculture devastated by Colbert's politics and that of English industry paralysed by the rigid constraints of the Statute of Apprentices – along with stringent criticism from physiocrats. In the second half of the eighteenth century, a Europe of enlightened monarchies developed which tried to apply the reforms devised by the physiocrats. Physiocracy contributed to the rise of a Europe of enlightened monarchies by proposing the doctrine of a "strong" State able to impose an economic natural order.

Both mercantilism and physiocracy contributed to the formation of a Europe of absolute monarchies where the great founding values changed profoundly: people enjoyed greater negative freedom (especially to trade) but less positive freedom (in the passage from commune-states to absolute monarchies); work and wealth became an expression of success or servitude; guilds became cages under government control; and community life declined. While in the Middle Ages everyone (individuals, communities and institutions) was called upon to contribute to the common good, in modern Europe this function was assumed by a sovereign endowed with absolute power. Individualism and absolutism became the two dominant features of modern Europe.

The hidden lesson during this era is that fundamental freedoms, such as religious or economic freedoms, cannot be violated or constrained without triggering a revolt that destroys the established order, whether it be medieval Christianity or subsequent despotic absolutism.

Notes

1 On the history of modern Europe, see Luzzatto (1934, 1960), Cipolla (1974), Schulze (1996), Blanning (2007), Greengrass (2015). On modern economic thought, see Zagari (2000), Bruni and Zamagni (2004), Bruni (2018).
2 See Berggren and Trägårdh (2011).
3 On the role of Catholicism and Protestantism in the formation of the spirit of Southern and Northern capitalism, see Bruni (2018), who takes up the work of Fanfani (1935). See also Bruni and Milbank (2019) and Santori (2021).
4 Kissinger (2014: 23) states:

> Richelieu's design would endure through vast upheavals. For two and a half centuries – from the emergence of Richelieu in 1624 to Bismarck's proclamation of the German Empire in 1871 – the aim of keeping Central Europe (more or less the territory of contemporary Germany, Austria, and northern Italy) divided remained the guiding principle of French foreign policy.

5 An important thinker, predating Hobbes, was Jean Bodin (1529–1596).
6 See Anderson (1979) and Hermet (1997: 33–34).

3

CLASSICAL POLITICAL ECONOMY AND A EUROPE OF LIBERAL NATION-STATES (1776–1870)

Introduction

Lucien Febvre (1944–1945 [1999]: 224–225, my translation from Italian) writes:

> And suddenly Europe was no longer spoken of as a homeland, as the home-
> land. It was spoken of only as the nation, and everything that it produced
> was national ... We saw this when, in 1789, everything that was royal became
> national. The army was national; the Assembly, national; finances, national;
> war, national; even the parish priests had to be national.

In only a few decades, we witnessed the epochal transition from a Europe
of absolute monarchies to a Europe of liberal nation-states, from Absolutism to
Liberalism. The years between 1776 and 1870 (two more symbolic dates) saw the
full emergence of a liberal Europe. In 1776, Turgot's physiocratic attempt to save
the *ancien régime* from bankruptcy failed. That same year the American Revolution
broke out, acting as a prologue to the French Revolution of 1789: enlightened
absolutism imploded and national sovereignty became the new principle of legitimacy proclaimed in France and exported to Europe on the bayonets of marching
armies. In revolutionary theory and practice, the old mercantilist credo resurfaced,
according to which, in the international arena, the national interest is defended by
aggressive protectionist policies. Following the defeat of Napoleon Bonaparte, the
Congress of Vienna restored the old social order based on the balance of power
between "legitimate" sovereigns. But the Revolution re-exploded in Europe in the
spring of 1848 and was still an uprising of peoples yearning for national independence. The process of forming a Europe of nation-states culminated in the unification of Germany and Italy in September 1870.

DOI: 10.4324/9781003188889-3

The years from 1776 to 1870 also comprised the golden age of classical political economy. In 1776, the year of the American Revolution, Adam Smith published *The Wealth of Nations*, the masterpiece that founded modern economic science and revolutionised European economic culture. Smith's thinking spread rapidly in England and on the continent. The Classical School was born, a community of economists who reflected on the nature and fate of capitalism, within which were formed two distinct and alternative streams of economic thought: an orthodox one represented by Say and Ricardo, and a heterodox one expressed by Malthus and Sismondi. In 1848, the year of the European revolution, J.S. Mill published his *Principles of Political Economy*, the work that, updated for the last time in 1870, offered a great synthesis of classical economic thought, a thought that generated a nascent liberalism as an alternative to the ever-resurgent neo-mercantilist nationalism.

In this chapter, we will try to determine what influence the ideas of the classical economists had on the formation of a Europe of liberal nation-states.[1]

We shall examine first of all revolution in Europe and resurgent nationalism, second, classical political economy and nascent liberalism, and third, a Europe of liberal nation-states.

Revolution in Europe and Resurgent Nationalism

On 8 August 1788, in a desperate attempt to get out of the serious economic crisis gripping the country, Louis XVI convened the Estates General of France. After despotic absolutism, enlightened absolutism also failed. It failed because of a crisis of legitimacy (it was no longer enough to reign in the name of God) and a consequent or parallel crisis of efficiency in governing the economy (while the court lived in opulence, the people starved to death). The enlightened reforms of the physiocrats ran aground in the swamp of the cross-vetoes of the affected classes. No one seemed to have the strength (or the authority) to impose the necessary reforms: neither the king nor his intendants.

The meeting of the Estates General became the unhoped-for occasion for revolution. On 20 June 1789, the deputies of the Third Estate (the bourgeoisie flanking the representatives of the clergy and nobility) met in the Tennis Court and swore to form a constituent National Assembly. On 4 August, in the aftermath of the storming of the Bastille on 14 July, the constituent Assembly abolished the feudal system and the Old Regime. In one night, centuries of abuses ended: *corvées*, censuses, tax privileges, rights of the nobles, personal servitude and ecclesiastical tithes. On 28 August, the Assembly, inspired by the American Declaration of Independence, adopted the "Declaration of the Rights of Man and of the Citizen". The first articles outline the principles of a new social order. In particular, Article 3 indicates national sovereignty as the new principle of legitimate power: "The nation constitutes the principle source of all sovereignty. No assembly or individual may exercise a power that does not derive expressly from the nation" (Schulze 1996: 155).

After setting out its principles, the Assembly approved reforms. These reforms were aimed at increasing internal economic freedom on the one hand and raising the level of external protection on the other. On 2 November, Church property to the value of 2 billion francs was expropriated and sold. On 14 June 1791, the Le Chapelier law was passed, abolishing the old arts and crafts guilds, banning trade unions and the right to strike, and establishing a regime of absolute freedom in the labour market. At the same time, in March that same year, a new customs tariff was approved which discouraged the import of manufactured goods produced domestically and facilitated the export of goods of secondary importance to French consumers.

A nationalistic feeling emerges among the revolutionaries. We have previously mentioned Rousseau's disappointment at the disappearance of true nationalists in Europe. In the *Philosophical Dictionary*, published by Voltaire (1764 [1900]: 132), another noble father of the Revolution, the entry "Europe" is missing altogether, but under "Fatherland" we read the following:

> To be a good patriot is to wish that one's city may be enriched by trade, and be powerful by arms. It is clear that one country cannot gain without another loses ... Such then is the human state that to wish for one's country's greatness is to wish harm to one's neighbours. He who should wish that his fatherland might never be greater, smaller, richer, poorer, would be the citizen of the world.

For Voltaire, as for Montaigne centuries earlier, a country cannot prosper except to the detriment of others. Despite reforms, the economic situation remained serious. In April 1792, the Assembly declared war on Austria and Prussia. It tried to solve its internal economic problems through external territorial expansion. On 21 January 1793, Louis XVI, who was denounced by public opinion as the real and hidden culprit of the nation's military and economic defeats, was guillotined. The European courts were appalled. Sovereigns reacted by forming the First Anti-French Coalition, led by Austria, Prussia and England. A costly war began that would force England in 1797 to suspend the gold convertibility of the pound, one of the pillars of its national economic system.

On 9 November 1799 – 18 Brumaire in the calendar of the Revolution that had broken out ten years earlier – General Napoleon Bonaparte, under the pretext of warding off a reactionary plot, abolished the Directory formed during the Terror, appointed three consuls and proclaimed himself First Consul. On that day, the French Revolution ended and Napoleon's dictatorship began.

In 1804, Napoleon crowned himself Emperor of the French and in 1806 forced Francis II to renounce the crown of the Holy Roman Empire and take the more modest title of Emperor of Austria. That same year, at the height of his success, Napoleon decreed the Continental Blockade, another restrictive measure which, by forbidding British ships to dock at French-controlled continental ports, forced the rival country to clear the land of declining fertility in order to obtain the raw materials and foodstuffs necessary to meet domestic needs. Following the disastrous Russian campaign, Napoleon was defeated in 1813 by the anti-French Sixth Coalition in the decisive Battle of Leipzig. There followed months of abdication, retirement and the decline of an Emperor who had changed history.

The Congress of Vienna in 1815, turning back the hands of history, restored the old order: the "legitimate" sovereigns returned to their thrones and undertook to maintain a "balance of power". In particular, they agreed to form a German Confederation comprising thirty-nine small states led by Metternich's Austria. Almost two centuries earlier, during the Thirty Years' War which culminated in the Peace of Westphalia, the Catholic Cardinal Richelieu, in order to defend France's national interest, had sided with the Protestant German princes against the emerging Catholic Habsburg Empire. Now, the victorious countries, in order to prevent a French *revanche*, were strengthening Habsburg Germany.

In Vienna, new understandings were born: The Holy Alliance of Austria, Prussia and Russia, which thus officially entered the "European concert", and the Quadruple Alliance, in which England also participated, to ward off possible French threats.

The most obvious result of the Congress of Vienna was the denial of the principle of national sovereignty. The revolt was not long in coming. The uprisings of 1820–1821 and 1830–1831 and, above all, the revolution that spread across Europe in 1848–1849, showed that the French lesson had not been, and could not be, forgotten: the peoples of Europe were demanding the right to national self-determination.

The neo-mercantilist nationalism that had emerged in revolutionary France resurfaced in victorious Restoration England. In 1812, in the midst of the Continental Blockade, the country had been forced to clear inferior land, which had raised the price of wheat to 126 shillings per quarter, swelling the landed estates of rich and often absentee landowners. Once Napoleon Bonaparte had been defeated and free trade with the continent had been restored, the price of grain and landed estates rapidly fell – to the delight of hard-working and enterprising industrialists. But in 1815, the English Parliament passed a law to protect agriculture, the Corn Law, aimed at halting the fall in agricultural prices and hence land rents. The interest of agriculture, it was argued, coincided with the interest of the country.

Between 1779 and 1848 – the age that Hobsbawm (1999) called "of revolution" – the national question thus emerged in Europe: nations existed and wanted to be sovereign. The historical–political problem that arises is how to regulate their relations. The choice is between a Europe of closed and aggressive nation-states and a Europe of open and cooperative nation-states.

It was during these same years that the great classical economists began their reflection.

Classical Political Economy and Nascent Liberalism

Adam Smith is the acknowledged father of classical political economy (and modern economic science). He was explicitly referred to by the other great economists of the time – Jean-Baptiste Say, David Ricardo, Thomas Robert Malthus, Jean Charles L.S. Sismondi, John Stuart Mill and many others – with one substantial difference. Keynes writes (1936: 32 and 1933: 120):

> Ricardo conquered England as completely as the Holy Inquisition conquered Spain ... If only Malthus, instead of Ricardo, had been the parent stem from which nineteenth-century economics proceeded, what a much wiser and richer place the world would be to-day!

Keynes thus reveals the substantial difference. Two souls are dwelling in the Classical School breast: an orthodox one represented by Ricardo (and Say), who describe capitalism as a self-adjusting economic system without incurring crises of general overproduction, and a heterodox one expressed by Malthus (and Sismondi) who, conversely, describe capitalism as an economic system afflicted by an auto-immune disease that, if neglected, generates periodic and serious crises arising from excessive capital accumulation.

In the following pages, we will attempt to summarise the most influential thinking of the orthodox classics, culminating in J.S. Mill's synthesis. Altogether, the classics elaborate a theory of economic development, and a consequent and coherent strategy of economic policy, which conveys a strong critique of resurgent nationalism and a powerful justification of the emerging economic liberalism.[2] The *Wealth of Nations* is a volume of over a thousand pages divided into five books. It is considered the first systematic treatise on political economy. Yet, it lacks a clear and explicit definition of both "wealth" and "political economy": Say called it a "chaos of right ideas". Nevertheless, there is an implicit vision of wealth, which is understood as a fund of material and exchangeable goods, which have the double characteristic of being tangible and therefore storable over time, and of having a market value and therefore being exchangeable with other products. The (implicit) definition of wealth is derived from the (explicit) definition of productive labour. For Smith (1776 [2005]: 270), it is productive: "the labour of the manufacturer fixes and realizes itself in some particular subject or vendible commodity, which lasts for some time at least after that labour is past", that is, work that presents the dual characteristic of materiality and exchangeability. On the other hand, work aimed at supplying services that are, by their nature, immaterial and therefore not stor-able in time is unproductive. Unproductive does not mean useless or harmful, but simply not productive of wealth understood as tangible and exchangeable goods. The (implicit) definition of political economy can be found in the title of the work: political economy is the science that studies "the nature and causes of the wealth of nations".

At the heart of it all is the question of the wealth and poverty of nations. For Smith, economic development essentially depends on two factors: labour productivity and the employment of productive labour, which in turn are related to the availability of capital.

Labour productivity, understood as the capacity to produce tangible and exchangeable goods, is associated with the "division of labour", that is, the break-down of the production process into stages and functions. Smith analyses the different and progressive forms of the division of labour: from the technical division within the factory, to the social division in the domestic and international markets. To explain the former, he uses the famous example of the pin factory, in which the manufacturing process is broken down into eighteen distinct phases entrusted to several workers. The average productivity of the work is two hundred times higher than in a traditional craftsman's workshop, that is, with the same number of working hours, two hundred times as many pins are produced. Labour productivity increases because workers' skills increase, downtime between operations is reduced and the introduction of machines that relieve and improve human labour is encouraged. A similar specialisation of production functions takes place in society. Smith (1776 [2005]: 18) is interested in explaining not only the advantages but also the origin, the limits and the ordering principle of the (social) division of labour. The origin is in the human inclination to exchange: "Nobody ever saw a dog make a fair and deliberate exchange of one bone for another with another dog". The limit is in the size of the market: in a small village where few visitors come, there is no place for the porter's trade. Anything that enlarges the market also extends the social division of labour. Again, Smith analyses the main factors that enlarge or restrict the market space. One factor is monetary stability: a stable currency, which maintains its purchasing power over time, favours internal and international trade (and vice versa). Another is a free trade regime: tariffs, quotas and any other form of protectionism restrict, *de facto*, the area of trade. A final, less intuitive factor is the availability of capital as a wage fund. A worker, Smith observes, can only specialise in the production of a good destined for the market if there is a capitalist-entrepreneur able to advance him the salary with which to buy the goods and services necessary for his livelihood. In the pre-capitalist economy, people consume what they produce; in the capitalist economy, thanks to the division of labour that is established in the market, they consume what they do not produce.

The social division of labour, like the technical division within the factory, raises the average productivity of labour, thereby increasing the wealth of nations: with the same inputs, with the same hours of work, you get more output. The mercantilists had described international trade as a zero-sum game in which a country can only win by taking away shares of the world's wealth from others. For Smith, on the other hand, trade, domestic and international, insofar as it accentuates the social division of labour, increases the overall world wealth from which all can benefit. In other words, it is a positive-sum game, a win–win activity in which everyone can potentially be a winner. Smith writes (1776 [2005]: 17):

> without the assistance and co-operation of many thousands, the very meanest person in a civilized country could not be provided, even according to, what

we very falsely imagine, the easy and simple manner in which he is commonly accommodated. Compared, indeed, with the more extravagant luxury of the great, his accommodation must no doubt appear extremely simple and easy; and yet it may be true, perhaps, that the accommodation of an European prince does not always so much exceed that of an industrious and frugal peasant, as the accommodation of the latter exceeds that of many an African king, the absolute masters of the lives and liberties of ten thousand naked savages.

Trade, both domestic and international, follows the intuitive principle of absolute advantages: each country tends to specialise in the production of goods requiring the least resources or the lowest cost of production. England only imports wine from Portugal if it incurs a higher internal cost of production.

Labour productivity is thus the first major lever of national economic development. It depends on the degree of division of labour, which in turn is related to the availability of capital.

The second major lever is the use of productive labour, that is, for the production of tangible and exchangeable goods. Smith (1776 [2005]: 270) states: "A man grows rich by employing a multitude of manufacturers; he grows poor by maintaining a multitude or menial servants". And he adds:

> The labour of some of the most respectable orders in the society is, like that of menial servants, unproductive of any value, and does not fix or realize itself in any permanent subject, or vendible commodity, which endures after that labour is past, and for which an equal quantity of labour could afterwards be procured.

The class of unproductive workers includes the sovereign and his court as well as clergymen, doctors and lawyers, and also actors, comedians and musicians.

Physiocrats considered only agricultural work to be productive because they believed that only in agriculture was a *produit net* formed. For Smith, all human labour is productive if it generates tangible and exchangeable goods, even the labour of the sterile physiocratic class. Productive labour "increases the value of the object". Productive labour, like labour productivity, depends on capital accumulation, that is, on the share of income that capitalist-entrepreneurs allocate to the wage fund rather than to the purchase of consumer goods.

Capital, for Smith (1776 [2005]: 276), is formed by saving, that is, by restraining unproductive consumption:

> Capitals are increased by parsimony, and diminished by prodigality and misconduct … Parsimony, by increasing the fund which is destined for the maintenance of productive hands, tends to increase the number of those hands whose labour adds to the value of the subject upon which it is bestowed.

Savings are always invested. In fact, capitalists transfer savings to entrepreneurs who use them to pay the wages of productive workers. In other words, the capitalists' savings are consumed, with the mediation of the entrepreneurs, by the productive workers. The fact that savings are always invested means that everything produced is always consumed; that is, there can never be a crisis resulting from an excess of global production or, which is the same thing, from a lack of global demand. Smith (1776 [2005]: 276) writes: "What is annually saved, is as regularly consumed as what is annually spent, and nearly in the same time too: but it is consumed by a different set of people".

The inquiry into the nature and causes of the wealth of nations raises the issue of the exchange value of goods. A man is rich or poor according to the goods at his disposal. In an exchange economy, each person obtains by his own labour only a small part of the goods he consumes. The rest he obtains through exchange and thus through the work of other men. A jeweller does not "consume" the diamonds he sells but if those diamonds have a high market value, in exchange for them he will be then able to obtain many goods he wishes to have. It therefore becomes essential to know the laws governing the exchange value of goods. Smith clearly distinguishes between use value and exchange value. Use value expresses the capacity of a good to satisfy a need, that is, its utility: water quenches thirst. Exchange value, on the other hand, expresses the purchasing power of a good on the market, that is, the quantity of other goods that can be obtained in exchange for it: in exchange for water, little or nothing is obtained.

Smith raises, but fails to resolve, the paradox of water and diamond. He asks why water, which is so useful, is worth nothing in the marketplace, while diamond, which is so superfluous, is worth a great deal. He deduces from this that the use value (utility) does not determine the exchange value (purchasing power) and sets out in search of a "measure" and the "cause" of the exchange value of goods.

The measure is always the quantity of other goods with which a good is exchanged on the market and thus the labour required to produce those goods. Smith defines the "measure" of the exchange value of a good as the labour that it can command, that is, that it can spare for the recipient of those goods. For example, a jeweller sells a diamond for a price equivalent to buying a house. The diamond "commands" the work that must be done to build the house and thus saves the jeweller the trouble of having to build a new house.

The "cause" of value, however, changes. In the pre-capitalist economy, where the worker is also the owner of the means of production and the land is free, "commanded labour" is determined by "embodied labour", that is, the labour time required to produce a good. Smith's example is decisive. A beaver is worth two deer simply because it takes, on average, twice as long to hunt a beaver as a deer. The labour embodied determines the labour commanded: a beaver "commands" (exchanges with) two deer simply because it "embodies" (requires) twice as much labour time. In the capitalist economy, where land is no longer free and the means of production belong to the capitalists, goods are no longer exchanged on the basis of the labour required. "Embodied labour" no longer determines "commanded labour". In fact, to the embodied labour, something more related to capital and natural resources must now be added. In this crucial logical step, an ambiguity emerges in Smith. It is not clear whether he intends to maintain that, even in the capitalist economy, labour remains the only cause of value, which then must be ceded in part to capitalists and landowners, or whether, on the contrary, he believes that value arises from the combination of three productive factors: nature, capital and labour.

Smith (1776 [2005]: 47) attempts to resolve the ambiguity by arguing that, in the capitalist economy, the labour commanded and hence the exchange value of goods is determined by the cost of production or natural price, which is equal to the sum of the normal compensations of labour, capital, and nature, or of wages, profit and rent:

> In every society, the price of every commodity finally resolves itself into some one or other, or all of those three parts; and in every improved society, all the three enter, more or less, as component parts, into the price of the far greater part of commodities. In the price of corn, for example, one part pays the rent of the landlord, another pays the wages or maintenance of the labourers and labouring cattle employed in producing it, and the third pays the profit of the farmer.

The market (or short-run) price is determined by the intersection of supply and demand but converges towards the natural (or long-run) price equal to the sum of the normal compensation of the production factors. That is, it converges towards the minimum average cost of production. The natural price is the new measure of commanded labour in the sense that, in a capitalist economy, the price of the production factors, the cost of production, determines the price of the final goods. One good is worth more than another simply because it costs more, because it requires a greater expenditure of resources. In a market economy, prices play an irreplaceable parametric role in guiding the choices of consumers and producers. The market registers the (changing) preferences of consumers and pushes producers to compete to satisfy them earlier and better than others. In this sense, an invisible hand leads individual players – motivated solely by the pursuit of their own advantage – to contribute to the common good.

In addition to coordinating consumption and production decisions, the market also fulfils a social function by making people freer and more equal. In feudal society, there were asymmetrical power relations between ruler and subjects, vassals and valvassours, lords and serfs. In the market, economic relations tend to be more impersonal and instrumental, but also more equal. In a commercial society, says Smith (1776 [2005]: 19), no one except the beggar is dependent on the benevolence of others:

> It is not from the benevolence of the butcher, the brewer, or the baker that we expect our dinner, but from their regard to their own interest. We address ourselves, not to their humanity, but to their self-love, and never talk to them

of our own necessities, but of their advantages. Nobody but a beggar chooses to depend chiefly upon the benevolence of his fellow-citizens.

The market therefore fulfils a dual economic and social function: it makes people wealthier and also freer and more equal.

Smith's analysis of the market, as we have just seen, assumes that the natural price, towards which market prices converge, coincides with the sum of the normal compensations of the productive factors. Here arises the crucial problem of income distribution between wages, profits and rents. Smith applies price theory to labour by distinguishing between a natural wage and a market wage. The first is the wage that ensures the survival of an average family with four children. It is a subsistence wage. The market wage, on the other hand, is determined by the intersection of labour supply and demand. The demand for labour is connected to the fund that capitalists allocate to workers' livelihoods (the so-called wage fund). The latter coincides with the number of workers in the market. The convergence of the market wage to the natural wage is ensured by (dramatic) population movements. The analysis of profit is different. Smith merely observes that normal profit includes a premium for the risk that the entrepreneur takes and cannot be lower than the yield offered by government bonds; otherwise, the entrepreneur would prefer to disinvest and live on an income. The profit rate tends to decline in advanced economies as capital accumulation proceeds and competition between firms increases, while it remains higher in developing countries. In the end, rent is simply the monopoly price of a scarce commodity such as land.

The economic policy proposal that emerges from *Wealth of Nations* is coherent and consistent with the stated theory of economic development. If wealth depends on labour productivity and the use of productive labour, which are in turn linked to the (technical and social) division of labour and capital accumulation, then action must be taken on those aspects of development. In concrete terms, Smith proposes a series of economic policy measures that can be summarised in a twofold course of action. On the one hand, obstacles to development must be removed by dismantling the mercantile system of constraints, controls and protections. This means deregulating and liberalising the economy. Smith proposed the reduction of customs tariffs that limit international trade, the abolition of the Poor Laws that hinder the mobility of labour, and the repeal of the Statute of Artificers which, by restricting production, limits the internal mobility of both labour and capital. On the other hand, he considers that, for political and social reasons, it is preferable not to liberalise either the credit market, regulated by usury laws, or the maritime trade market, monopolised by the Navigation Act. Moreover, the government should provide the essential public services that cannot be provided by private entrepreneurs but are essential for the proper functioning of the market: defence, justice, public order, infrastructure.

Hence, for Smith, the wealth of nations depends on labour productivity and productive labour, both of which are related to the division of labour and capital accumulation. The division of labour conforms to the principle of absolute advantages (everyone specialises in the production of goods that require a lower absolute cost) while capital is formed through savings and savings are always invested; that is, capitalism is an economic system potentially capable of developing in equilibrium. The distribution of income influences the accumulation of capital and thus economic growth. At the origin of the wealth of nations is human labour, the "source of wealth".

Smith is the first great theorist of the market understood as a spontaneous order that coordinates, through price movements, the decisions of millions of agents. In his first major work, the *Theory of Moral Sentiments*, he had presented a catalogue of human impulses and virtues. The lowest virtue was self-interest or "well-meaning selfishness" because it was tempered by sympathy, that is, the ability to empathise with the motives of others, to put oneself in their shoes. The supreme virtue was benevolence, which evoked the medieval *caritas*. Benevolence was in fact the innate desire to promote, directly and intentionally, the collective good. In the *Theory of Moral Sentiments*, Smith focuses on the higher virtues. In the *Wealth of Nations*, he wants to show how the lower virtue of self-interest also leads, albeit unintentionally, to the common good.

The *Wealth of Nations* provides a systematic explanation of primary economic phenomena: development, value, distribution, economic policy. At the heart of economic analysis is the theory of value and distribution. And it is here that the greatest fibrillation occurs. Smith proposes a circular theory of prices: he explains prices by prices. Indeed, the natural price towards which the market price converges is equal to the sum of the average or normal wages, profit and rent. But, to calculate the natural wage, we must know the prices of the consumer goods that comprise the basket of subsistence goods of an average household. To calculate the natural price of wheat, one must know it already. At the root of this aporia is Smith's "ambiguity" about what generates the value of goods in a capitalist economy in which the worker no longer owns the means of production, that is, whether the value is still generated by labour alone or whether it also flows from the contribution of nature and capital.

Say and Ricardo, following opposite directions, seek a solution.

Say comes out of the "right-wing" ambiguity with a theory of value that places the triad of productive factors on the same level and by enunciating a "law of outlets" that considers capitalism immune to crises of general overproduction.[3]

For Say, political economy is the science that studies the way in which national wealth is produced, distributed and consumed. This partition, introduced in the *Traité* of 1803, was adopted until World War II in the main manuals and treatises around the world. Social wealth encompasses all useful goods that have an exchange value (not necessarily preservable over time) and require a sacrifice. Goods are produced with the help of three agents – nature, capital and labour – and their compensations form the production costs that delimit the minimum offer price: no producer would be willing to offer a good at a price that did not cover at least the production costs. The market price converges towards the production costs, which measure the sacrifice people are willing to make in order to obtain useful goods. In a free market, competition among producers pushes the effective price to the level of the minimum price, corresponding to the production costs.

Production, for Say, is the accretion or creation of utility: all human labour that generates utility, even immaterial services, is productive. In this way, Say takes a decisive step forward from the "materiality" of both the physiocrats and Smith.

Production always finds an outlet in the market: "every supply creates its own demand". The meaning of this famous phrase, known as the "law of outlets" (*Loi des débouchés*), is that man, as long as he is on earth, will live in a condition of structural disproportion between perceived needs and available goods. In this sense, there can never be a general over-production, an excess of all the goods useful to satisfy human needs. Man, on earth, will live in a condition of perpetual scarcity and will have to wait until he returns to Eden to experience the economy of abundance. What can happen, and frequently does happen in a market economy, is a series of partial imbalances. While some goods abound, others become scarce or, as Say pointed out, some goods abound because others have failed.

The market is like a system of communicating vessels: the water that escapes from one pool pours into others. That is, in markets where there is an excess of supply over demand (an abundance of goods), prices fall, profits contract and producers, if the market is free of impediments, are urged to move to markets where there is an excess of demand (a shortage of goods) and a consequent and inverse rise in prices and profits. In this sense, each supply creates its own demand: products are exchanged for products (currency is a mere intermediary), and there is never any danger of a global imbalance. Say also applies the law of outlets to the international market. The maxim "products are exchanged for products" becomes "imports are paid for by exports". The English will not be able to export their manufactured goods to Italy if the Italians are not free to export their foodstuffs to England. In fact, only in this way will the Italians be able to obtain the necessary pounds to buy English manufactured goods: imports are paid for by exports.

For Say, the distribution of wealth is also governed by the utility of final goods. It is the demand for bread that makes the price of grain rise or fall and therefore also the land rent. Say, without admitting it, turns Smith around again: it is the price of final goods that determines the price of productive factors (and not vice versa).

Lastly, consumption is utility destruction, but there is unproductive consumption to satisfy present needs and reproductive consumption to satisfy future needs. Public spending is an unproductive consumption.

In brief, for Say, the process of production, distribution and consumption of wealth is governed by the utility that consumers attach to final goods. Economic development is limited by the availability of productive resources and by the obstacles that governments place in the way of products. Economic policy should protect freedom of trade and curb unproductive State consumption: in a competitive economy, the market price converges towards a natural price that includes the remunerations of all agents, including landowners and producers of intangible services. Say breaks out of Smith's ambiguity from the "right" by arguing that at the origin of wealth lies a triad of productive factors: nature, capital and labour. He also grasps the importance of the utility factor in the relationship between factor and commodity prices, but fails to formulate a satisfactory theory of value and falls into the same trap as the Smithian natural price.

Ricardo escapes the "left-wing" ambiguity with a pure labour theory of value.[4]

Ricardo accepts Smith's framework: economic development ultimately depends on the accumulation of capital and thus on the profit rate, which is the crucial variable in investment decisions. For this reason, he considers political economy to be the science that studies income distribution. In fact, Ricardo is only interested in studying income distribution in relation to the central problem of economic growth. In order to explain the development of profit, he believes he must reformulate the Smithian theory of value and distribution. For Ricardo, the theory of "labour embodied" value, which Smith considers valid only in a pre-capitalist economy where all the product of labour belongs to the worker, remains valid even in a capitalist economy marked by the separation of ownership of the factors of production. In fact, capital is nothing but indirect labour, expended in the past to build the plant and equipment that comprise physical capital in the hands of the capitalist-entrepreneurs, while rent does not become part of the price of goods. Rent, in fact, is the compensation paid to the owner for the use of the land. On all land an annuity is paid, which the rightful owner demands, but not on all land is a pure annuity paid. For Ricardo, the pure rent is the compensation due for the soil's natural and indestructible qualities; that is, it is a differential rent paid only on the most fertile land. In agriculture, the harsh law of diminishing returns applies. The rent is not part of the price of, say, wheat, because the price is determined by the cost of production incurred on the less fertile or marginal land on which no pure rent is paid (only a rent for the landlord's rights). If the price were lower, the marginal land could not be cultivated, there would be an excess of demand for wheat over supply and the price would rise. The price of wheat, says Ricardo (1821 [2001]: 44), tends to rise because of increasing "difficulties of production", that is, the need to cultivate less fertile land. The rent is thus the effect and not the cause of a high grain price:

> The reason then, why raw produce rises in comparative value, is because more labour is employed in the production of the last portion obtained, and not because a rent is paid to the landlord. The value of corn is regulated by the quantity of labour bestowed on its production on that quality of land, or with that portion of capital, which pays no rent. Corn is not high because a rent is paid, but a rent is paid because corn is high.

Ricardo believes that he has corrected the original Smithian theory of embodied labour by making possible its extension to the capitalist economy characterised by the separation of ownership of the means of production. Like wheat, other commodities are exchanged on the basis of the labour, direct and indirect, required to produce them, while rent is only an effect, and not a component, of price. Ricardo believes he has thus solved the value paradox that Smith had stumbled upon: water has little or no exchange value simply because it is a free good, which everyone can obtain without having to employ labour, while diamond has a high exchange value because it requires much direct and indirect labour to be available. Ricardo notices the existence of a "curious effect", which occurs when a change in the destruction of income between wages and profits changes the exchange value between two goods with a different combination of labour and capital without changing the amount of labour contained in the two goods. But he considers it a second and secondary cause of exchange value. Stigler called this solution the 93% labour theory of value.

Ricardo introduces a key distinction, whose crucial relevance for classical economic theory and policy has perhaps not yet been fully realised. He distinguishes between domestic market and international market. In the former, the factors of production, capital and labour, circulate freely, whereas in the latter there is partial or imperfect mobility of inputs: in England, for example, workers and capital move easily from York to Birmingham while the same does not happen between England and Portugal. Ricardo welcomes the existence of limited international mobility of factors of production and hopes that everyone can continue to live in their own country. In the domestic market, goods are traded on the basis of absolute costs measured in terms of embodied labour, while in the international market they are traded on the basis of comparative production costs expressed as the ratio of the absolute cost of producing two goods within the same country.

Ricardo developed the revolutionary theory of comparative costs (or advantages). For Smith, as we have seen, the international division of labour conforms to the intuitive principle of absolute advantages: England and Portugal specialise and exchange wine (foodstuffs) and cloth (manufactured goods) only if one country produces a good at a lower absolute cost than the other. For Ricardo, on the contrary, international trade is possible and mutually beneficial even if a country is able to produce both goods at a lower absolute cost, that is, even if Portugal – which Ricardo, like a good gentleman, assumes to be superior to England – is able to produce both wine and cloth at a lower absolute cost. Each country should specialise *not* in what it does best in absolute terms (Portugal makes wine and cloth best) but in what it does *relatively* best; that is, it should specialise in the production of goods that require a lower comparative cost and therefore a lower sacrifice of the alternative good that could be produced with the resources devoted to the production of the chosen good.

The "miracle" of international trade (or trade gains) is that, with the same inputs, more output is obtained from which the trading countries can benefit, often to varying degrees. The crucial hypothesis is that there is an imperfect mobility of production factors in the international market; otherwise, the Smithian principle of absolute advantages applies again and all production (of wine and cloth) is relocated to Portugal. The economic message is revolutionary. If there is an imperfect international mobility of production factors, only one economic freedom is needed to maximise global and national gains from international trade: that of trade in goods and services. If, on the other hand, perfect international mobility of both inputs and outputs is established – what we now call economic globalisation – the international market becomes equal to the domestic market, individual countries become like regions of the same state, and in order to maximise global and national wealth, the sole freedom to trade goods and services is no longer sufficient.

The example of Ricardo is enlightening and worth quoting briefly. Let us suppose that in Portugal, 80 workers are needed to produce 1 unit of wine and 90 workers are needed to produce 1 unit of cloth, while in England, 120 and 100 workers are needed, respectively. Portugal, as we can see, has an absolute advantage in the production of both goods: to produce 1 unit of wine requires 120 workers in England and only 80 in Portugal, while to produce 1 unit of cloth requires 100 workers in England and only 90 in Portugal. So there do not seem to be any conditions for specialisation and exchange. Things change if we look at comparative costs (and the terms of trade). The comparative cost of wine is 0.88 (= 80/90) in Portugal and 1.2 (= 120/100) in England: producing 1 unit of wine means, in fact, giving up 0.88 units of cloth in Portugal (the quantity that can be obtained by employing 80 workers) and 1.2 units of cloth in England (the quantity that can be obtained by employing 120 workers). The comparative cost of cloth is 1.12 (= 90/80) in Portugal and 0.83 in England (= 100/120). Portugal has an absolute advantage in the production of both goods but has a comparative advantage in the production of wine just as England has a comparative advantage in the production of cloth.

The two countries are better off specialising in the production of the good that requires a lower comparative cost and importing the other: Portugal is better off specialising in wine production and England in cloth production. For example, if the terms of trade were 1 (1 unit of wine = 1 unit of cloth), Portugal could obtain 1 unit of cloth, which requires 90 workers at home, by giving up 1 unit of wine, which only requires 80 workers. Portugal is better off importing cloth from England, rather than producing it domestically, simply because it is cheaper: it costs the labour of the 80 workers needed to produce 1 unit of wine to exchange for 1 unit of English cloth. They cost 80 workers instead of 90. Equally, England could obtain 1 unit of wine, which employs 120 workers at home, by giving up 1 unit of cloth, which only requires 100 workers.

Thus, in the international market, the labour of 80 Portuguese (necessary to produce 1 unit of wine) can be exchanged with the labour of 100 English (necessary to produce 1 unit of cloth): "Such an exchange – writes Ricardo (1821 [2001]: 91) – could not take place between the individuals of the same country. The labour of 100 Englishmen cannot be given for that of 80 Englishmen" (goods are exchanged according to the content of labour or absolute cost in the domestic market). In Ricardo's example, we can see the "miracle of trade", the so-called gains from trade.

The "miracle" can also be seen from another, more problematic perspective: the same output is obtained with fewer inputs (see Montani 1996). If the two countries choose self-sufficiency instead of exchange, then to produce 1 unit of cloth and 1 unit of wine, England needs 220 men (100 + 120) and Portugal 170 men (80 + 90) for a total of 390 men. If, on the other hand, they choose an exchange, England employs 200 men (to produce 2 units of cloth) and Portugal 160 workers (to produce 2 units of wine) for a total of 360 men. If, in the end, the barriers to the free movement of inputs fall, the international market becomes like the domestic market and all wine and cloth production is located in Portugal: in this case, only 340 men (170 × 2) would be sufficient. Here is the "problematic miracle": economic efficiency increases but geographical imbalances arise between a region that is populated (Portugal) and one that is depopulated (England).

With the renewed theory of value, Ricardo can finally reformulate the theory of income distribution (which he considers the heart of economic science) and predict the fate of capitalism. According to Ricardo, in the absence of appropriate economic policies, capitalism tends to slide into a steady state, an economic scenario in which capital accumulation and hence wealth growth is halted. In the background, we can see the political events of England at the time, forced to limit the import of raw materials and foodstuffs, first by the Napoleonic Blockade and then by the protectionist Corn Laws passed by Her Majesty's Parliament. A country unable to obtain supplies from abroad, where the population increases, is forced to cultivate the land of decreasing fertility: the cost of production on marginal (less fertile) land increases, the cost of living rises, real wages remain at a historically determined subsistence level and the increase in rents, by squeezing profit margins, reduces the propensity to invest, pushing the economy towards a stationary state.

Ricardo outlines an organic economic policy to save capitalism from the spectre of stagnation. The intermediate objective, functional to the final one, is to widen the profit margins necessary to reactivate the process of capital accumulation. The agenda comprises four main economic policy actions appropriate for every country.

First of all, the country needs a free trade policy, including the abolition of the Corn Laws passed by Parliament in 1815 to stop the fall in agricultural prices following the end of the Continental Blockade. Import restrictions had forced the British to farm less fertile land, causing rents to rise and profits to be squeezed. The same restrictions had prevented continental countries from exporting agricultural products to England and then importing English manufactured goods. Free trade would have solved the double problem: England could have bought cheap grain from the continent and could have sold manufactured goods on the continent at competitive prices.

Second, a monetary policy geared to exchange rate stability and domestic price flexibility is needed. To ensure the gold convertibility of sterling, Ricardo proposes imposing a quantitative limit on paper circulation so that the total money supply varies in relation to the availability of gold reserves (price-species flow mechanism).

Third, Ricardo suggests a fiscal policy of balancing the public budget. In fact, it is equivalent to financing public expenditure by deficit or by tax increases. In the first case, taxpayers know that they will have to pay more taxes in the future: they will therefore increase their propensity to save, cancelling out the expansionary effect of public spending (the so-called Ricardian equivalence). Moreover, a tax system that does not penalise profit-earners is necessary.

Lastly, he recommends a welfare policy outside the market that does not interfere with the decisions of economic agents. Ricardo (1821 [2001]: 68) is against the poor laws and criticises the experience of cooperative villages:

> instead of making the poor rich, they are calculated to make the rich poor; and whilst the present laws are in force, it is quite in the natural order of things that the fund for the maintenance of the poor should progressively increase, till it has absorbed all the net revenue of the country, or at least so much of it as the state shall leave to us, after satisfying its own never failing demands for the public expenditure.

Poverty is combated by economic development and a form of public assistance can only be justified in extreme cases.

Ricardo accepts Smith's theory of economic development but corrects the underlying theory of value and distribution. The most significant change, for our purposes, is the introduction of the revolutionary principle of comparative advantage. The economic message is that international trade is inclusive, generates wealth and creates mutual benefits. Both strong (efficient) and weak (less efficient) countries can benefit from international trade. Each has the advantage of specialising not in what it does best in absolute terms but in what it does relatively best: wine in Portugal and cloth in England. The political message is that it is possible to harmonise and reconcile national interests. Both England and Portugal defend their national interest by opening up to trade and economic integration. International trade makes it possible to maximise global wealth and national wealth at the same time. This is subject to two basic conditions: that the canons of classical economic policy are respected and that there is relative international immobility of the factors of production.

In 1848, the year of the Revolution in Europe, Mill published his *Principles of Political Economy*, which was to remain the Bible of economics until Alfred Marshall's treatise appeared in 1890. Mill presented himself as a simple systematiser of the classical citadel, of which he only wanted to build the bridges and clear the roads. In reality, however, he tears down walls and opens up new paths. Mill is an innovator, an "orthodox heretic".[5]

Mill, like Say, considers political economy to be the science that studies the production, distribution and consumption of national wealth. Smith and Ricardo, as we have seen, considered production and distribution inseparable. Indeed, the distribution of income, especially in Ricardo's view, had to be functional to the accumulation of capital and thus to economic development. For Mill, on the other hand, production and distribution of wealth can and must be separated. Production must conform to the strict laws of the market and favour, as far as socially possible, the accumulation of capital. But, once things have been produced, they can be redistributed according to criteria of greater or lesser equity established by human institutions. Mill writes (1848 [2009]: 182):

> The laws and conditions of the Production of Wealth partake of the character of physical truths. There is nothing optional or arbitrary in them. It is not so with the Distribution of Wealth. That is a matter of human institution solely. The things once there, mankind, individually or collectively, can do with them as they like. They can place them at the disposal of whomsoever they please, and on whatever terms. The Distribution of Wealth depends on the laws and customs of society.

Production, Mill argues, always takes place with the use of two original factors: labour and natural resources. Like Ricardo, he distinguishes between direct and indirect labour and, like Say, tends to value intangible services. By productive labour, Mill means those kinds of activities which produce utilities embedded in material objects: The teacher who trains a worker to produce material goods is indirectly productive, while workers such as actors, singers and preachers, who have no connection with the production of tangible goods, remain unproductive.

Still on the subject of production, Mill makes a decisive contribution to the classical theory of international trade and thus to the patterns of productive specialisation of individual countries. The specific contribution concerns the way in which the gains from trade are distributed among trading countries, but in reality Mill re-exploits, in a brilliant and persuasive way, the entire Ricardian theory of comparative advantages. First of all, he makes it clear that, for a country, the direct advantage, even "the only direct advantage" of foreign trade, consists in the possibility of importing goods which it would otherwise not have or which it would have to produce at a higher cost. The advantage is therefore in imports and not, as mercantilists wrongly claim, in exports. The value of a good always depends on its cost: but the cost of an imported good corresponds to the cost of the exported good given in exchange, and it is this cost that is lower than the domestic cost of production. In Ricardo's example, Portugal pays for the import of English cloth with the export of Portuguese wine by incurring a lower cost (80 workers) than that required to produce domestic cloth (90 workers). The gains from trade are shared between the two countries according to the terms of trade, which may be more or less favourable to one country/good or the other. Mill (1848 [2009]: 463) clarifies that the terms of trade depend on the reciprocal demand for goods expressed by the two trading countries:

> It may be considered, therefore, as established, that when two countries trade together in two commodities, the value of exchange of these commodities relatively to each other will adjust itself to the inclinations and circumstances of the consumers on both sides, in such manner that the quantities required

by each country, of the articles which it imports from its neighbor, shall be exactly sufficient to pay for one another.

Mill then addresses the issue of the distribution of the income produced among wages, rents and profits: wages are the compensation for work, rents are the landowner's compensation for the increased fertility of the land, and profits are the capitalist's compensation for foregoing present consumption. Mill innovates the theory of the wage fund already outlined by Adam Smith. The market wage, as we have seen, is the quotient between the "wage fund" made available by capitalists and the number of workers in the market. The lesson that Mill draws and, above all, imparts is that in the short-run trade unions can do nothing and must accept the market wage that ensures full employment. In the long run, on the other hand, workers' representatives should fight for an increase in the supply of labour (linked to demographic dynamics) that is proportional to the increase in the demand for labour (linked to the increase in the wage fund).

In a book published in 1869, another classical economist, W. T. Thornton, argued that the theory of the wage fund lent itself to anti-union use by prefiguring a bronze law of wages. Reviewing the book, Mill conceded that, through appropriate redistributive policies, it was possible to increase the wage fund and thus raise wages without reducing employment. In particular, the fund could be increased by tax policies aimed at hitting luxury consumption and raising the propensity of capitalists to save, and by measures to encourage workers' participation in company profits and the formation of cooperative enterprises which, by their nature, tend to set aside profits to be reinvested in production.

Lastly, with reference to the final act of consumption, Mill, unlike Ricardo, considers the stationary state a positive scenario. With the increase in wealth, generated by capitalism, basic human needs are amply satisfied; the penury of saving, and thus the compensation for abstinence from present consumption, is reduced; and the economic system settles into a state of quiet or simple reproduction (today we would say of happy degrowth) in which, after having solved the problem of maximum production, it will be possible to solve the problem of the best distribution of national wealth.

Mill's analysis reinforces the economic policy strategy outlined by Ricardo. Development depends on the international division of labour and capital accumulation. Each country should specialise in the production of goods that require a lower comparative cost. Exchange is possible and mutually beneficial if there is a gap in comparative costs and if the terms of trade (the relative price) take on a value intermediate to the gap. The terms of trade depend on reciprocal demand and fluctuate by keeping trade balances in equilibrium. If, for example, a country runs a trade deficit, the relative price (the terms of trade) increases, imports decrease, exports increase and the trade balance returns to equilibrium. Money does not alter this mechanism. It simply envelops it in a veil. The trade deficit causes an outflow of money, a reduction in domestic prices and a consequent rebalancing of the trade balance – as if money did not exist. The external balance of payments equilibrium is thus automatically ensured by a mechanism, devised by Hume and Ricardo, known as the price-species-flow mechanism.

In particular, the idea that two major social institutions are needed to ensure balanced and stable (today we would say sustainable) economic development is reinforced: a free trade regime and a gold-based monetary system. In this sense, Mill is orthodox. However, he is also a heretic: after having defended a redistributive policy in favour of workers, he also legitimised a partial protectionist policy by circumscribing the cases in which it could be justified, starting with the temporary protection of infant industries.

There are three major "heresies" of Mill with respect to the earlier or contemporary classical tradition. The first is the distinction between production, subject to the naturalistic laws of the market, and distribution, open to voluntary human decisions. The second is the interpretation of the stationary state of zero growth as a positive scenario in which to operate a better distribution of wealth. The last is a more discretionary economic policy that justifies an economic role for trade unions and cooperation, the use of redistributive measures in favour of the poorer classes and the adoption of protectionist measures for economic growth. Mill is considered the initiator of modern liberalism which, unlike classical liberalism, is rigidly anchored to the respect of certain rules (free trade and gold standard) and prefigures and justifies partial discretionary government interventions in the economy.

In short, the main political message of the classics, for the topic at hand, is that national interests are defended by developing a free and integrated world market. Economic nationalism, by contracting international trade, ultimately harms national interests themselves. International market cooperation can only develop with appropriate social institutions, which can be traced back to a free-trade regime and a gold-based monetary system. These institutions promote economic development in line with the spontaneous division of labour and capital accumulation, on the crucial assumption that there is an imperfect mobility of labour and capital in the international market.

The classics offer a systematic explanation of the functioning of an abstract market economy and a concrete capitalist system, that preceding the first globalisation at the end of the nineteenth century. The main limitations concern the labour theory of value, taken up by Marx and abandoned by neoclassical economists, the failure to distinguish between "absolute and relative" gains from international trade (everyone gains but some more than others and inequality grows) and the underestimation of the effects of free international trade in the case of perfect mobility of production factors, that is, the phenomenon that would later be called economic globalisation.

A Europe of Liberal Nation-States

The Vienna order (or system) began to crumble with the Crimean War of 1853–1856, which broke the (Holy) alliance between Austria, Prussia and Russia. After the Crimean War, Napoleon III's France and Bismarck's Prussia tried to demolish the Vienna order. Kissinger (1995: 104) writes:

> Napoleon III hated the Vienna system because it had been expressly designed to contain France ... Bismarck resented Metternich's handiwork because it locked Prussia into being Austria's junior partner in the German Confederation, and he was convinced that the Confederation preserved so many tiny German sovereigns that it shackled Prussia. If Prussia were going to realize its destiny and unify Germany, the Vienna system had to be destroyed.

The political order of Vienna finally dissolved at the Battle of Sedan on 2 September 1870, with the victory of Bismarck's Germany and the capitulation of Napoleon III's France.

Between 1776 and 1870, in just under a century, we witnessed the epochal transition from a Europe of absolute monarchies to a "Concert" Europe of liberal nation-states, from enlightened absolutism to national liberalism.

The ideas of the classical economists are helping to change Europe. Of course, care must be taken not to fall into the trap of naive idealism: ideas alone cannot change the world. Enlightened absolutism, like despotic absolutism, implodes because it dashes the population's hopes for prosperity and freedom. There is, first of all, a failure of experience, which reason records and validates.

Classical economists accompany and evaluate Europe's transformation process. It is not easy to document the political influence of the classics. But there was an influence. The classics helped to eradicate, in English and continental public opinion, the belief that agrarian protectionism was in the interests of the nation. In 1836 Richard Cobden, a staunch follower of Ricardo, founded the Anti-Corn Law Association, which waged a long and successful campaign for the repeal of the Corn Laws. Cobden himself, together with the French economist Chevalier, drafted the trade treaty between England and France in 1860 that opened the short but intense season of free trade in Europe. Moreover, influential economists, such as Ricardo and Mill, sat in Parliament and other economists held important political posts.

Liberal Europe is very much like the Europe envisaged by classical economists.

Between 1776 and 1870, the historic liberalisation of the European economy took place. First, the internal barriers, which hindered the free movement of labour and capital, fell; then the external barriers, which restricted the free movement of goods, were torn down. An economic revolution began in the two leading countries – France and England – but in different ways. In France, it began from the top, with a rationalistic act of empire: the 1791 Le Chapelier law cancelled the arts and crafts guilds and banned all associations for economic purposes. In England, on the other hand, the revolution began from below with the peaceful circumvention of the Statute of Artificers – Einaudi calls it the "outburst" – followed by its formal abrogation in 1813–1814. Still in England, in 1832, Parliament approved the New Poor Law, a measure prepared by a commission chaired by the classical economist

Senior, which, by restricting public assistance to the workhouses, drove floods of poor people towards the factories in the cities. Einaudi (1949 [1975]: 127–128, my translation from Italian) writes:

> The outlet was found in two typically different ways. One is the revolutionary means, French-style. After a first attempt at abolition made by the minister Turgot in 1776 and soon disavowed by the weak Louis XVI, the Chapelier law of 1791 abolished them definitively at the time of the revolution and, going ahead in reaction to the abuses of corporatist decadence, declared illicit any kind of workers' or employers' association aimed at achieving a variation in working conditions, an increase in prices or, similarly, by abandoning work (strike) or closing factories (lock-out). The other way is the typically English way of peaceful circumvention.

External liberalisation began in England and spread across the continent along the dual lines of free trade and the gold standard. In 1846 England repealed the Corn Laws and in 1849 the Navigation Act, the two symbols of protectionism, and in 1860 it stipulated a free trade treaty with France that inspired similar measures in other European countries. This is how Luzzatto (1960: 280, my translation from Italian) recalls the years following the publication of Smith's *Wealth of Nations*:

> In the ten years following the first publication of his work, it seemed that a wide breach was to be made in the British commercial system, and in 1786, under the presidency and at the express will of Pitt junior, a passionate and convinced reader of the *Wealth of Nations*, the Treaty of Eden was concluded with France, which, by abolishing the old discriminations against French imports, and in particular against wines, tripled in three years the trade between France and England. Perhaps we would have proceeded even more courageously along the same path if the Revolution and the state of war which lasted for 22 years between the two countries had not only precluded any possibility of new applications of the principle of freedom of trade, but with the blockade and counterblockade had not brought back into force the most prohibitive methods of past times.

At the end of the war, while Ricardo, with the aforementioned theory of comparative costs, was laying the scientific foundations of the theory of international trade and thereby gaining new adherents to the principle of freedom of trade, an ever-sharper conflict emerged in this relationship between the interests of industry in rapid transformation and development and the interests of agriculture. Agriculture, in the name of which, at the beginning of the eighteenth century, the reaction against mercantilism had begun, accused of stifling it in order to help the often-artificial development of industry, now felt the need to be protected against the threatening fall in prices, while big industry felt the damage caused to it by the narrowness of the market, by the obstacles which stood in the way of its expansion, increasing day by day.

In the mid-nineteenth century, England, the only large industrial country in the world, felt the vital need to have a free and large continental market in which to procure the necessary raw materials and foodstuffs and in which to place its abundant industrial production. The countries of the continent, in order to buy British manufactured goods, had to be put in a position to sell their agricultural products to the British. In other words, the Corn Laws had to be abolished which, by limiting the ability of the continental countries to export agricultural products to England, also limited their ability to import English manufactures. This was the favourite argument of the Cobden League: "the League availed itself of all legal means of agitation", writes Luzzatto (1960: 284, my translation from Italian),

> newspapers, pamphlets, conferences, rallies. Having entered the House of Commons in 1842, Cobden, who could already count on a large current of public opinion throughout England, declared that he did not wish to bind himself to either of the two traditional parties, but demanded the acceptance of free trade from both the Whigs and the Tories. Whether it was the effect of his propaganda or for some other political reason, Sir Robert Peel, leader of the Conservative party, which had then regained power, began to convert to the cause of free trade.

After some initial hesitation, in the autumn of 1845, as fears spread of a new famine starving the people, Peel decided to abandon agricultural protectionism. In 1846 the Corn Laws were repealed and in 1849 the Navigation Act – the two symbols of English protectionism. In 1860, a free trade treaty was signed between France and England which inspired similar measures adopted by the major European countries. Luzzatto (1960: 285, my translation from Italian) remarks:

> Thus, between 1845 and 1860, both with the laws reforming the English tariff and with the trade treaties that were stipulated with France and with the other states of the continent, prepared in part by the propaganda work carried out after 1846 by Cobden himself, the triumph of free trade in England can be said to be complete, and it becomes a model that inspires, for more than twenty years, the commercial policy of most European states.

During the Restoration, a debate developed in England on the monetary question, with two schools of thought opposing each other: the Banking School and the Currency School. In 1821, the gold convertibility of sterling, which had been suspended in 1797, was restored and the country returned to a gold-based monetary system, codified in 1844 with the Bank Charter Act by Peel, inspired by Ricardo's ideas and the principles of the Currency School. The two schools agreed on the need for a monetary system based on the gold convertibility of paper money. For the Banking School, this was a necessary and sufficient condition because the banks, knowing that they had to guarantee the convertibility of banknotes into gold, would avoid issuing an excessive amount. On the other hand, for the Currency School, convertibility was a necessary but not sufficient condition because banks, trusting in the inattention of their customers, might have given in to the temptation to make a profit by lending too much. It was necessary to add, as Ricardo suggested, a quantitative limit to the issue of paper money proportional to the availability of gold reserves. Bresciani Turroni (1958, vol. II: 94, my translation from Italian) wrote:

> The theories of the "currency school" are based on the Ricardian conception according to which the *limitation of the quantity* of money in circulation is the fundamental condition for the stability of the value of money itself ... it is necessary to ensure that the quantity of banknotes in circulation varies in exactly the same absolute measure in which circulation would vary if it were made up only of gold.

The banking law passed in England in 1844 (Peel's Bank Charter Act) implemented the principles of the Currency School:

> The quantity of banknotes that could be issued without gold cover – to which corresponded English government bonds for an equal value – was fixed at 14 million pounds ... Beyond this limit each note had to be entirely covered with gold ... The Bank of England was divided into two departments: the Issuing Department, whose task was merely to regulate the issuing of notes in the above-mentioned manner, and the Banking Department, which was to deal with ordinary banking operations.
>
> *Bresciani Turroni 1958, vol. II: 97, my translation from Italian*[6]

Between 1776 and 1870, the liberal revolution spread across Europe, thanks also to the contribution of the classical economists. However, it took root and flourished in different forms, reinforcing the diverse yet common identity of the three Europes. In Western Europe (England and France), homogeneous nation-states were consolidated, developing a policy of openness and peaceful cooperation: a form of "liberal nationalism", as Mises called it, or, if you prefer, "national liberalism". In Central and Eastern Europe, on the other hand, due to the widespread presence of strong linguistic minorities (Germans, Poles, Hungarians and Czechs scattered everywhere), it is impossible to build cohesive nation-states. A twofold solution to the national question emerged: after the defeat at Sadowa (1866), the newly formed Austro-Hungarian Empire set out to become a multinational state, while after the victory at Sedan (1870), the newly formed Second Reich set out to establish a German nation-state.

In Short

Between 1776 and 1848, the age of revolution, the national question exploded in Europe and a nationalistic solution emerged in the thought of the influential fathers of the Enlightenment and the French Revolution (Voltaire and Rousseau) and also in the political choices of both the revolutionary French government and Queen Victoria's British government.

Between 1776 and 1848, the great classical economists – Smith, Say, Ricardo and Mill – developed a theory of economic development and a consequent, coherent strategy of economic policy that conveyed a central political message: a European order based on free trade and the gold standard was in the interests of everyone, that is, of individual nations and of Europe as a whole. Cooperation is worthwhile and possible. It is worthwhile because the international division of labour maximises global and national wealth. It is only possible if common rules and institutions are respected and, above all, on the crucial assumption that limited international mobility of production factors is maintained. The dismantling of the mercantile system and the internal and external liberalisation of the economy transformed Europe into a collection of cooperating nation-states.

What role, then, did the ideas of the classical economists play in the epochal transition from a Europe of absolute monarchies to a concerted Europe of liberal nation-states?

According to Lucien Febvre, the Restoration failed to realise that, after the advent of nations, it was no longer possible to return to the Europe of kings. From what we have seen, we can perhaps affirm that the classical economists contributed to the formation of a Europe of liberal nation-states, first by refuting the myths of mercantilist and physiocratic absolutism and then by developing the principles of a harmonious spontaneous order. The classics, starting with Smith, demonstrate the fallacy both of the mercantilist creed, according to which a kingdom becomes rich by accumulating precious metals through a protectionist policy, and of the physiocratic doctrine, which assigns to the enlightened sovereign, endowed with absolute power, the task of realising a predefined economic order, existing in nature. The classics, again starting with Smith and in parallel with the theorists of constitutionalism, elaborated and spread (in Europe and elsewhere) the idea that, under certain conditions, an economic order can be achieved that enables the harmony of individual and national interests. The basic condition is the presence of institutions, both formal and informal, that protect individual, and in particular economic, freedom of action and cooperation among nation-states by establishing appropriate trade and monetary agreements.

In the century of revolutions, partly due to the influence of the classical economists, the constituent values of Europe changed. *Libertas* became more individualistic, no longer bound to the direct and intentional pursuit of the common good by each subject. After the end of the *ancien régime*, the sphere of both negative liberty (with the recognition of economic rights) and positive liberty (with the progressive extension of political rights) was enlarged, but new trade-offs arose: for example, the freedom of economic enterprise corresponded to the prohibition to form workers' associations (which would only be restored in 1871). The idea, almost the ideal, according to which each person, by pursuing his own advantage, contributes, indirectly and unintentionally, to the common good of society, was affirmed. The transformation of private interest into general interest is entrusted to an invisible and impersonal mechanism, the market, which coordinates individuals' consumption and production decisions. Human labour (*opus*) becomes the source of wealth or a factor of production alongside capital. Lastly, the community (*communitas*) also underwent a transformation, with the decline of corporations and communes and the rise of nations which some, decades later, would define as "imaginary communities" – but communities nonetheless.

One lesson we can draw from this story is that, under certain conditions, cooperation between nation-states (and among individuals) is possible and mutually beneficial.

Notes

1 On the history of liberal Europe, see Schulze (1996), Hobsbawm (1999), Blanning (2007), Evans (2017), Zamagni (2017). For an overview of classical political economy, see Roggi (1978), O'Brien (1984), Landreth and Colander (1994, Part II), and Montani (1996).
2 On Adam Smith's life and work, see Phillipson (2010).
3 On J.-B. Say (1767–1832), see Schoorl (2013).
4 On David Ricardo (1772–1823), see Weatherall (2011).
5 On J.S. Mill (1806–1873), see Capaldi (2009).
6 On Ricardo's monetary theory, see Marcuzzo and Rosselli (1990).

4

NEOCLASSICAL ECONOMICS *VS.* ETATISM AND A EUROPE OF EMPIRES (1871–1918)

Introduction

In 1871, the British statesman Benjamin Disraeli, a contemporary of Bismarck, commented on the German victory over France: "The war represents the German revolution, a greater political event than the French Revolution of the last century" (Kissinger 1995: 134).

Before 1871, as we have seen, the European order had always rested on two pillars, more or less solid and visible: the medieval order on divine legitimacy and fragmented sovereignty (a stateless society); the Westphalian order on the balance of forces between sovereigns legitimised to exercise absolute power by the need to ensure peace (the Leviathan); and lastly, the Vienna order on a Concert of nation-states re-legitimised to rule by tradition (by the grace of God) and by national interest (by the will of the nation).

With the unification of Germany, a New European Order was in fact born: an order without divine or popular legitimacy that rested only on a precarious balance of power among the five great powers that had survived the Napoleonic tornado: Austria-Hungary, Germany, Russia, France and Great Britain. The order held as long as Bismarck ruled, but when, in 1890, the Iron Chancellor was forced to resign by the new Kaiser Wilhelm II, the order first faltered and then imploded. Between 1871 and 1918, in only fifty years, Europe went from being a concert of cooperating nation-states to a theatre of war among warring factions.

In those same years, between 1871 and 1918, a parallel battle of ideas was fought between a new orthodoxy, neoclassical economics, and a new heresy, historicist and Marxist etatism, both claiming descent from a common classical tradition.

In this chapter, we ask what influence the great economic ideas had on the epochal transition from a Europe of peaceful nations to a Europe of belligerent

DOI: 10.4324/9781003188889-4

empires.[1] We shall examine first of all the decline of Liberal Europe, second, Neoclassical economics and Etatism, and third, a Europe of empires at war.

The Decline of Liberal Europe

The 1870s were marked by a profound political and economic crisis and a consequent and final turning point in economic policy. Prior to German unification, the European order had rested on the Concert of Five Great Powers: Austria, Prussia and Russia, united in the Holy Alliance; Great Britain, returned to "splendid isolation" but ready to intervene, with the Quadruple Alliance, to defend the European balance; and France, returned to its "legitimate" sovereigns.

The founding of the Second Reich breaks the "peaceful spell" and generates a series of latent conflicts. Germany came into direct conflict with France and Austria. From the former, beaten on the battlefield of Sedan, it took Alsace-Lorraine, triggering a desire for *revanche* that would dramatically mark twentieth-century European history. The second, excluded from the Germanic Confederation, took away the leadership of the German world, triggering a competition for hegemony in Central Europe. Lastly, by forcing Austria to seek expansion into the Balkan area, a united Germany indirectly generated a conflict between Austria and Russia, which was also interested in the Balkans as a gateway to the Mediterranean. In the spring of 1877, the Russo-Turkish war broke out over control of territories belonging to the Ottoman Empire. The war ended the following year with the birth of new states – Serbia, Romania, Montenegro, Bulgaria – which broke away from the Ottoman Empire but entered the Russian orbit. The balance of power threatened to break down.

During the same years, Europe was shaken by a severe and unprecedented economic crisis known as the "Great Depression of 1873". The crisis began in 1873 and lasted until 1896. But it is a strange crisis, which could perhaps be described as a crisis of growth or, in Schumpeterian terms, of the "creative destruction" of capitalism. On the one hand, European agriculture was in crisis because of American and Russian competition and parallel deflation, but on the other hand, new product and process innovations were adopted that marked the beginning of the second industrial revolution.

Germany is at the epicentre of the political and economic crisis and the resulting turnaround in economic policy. In 1878, Bismarck had a series of laws passed against socialists but in favour of workers: this was the start of a social policy aimed at beating the nascent workers' movement. That same year he presided over the Congress of Berlin, which was called to scale down Russian conquests in the Balkans and to reshape Europe. The Congress marked a turning point in the economic order. Until then, European nations had limited themselves to acquiring raw materials and foodstuffs from regions in Africa and Asia on favourable terms. The Congress outlined, among the European powers, a systematic action of political subjugation and economic exploitation of the Afro-Asian area. We move from colonialism to imperialism.

Bismarck was fond of repeating that, in a world of five, it is better to be in three. And since Great Britain was isolated and France hostile, Germany was better off with Austria and Russia. In 1873, he promoted the League of the Three Emperors (of Austria, Germany and Russia). After the Congress of Berlin, aware of Russian resentment, he signed a Dual Alliance with Austria-Hungary, which later became the Triple Alliance with the accession of Italy in 1882, and at the same time concluded the Reinsurance Treaty with Russia to maintain good diplomatic relations. Lastly, in July 1879, Bismarck had a new customs tariff approved by the *Reichstag* in favour of both agriculture and industry. In 1878–1879, Bismarck and Germany were the architects of a change in European politics when they initiated the social policy, comprehensive protection (of agriculture and industry) of the national economy and political and economic imperialism.[2] This was only the beginning. Europe could still choose between openness and closure, between cooperation and antagonism, between national liberalism and nationalist imperialism. But it was no longer the Europe of the Concert of open and peaceful liberal nation-states.

Neoclassical Economics and Etatism

In the early 1870s, three unknown or little-known economists published their treatises, each unbeknownst to the other. In 1871, the *Fundamental Principles of Economics* by the Austrian Carl Menger (1840–1921) was published, as well as *The Theory of Political Economy* by the Englishman William Stanley Jevons (1835–1882), and three years later, in 1874, of *Elements of Pure Political Economy* by the Frenchman Léon Walras (1834–1910).

While Disraeli was well aware of the political revolution that Bismarck effected before his very eyes, few economists realised the revolutionary significance of those treaties. The 1870s were still dominated by classical political economy in public and scientific debate. Then, the revolution exploded, under the name of "marginalism". Historians still wonder whether it was a real revolution, what links it maintained with the classical tradition and why it exploded almost a decade late.

In those same early 1870s, another uprising smouldered under the ashes. In the spring of 1871, the Paris Commune was born and on which Marx commented in *The Civil War in France*. Marx was already known as the author, together with Engels, of the 1848 *Manifesto of the Communist Party*, as the inspirer of the First Workers' International founded in London in 1864 and as the author of the First Book of *Capital*, which appeared in 1867. In 1871, he began work on a new edition of the First Book, to be published in 1873, and continued to influence the internal and external affairs of the emerging workers' movement by proposing a revolutionary solution to the social question. In October 1872, a group of German economists, known as "chair socialists", founded the *Verein für Sozialpolitik* (Association for Social Policy) in Eisenach, a small German town, outlining a reformist or interventionist perspective to the same social question.

In 1871, the English Parliament passed the Trade Union Act, a law that fully legalised trade unions and strengthened the action of the organised labour movement.

What took place between 1871 and 1918 was a complex battle of ideas, perhaps even more enigmatic than the one fought between the chancelleries of the main European capitals. To the acknowledged founders of the marginalist orientation – Jevons, Menger and Walras – we should add a fourth, the Cantabrigian Alfred Marshall (1842–1924), who in the early 1870s distributed among friends and colleagues some writings of marginalist inspiration, which then merged into the major work that appeared in 1890. The initiators were also the founders of distinct, authoritative and influential schools of economic thought. Menger is the founder of the Austrian School, which was joined over time by Böhm Bawerk, von Wieser, von Mises, von Hayek (Nobel Prize for Economics in 1974) and many contemporary economists. Walras was the founder of the Lausanne School, which was joined by Vilfredo Pareto and, after him, by other economists attracted by the rigour of mathematics. Lastly, Marshall, who compared himself with his fellow countryman Jevons, was the founder of the Cambridge School, which trained J.M. Keynes and, with him, a whole generation of new economists.

Space limitations make it impossible to detail the variety of approaches of the three schools, the results obtained, the obstacles overcome, the unsolved problems. In the same way, within the heretical or heterodox tradition, a heated debate develops between Marx's heirs and among the adherents of the *Verein*. Likewise, it is impossible to revisit that complex and rich debate. I will only try, in a risky attempt at synthesis, to capture some common and distinctive features of both the new marginalist or neoclassical orthodoxy and the new etatist heresy by briefly dwelling on the two economists who, within the neoclassical tradition, have exerted the greatest influence on economic culture: Carl Menger and Alfred Marshall.[3]

The common and distinctive features of neoclassical economics

What the economists of the marginalist tradition – which, starting with Marshall, became neoclassical – have in common is, first and foremost, a new method, a new way of looking at economic phenomena. The classical economists, as we know, took a holistic view of reality. To understand and explain the functioning of the market and the dynamics of capitalism, they looked at the interests and choices of three major social classes: landlords, capitalists and workers. For marginalists, on the other hand, economics is such a general science that it should also be able to explain the choices of an isolated individual. The favourite metaphor of the new economists, especially the Austrian ones, is the castaway who lands on a desert island: Robinson Crusoe. There are no social classes, there is no currency and no government. And yet *the* economic problem is very much felt, taking the essential and structural form of the scarcity of resources compared to the needs that one would like to satisfy. This is where one can understand the true nature of the science of economics, which studies man's rational choices when he must decide how to allocate the scarce resources available to satisfy a multiplicity of ends and needs. Crusoe also has to choose, possibly rationally. He must decide how much time to devote to work and how much to rest and, during work time, how much to build a boat (his capital) and how much to fish (his production of consumer goods). But, starting from the choices of an isolated individual, marginalists want to explain the functioning of an entire economic system. Thus, on the desert island, Friday and other castaways arrive who specialise in producing specific production and consumption goods that they exchange within individual markets, and the economy is conceived as a system of interconnected markets. It is a compositional method that, starting from individual choices, goes back to the functioning of the whole economic system.

The new method, known as "methodological individualism", also introduces a new object of investigation. As we have seen, the focus of the classics' analysis is on the wealth of nations and thus on long-term economic development. Smith, Ricardo and Mill are concerned with determining why some nations become richer and richer over time while others remain in a state of structural backwardness and poverty. The marginalists are attracted by another empirical–theoretical problem. They want to determine the conditions of economic equilibrium, that is, the optimal allocation of scarce resources. They want to determine when Crusoe can go to bed satisfied with having made good use of the limited time at his disposal and, by analogy, when the inhabitants of the desert island can be satisfied with having made good use of the scarce resources at their disposal and, again by analogy, when a country, a continent or the whole world can be satisfied. This does not mean, as has sometimes been thought or written, that the marginalists were purists locked in an ivory tower, intent on constructing formalised mathematical models and uninterested in the historical problems of their time. On the contrary, they intervened in the issues related to protectionism and imperialism prevailing in Europe. The fact is that, when addressing these issues, they simply used the classical theory of economic development, which, not surprisingly, was saved by the marginalist revolution. Like the classics, the marginalists thought that development depended on labour productivity and the employment rate and required a liberal policy based on free trade and gold money to promote it.

The new object of analysis, economic equilibrium, re-proposes the ancient and unresolved question of the exchange value of goods and the related theory of distribution. For the classics, as we have seen, the exchange value of a good ultimately depends on the cost of production, while the income produced is distributed among wages, rents and profits according to different criteria: the wage is the price of labour, the pure rent is related to the different fertility of the land, and the profit is the residual income. Marginalists develop a new theory of value. Whereas Smith had considered use-value, utility, only as a prerequisite for exchange value, for marginalists utility is what determines or contributes to exchange value. Not generic utility, but the utility that provides the last available dose of a good or marginal utility. This is how they think they can explain the classic paradox of water and diamond: in the desert, in a condition of extreme scarcity, no one would give up a bottle of water to get a diamond in exchange. What gives (exchange) value to a good is its recognised (marginal) utility. Marginalists also elaborate a new theory of distribution by considering the factors of production (nature, capital and labour) as a special category of goods (those of production) and their rewards as a special category of prices. Following different paths, they search for a unitary criterion that, in the end, is identified in the principle of marginal factor productivity, according to which each agent receives a compensation commensurate with the contribution made to the production value of the final goods.

Thus, what the marginalists of each school have in common is a new method (methodological individualism), a new object of investigation (economic equilibrium), a new theory of value (marginal utility) and distribution (marginal productivity). These three elements, which unite the marginalists, also mark their distance or discontinuity from the classical economists, who share a holistic method, an exclusive cognitive interest in the subject of economic development, a theory of value-cost of production and a differentiated and intrinsically conflicting theory of distribution. In this sense, marginalism represents a scientific revolution. At the same time, however, marginalists maintain a solid link with the classical tradition on the subject of economic development and its related liberal economic policy.

The main differentiations or characterisations within the marginalist orientation can be (simplifying and schematising a great deal) traced back to the great theme of exchange value, which remains central to explaining the functioning of a market economy. For the classics, as we have said, value depends on the cost of production. For marginalists, as we have just seen, it depends (also) on the marginal utility of goods. Utility and cost are therefore the two factors that come into play in determining value. Menger and the Austrian School attempted to expunge the cost factor from economic analysis, reducing the entire explanation of economic phenomena to the utility factor. After all, they thought, cost is nothing more than sacrificed utility. For Robinson Crusoe, the cost of a fish is the hour he could have spent hunting a rabbit, it is the (sacrificed) utility that the rabbit would have provided: it is an opportunity cost.

Walras imagines that one hundred castaways land on Crusoe's island and immediately divide up the work and organise markets. The essence of the economic phenomenon lies in the interdependence of all the markets comprising an economic system. What happens in one market reflects, instantaneously, on the others, and the only way to describe the functioning of a network of interconnected markets is through a system of simultaneous equations called the "theory of general economic equilibrium". Pareto, who succeeded Walras as head of the Lausanne School, sought to expunge the utility factor from economic analysis by relying exclusively on the detection of individual preferences. Pareto distinguishes between ofelimacy (that which, by giving pleasure, satisfies a felt need) and utility (that which is useful). Learning to read is not ofelimous for a child, yet it is useful. Conversely, tobacco is ofelimous (gives pleasure) but is not useful at all (in fact, it is harmful to one's health). In order to describe the choices of individuals, it is sufficient to detect and order their preferences without resorting to the ambiguous category of utility. It is enough to assume not that the individual chooses what is useful but that what the individual chooses is useful. This approach marks the transition from cardinalism to ordinalism.

Lastly, Marshall and the Cambridge School try to hold together the cost factor, which affects the production choices of firms, and the utility factor, which affects the consumption choices of individuals and households.

The three schools come up against a number of analytical obstacles which it is not possible to examine here. Let us limit ourselves to examining, again synthetically, the thought of Menger and Marshall who, as we have said, exerted a greater and more lasting influence on European economic culture.

Menger's economic reflection began, almost by chance, as a journalist investigating price trends in the Vienna market.[4] Menger realised that the classical theory of labour-value was inadequate to explain the actual development of prices and markets. From this realisation of the heuristic failure of the classical theory, he developed the conviction that economic science needed to be rebuilt from scratch.

For Menger (1871 [2007]), economics is the science that studies human action aimed at the rational use of scarce and useful goods to satisfy a variety of needs. The entire investigation revolves around a comparison between economic goods (useful and scarce) and subjective needs (present and future). Scarcity is a relative concept precisely because it arises from a subjective comparison between goods and needs. A useful good becomes economic when it is scarce with respect to the needs it can satisfy but reverts to a good or thing when the scarcity disappears either because the need is no longer felt or because the good is no longer scarce. Tobacco, for example, ceases to be an economic good for a community that no longer feels the need to smoke. Menger distinguishes between consumer goods (or first-order goods) and capital goods (or higher-order goods). Bread, for example, is a consumer good, which directly satisfies the need to feed oneself. The flour, the wheat, the plot of land, and everything else that contributes to the production of bread belongs to the chain of instrumental or higher-order goods. For the classics, as we know, it is the value of capital goods that determines, according to an approach that today we might call top-down, the value of final goods (things are worthwhile because they cost). Menger overturns the value scale by arguing that it is the value of final goods that, going upwards (bottom-up), determines the value of capital goods (worthwhile things have a cost). With the "table" that bears his name, Menger shows how the individual tends to distribute the goods he can dispose of (i.e. income) in such a way as to leave equally unsatisfied the perceived needs or to balance the marginal utilities of the goods (although he does not use this expression). This is the rational allocation of resources. The value of instrumental goods, that is, the inputs used to produce final goods, is resolved in the "predictable value" of consumption goods. If, to use the same example, consumers attach great importance to tobacco, then all the inputs used in the production of tobacco will, in total, receive a high return. Menger explains the distribution/imputation of the income produced among the different inputs used by the so-called loss principle: that is, the value of an input can be determined by calculating the loss that the production value of the final good would suffer if one unit of the input in question were subtracted from the production combination: for example, the wage can be determined by calculating the loss of value of tobacco production if a worker were to be laid off. This principle is not entirely satisfactory, for reasons we cannot go into here, but it prefigures the more coherent and shared (by the neoclassical economists) principle of marginal factor productivity, according to which each input receives a compensation commensurate with its contribution to production. The significant conclusion is that, for Menger, the value of consumer goods depends on the marginal utility that consumers assign to the goods and that same utility determines the distribution of income among the productive factors. In other words, everything depends on the subjective and changing preferences of consumers.

Among Menger's heirs, Eugen von Böhm-Bawerk (1851–1914) is the author of an original theory of interest. For Böhm, interest is the reward for renouncing the preference for present goods. There are present goods (a supply of food) and future goods (a boat to be built). Individuals, for a variety of reasons, prefer present goods to future goods. The psychological reasons are that individuals tend to overestimate the availability of future goods and underestimate the intensity of future needs. That is, they are optimistic. But there is also a technical reason: present goods can be used to finance/support workers engaged in the construction of machines that increase the productivity of human labour. In other words, surplus assets represent savings that can be used to finance productive investments. For these reasons, those who own present assets are only willing to give up part of them in exchange for an appropriate compensation, which is called interest. If a community has many present goods, which largely satisfy the needs felt in the present, the owners of those goods will be willing to give up part of them to the demanders in exchange for a low compensation. If, on the other hand, present goods are scarce, that is, there is a shortage of savings, they will demand a higher payment. The interest rate is an indicator of the relative abundance or scarcity of existing goods or savings. A high interest rate signals a marked preference of individuals for present goods over future goods or a scarcity of savings (and vice versa). Consequently, a lower interest rate signals a higher availability of savings and a higher preference for future goods. However, in the modern economy, central banks have the discretionary power to set a monetary interest rate that guides the choices of both consumers and firms. Böhm's message is that it is dangerous to manipulate the "natural" interest rate, that is, the rate that would be set in an economy without money. For example, by lowering the money rate below the natural rate of interest, banks are inducing firms to invest more than they save or to produce fewer present goods and more future goods, even though the composition of consumer demand has not changed. By doing so, they generate an imbalance in the economy.

For the Austrian School, as can be seen, there is only one guiding principle of the economy: the subjective utility of consumers, which guides the present and future production of companies.

Alfred Marshall, founder of the Cambridge School, attempts a synthesis between the classical tradition and the marginalist revolution.[5] For Marshall, economics is the science that studies human behaviour as a calculation between satisfaction and effort. One could also add as a comparison between utility and cost. The neoclassical synthesis, of which he is the creator, consists in harmoniously combining the cost factor of the classical tradition with the utility factor of the marginalist revolution.

Marshall titled his treatise *Principles of Economics* instead of *Principles of Political Economy*, as it was used until then. For the first time, the word economics replaces political economy, even though Marshall can be considered a political economist in his own right. His aim is to be read by businessmen and to influence public opinion. Overall, he aims to explain the economic equilibrium and then the cyclical instability of capitalism. With the first attempt, he actually founded modern microeconomics; with the second, he launched a research programme which, taken up by Keynes, founded modern macroeconomics.

Marshall places marginal utility (of the marginalists) as the basis of the market demand curve and production cost (of the classics) as the basis of the market supply curve. After constructing the market curves, he studies the functioning of the market using the so-called partial equilibium and period analysis. Partial equilibrium in the sense that he adopts the clause of *ceteris paribus* ("all other things being equal"), analysing the functioning of a market under the hypothesis that what happens in the other markets remains unchanged. Period analysis because market equilibrium is represented in the short, medium and long term. Marshall draws a typical demand curve, with a negative slope, coinciding with the decreasing marginal utility curve. The underlying idea is that an individual, considering the decreasing marginal utility of the good, will be willing to buy increasing quantities only at decreasing prices. However, utility is purely subjective and therefore difficult to measure. Marshall then resorts to the concept of "willing to pay": marginal utility can be measured in terms of the amount of money a person is willing to sacrifice to obtain one more unit of the good. That is, at each point on a typical demand curve, we find the maximum purchase price that the individual consumer is willing to pay for that unit of a good. The lower the price, the higher the demand (and vice versa). Market demand is simply the horizontal sum of the different individual demands in the market. The Cambridge economist drew up the demand sheet and the corresponding curve that we still use today in a standard microeconomics course. Demand is an inverse relationship between price and quantity and depends on a number of other exogenous variables (income, preferences, price of substitute and complementary goods) that determine the position and movements of the demand curve. He then developed the concepts, still used today, of consumer surplus and price elasticity of demand.

Marshall then constructs a symmetric supply curve with a positive slope. Today, we use a simple production function to indicate the relationship between inputs and outputs. In the simplest version, we assume that two inputs – labour and capital – are needed to produce a good, and we assume that in the short run one input, usually capital, is fixed or invariable. From this, we derive the distinction between fixed costs, which do not vary with changes in production, and variable costs, which are proportional to changes in production. Total cost is simply the sum of the two and marginal cost is the change in total cost resulting from the increase of one unit of output. Marshall draws a typical supply curve, with a positive slope, coinciding with the upward slope of the marginal cost curve. The rising marginal cost curve reflects the rising cost of both labour and capital. The entrepreneur must compensate for the increasing efforts of the workers and the increased "waiting" of the capitalists who, by saving, postpone any consumption decision. Like the demand curve, it formulates the concepts of producer surplus and price elasticity of supply, completing the analysis of supply with the innovative category, still used today, of "economies of scale" (internal and external).

Marshall is therefore able to put forward a proposal to reconcile the classical tradition with the marginalist revolution and to solve the conundrum of exchange value. Value depends neither on cost alone, as the classics claim, nor on utility alone, as the marginalists claim, but simply on both. Exchange value is in fact determined at the point of intersection of market supply and demand, and at that point, the marginal utility underlying the demand curve coincides with the marginal cost underlying the supply curve. Value is like a sheet of paper cut by the two scissor blades. Marshall (1890 [1930]: 348) writes: "We might as reasonably dispute whether it is the upper or the under blade of a pair of scissors that cuts a piece of paper, as whether value is governed by utility or cost of production". Supply and demand thus determine the exchange value of a good simultaneously. However, historical time is a crucial variable. Marshall analyses market equilibrium by distinguishing between market (or short), medium and long periods.

If Menger and the Austrians try to recapitulate the entire economic analysis in the subjective factor of marginal utility, Marshall and his Cambridge students try to harmonise the objective factor of production cost, inherited from the classics, with the subjective factor of marginal utility introduced by the marginalists.[6]

The two faces of Etatism

Mises (1944: 44) writes:

> The most important event in the history of the last hundred years [since 1848] is the displacement of liberalism by etatism. Etatism appears in two forms: socialism and interventionism. Both have in common the goal of subordinating the individual unconditionally to the state, the social apparatus of compulsion and coercion.

In fact, in the same years in which the marginalist revolution exploded, a parallel and alternative revolution broke out: the etatism revolution. Etatism, as Mises argues, has two faces: the more radical face of socialism and the more reassuring face of interventionism. Both have in common a critique of classical liberalism adopted, without substantial variations, by neoclassical marginalists. Both, however, propose their own solution to the social question that exploded in Europe in the decades following the revolution of 1848.

Socialism aims at the destruction of the key institutions of capitalism and European civilisation: private ownership of the means of production and the market economy, to be replaced, in the idealised society of the future, by state ownership of the means of production and a centrally controlled planned economy.

The recognised theorist of socialism is Karl Marx who, in his analysis of capitalism, begins with the classics. In particular, he uses their labour theory of value to predict the inevitable fall in the profit rate and, with it, the inevitable collapse of capitalism. Marx believed that the fall in the profit rate would occur in any case: whether goods were sold at their labour-values (or production prices) or whether it was impossible to sell goods at those values because of a series of imbalances inherent in the market. The classics had tried to save capitalism: both the theorists of the congenital crisis, such as Malthus, who justified unproductive expenditure, that of landowners, to absorb the excess production of consumer goods, and the theorists of the final crisis, such as Ricardo, who proposed the abolition of corn laws to squeeze rents for the benefit of profits. For Marx, however, capitalism is unworkable and can only commit suicide. The capitalist, in fact, by pursuing his own interest, deals a fatal blow to the whole system. The capitalist, in order to maximise profit, substitutes machines for human labour but, in so doing, reduces the amount of labour socially necessary to produce the commodities that generate surplus value and thus the overall profit that the capitalist class appropriates. It kills what Marx calls the "golden goose". In this sense, Smith's philosophy is reversed: an invisible hand, instead of transforming the personal gain of the capitalist into the common good of the consumers, destroys the entire class of capitalists and paves the way for a classless society.

Marx's theory passionately animates the debate within the First (1864–1876) and Second (1889–1916) Workers' International. The debate revolves around the dual hypothesis of the falling rate of profit. If the fall is unstoppable, then it is only a question of hastening the end of capitalism with a revolutionary policy. If, on the other hand, the crisis stems from market imbalances, examined by Marxists with the schemes of simple and extended reproduction, then there is room for a policy of social reform. The alternative, which will dramatically mark the history of the workers' movement, is between revolutionaries and reformists, between communists and social democrats.

The other face of etatism, the more reassuring one, is interventionism. Interventionism does not aim to destroy the institutions of capitalism and Western civilisation – private property and the market – but to complement and regulate them. Interventionists defend the right to private property and economic freedom, but believe that public regulation is necessary.

The first theorist of interventionism was Friedrich List (1789–1846), who published *The National System of Political Economy* in 1841. List, like Marx, began with the classics, in particular with Smith, but, unlike Marx, did not consider or underestimate the contribution of Ricardo. For List, the classics have elaborated a great universal economic theory that explains the conditions for increasing the welfare of individuals and humanity but not of nations. This is List's great criticism of the classics, or rather of Smith who, in his opinion, did not realise that between the individual and the world there is an intermediate entity, the nation, which has its own characteristics and which must become the object of study of political economy. Not having considered the theory of comparative advantages, List could not appreciate the attempt made by Ricardo to show precisely the possible conditions for a harmonisation of the various national interests.

List proposed free trade within a country or region and external protectionism to defend infant industries. His ideas inspired the creation in 1834 of the *Zollverein*, the customs union between the states, excluding Austria, of the Germanic Confederation.

List can also be considered a precursor of the German Historical School, a current of thought dominant in Germany and elsewhere in the years when, to use Mises's expression, etatism took over from liberalism. In particular, between 1870 and 1918, Schmoller and Wagner were the most authoritative and influential exponents of the so-called Young or New Historical School, which advocated a policy of public intervention in defence of the national economy. Mises argued that it was the ideas of the historicists that inspired a policy, initiated first and foremost by Bismarck, aimed at creating large and self-sufficient economic areas – a policy that would shortly afterwards take the inauspicious name of *Lebensraum*. Mises (1944: 76) writes:

> The representative literary champion of modern German protectionism was Adolf Wagner. The essence of his teachings is this: All countries with an excess production of foodstuffs and raw materials are eager to develop domestic manufacturing and to bar access to foreign manufactures; the world is on the way to economic self-sufficiency for each nation. In such a world what will be the fate of those nations which can neither feed nor clothe their citizens out of domestic foodstuffs and raw materials? They are doomed to starvation.

Historicists, according to Mises (1944: 76), were aware of the limits of protectionism and aimed at national self-sufficiency:

> The remedy they recommended was conquest of more space – war. They asked for protection of German agriculture in order to encourage production on the poor soil of the country, because they wanted to make Germany independent of foreign supplies of food for the impending war. Import duties for food were in their eyes a short-run remedy only, a measure for a period of transition. The ultimate remedy was war and conquest.[7]

Hence, between 1870 and 1890, two parallel revolutions took place: the marginalist revolution which, with Marshall's neoclassical synthesis, became the new orthodoxy, and the etatist revolution which, in the dual version of socialism and interventionism, represented the new heresy.

A Europe of Empires at War

The decades at the turn of the nineteenth century, roughly between 1890 and 1918, were an extraordinary time of glaring light but also of dark shadows: the years of the *belle époque* before the Great War.

In 1890, Bismarck handed in his resignation to Kaiser Wilhelm II. The fragile balance of power on which a European order without further legitimacy (divine or popular) rested broke down. In 1891, Germany did not renew the Reassurance Treaty with Russia, which was thus pushed closer to France, while Great Britain, after 1904, abandoned its "splendid isolation" to join the Entente Cordiale of France and Russia.

Europe was now divided into two opposing camps: on the one hand, the Triple Alliance, formed by Austria, Germany and Italy, and on the other, the Triple Entente, perfected in 1907, comprising France, Great Britain and Russia.

In the last decades of the century, the European economy entered the First Globalisation, as it was later called by historians. Everything moves. Thanks to technical, transportation and financial advances, people and capital began to move alongside goods. Between 1870 and 1900, millions of people left Europe for the United States, Latin America, Canada, Australia, New Zealand and South Africa. The Ricardian hypothesis of an international market characterised by the imperfect mobility of productive factors fell. The hypothesis of a possible reconciliation of national interests based exclusively on the free trade of goods and on the gold standard currency, therefore, also falls.

How are the major European countries responding to the challenge of the First Globalisation?[8]

To simplify, one could say that etatism prevails over neoclassical liberalism. In particular, historicist interventionism prevails, while socialism takes root in only one large country: in Bolshevik Russia with the October 1917 Revolution.

Germany became the leading country in Europe. In 1879, Bismarck had adopted complete protectionism, defending both industry and agriculture. A similar tariff was adopted in Russia in 1881, Italy in 1887 and France in 1892. Europe abandoned free trade and took refuge in protectionism. England was the only country that officially and apparently did not renounce its fathers' doctrine. In reality, it too was thinking of a form of protection. In 1903, Colonial Minister Chamberlain proposed an "imperial Zollverein", a customs union between the mother country and the colonies, with preferential tariffs towards the colonies and a common, higher tariff towards the outside, while Premier Balfour coined the expression "island free trade" to indicate a preference towards the Empire and a negotiating pressure on rival countries to abandon protectionism.[9]

In 1890, the United States passed its first antitrust law: The Sherman Act. In Germany, on the other hand, myriad trusts and cartels proliferated without sanctions: in 1910, more than 360 trusts and cartels were registered (Hartwich 2009: 13 and Gerber 1998 for in-depth analysis).

The neoclassical economists proposed the old recipe again: free trade and gold standard. On 15 August 1903, *The Times* published a letter signed by 16 British economists, among them Cannan, Edgeworth, Pigou and especially Marshall, where one can read the following:

> we think that any system of preferential tariffs would most probably lead to the reintroduction of Protection into the fiscal system of the United Kingdom. But a return to Protection would, we hold, be detrimental to the material prosperity of this country, partly for reasons of the same kind as those which, as now universally admitted, justified the adoption of Free Trade – reasons which are now stronger than formerly, in consequence of the greater proportion of food and raw materials imported from foreign countries, and the greater extent and complexity of our foreign trade.
>
> *quoted by Klein 2010: 158–159*

The classic proposals of the neoclassical economists were not accepted in England or elsewhere. A line of interventionist economic policy prevails, which seems to be sliding down a slope at the end of which is the precipice of war. The steps down the slope are protectionism, the formation of trusts, the creation of empires or self-sufficient economic areas.

Mises, again, proposed an interpretation of these events: a strong interpretation, worthy of being known but also verified.[10] For Mises, the origin of the war was interventionism, the Austro-Hungarian Empire of Franz Joseph, which implemented a policy of discrimination against linguistic minorities, exacerbating nationalistic conflicts, and above all Bismarck's Germany. Bismarck, according to Mises (1919: ch. II), instead of recognising the free movement of goods, people and capital, sought to ensure a high level of prosperity for a population in excess of Germany's resources. First and foremost, Germany introduced a working-class *Sozialpolitik* that raised production costs and made it necessary to protect the national economy in full. Protectionism, in turn, undermined the country's international competitiveness by forcing the government to support or encourage the formation of cartels between companies to implement a policy of multiple pricing: higher in the domestic market and lower in international markets. Over time, Germany's ultimate goal became to conquer the living space (*Lebensraum*) necessary to achieve economic self-sufficiency. The creation of large economic spaces led to the inevitable war conflict.

This is also the background to the debate on the future of Central Europe (*Mitteleuropa*) initiated by Naumann's 1915 book. The alternative is between those who want a Middle Europe led by Austria and Germany (including Naumann himself) and those who, like Masaryk, imagine an area of small independent states freed from both Austrian-German and Russian domination.[11]

In Short

Liberal Europe, understood as a Concert of cooperating nation-states, came to an end in the 1870s, after the proclamation of the Second German Reich, faced with a crisis of legitimacy (the balance of power was no longer sufficient) and a great economic depression. In the same decade, and in the following one, economic science underwent two parallel scientific revolutions that gave rise to a new orthodoxy: the neoclassical one that re-proposed classical liberalism, and the etatist one that took on the double face of Marxist socialism and historicist interventionism. In the last decades at the turn of the century, after Bismarck's exit from the scene, the major European countries adopted an interventionist economic policy aimed at creating large, closed economic spaces.

So what influence did the great economic ideas have on the transition from a Europe Concert of liberal nation-states to a Europe of warring empires?

One can perhaps say that neoclassical economics conquers science but not society, where clearly etatist ideas and policies prevail. Nationalist imperialism also feeds on economic ideas which, by repudiating the classical harmony of individual and collective interests, emphasise the antagonism between class and national interests. The constitutive values of Europe change yet again. *Libertas* returns to be subject to greater control by *potestas*: positive freedom of participation is extended, thanks to an extension of the right to vote and the foundation of parties and trade unions but, at the same time, negative freedom of action is restricted, conditioned by the presence of trusts, trade unions and measures restricting individual economic initiative. Work (*opus*) was better protected both by trade unions and by the nascent welfare state, while new communities (*communitas*) emerged in society, such as trade unions, cooperatives and political parties, and the feeling of belonging to a national community degenerated in nationalism.

The historical lesson is that, at the time of the First Globalisation, when people and capital began to circulate along with goods, the European economy entered a great depression that called for the defence of national interests: a defence that was guaranteed neither by traditional free trade, which everyone abandoned, nor by imperialist etatism, which unleashed a destructive war. One might even say neither by the free market nor by the absolute State.

Notes

1 On the history of Europe in the age of imperialism, see Kemp (1969), Fieldhouse (1980), Kennedy (1980), Wood (1983), Feuchtwanger (1985), Massie (2007), Hobsbawm (1996), Cain and Hopkins (2002), Evans (2017). On neoclassical economics, see Landreth and Colander (1994, Part III), Screpanti and Zamagni (2005, chs. 5–6); on etatism, see Mises (1922, 1929, 1944).
2 See Stürmer (1986).
3 On the spread of Marxism, see Colletti and Napoleoni (1970), Zanardo (1972); on the spread of Historical School, see Cardoso and Psalidopoulos (2016); on *Verein*, see Roversi (1984); on the origin of the clash between Marxism and Marginalism, see Böhm-Bawerk, Hilferding, Bortkiewicz (1971).
4 On Carl Menger (1840–1921) and the Austrian School, see Wasserman (2019).
5 On Alfred Marshall (1842–1924), see Groenewegen (1995).
6 Another attempt at neoclassical synthesis is made by Maffeo Pantaleoni, who argues that marginalism permits a generalisation of the main theorems developed by the classics.

These theorems may in fact be expressed, indifferently, in terms of utility or of cost. That is so because the exchange value of a good originates from the utility of the last available dose of the good itself, or its final degree of utility, but its available quantity depends on its cost of production. At the margin, cost and utility coincide: "In this sense the cost of production of something is first of all *merely another term for its final degree of utility*" (Pantaleoni (1889 [1931]: 232, original italics, my translation from Italian).

7 For a general critique of interventionism, see Mises (1929). Franz Neumann (1942), too, in his classic work on National Socialism, considers List and Wagner precursors of the idea of living space. Neumann (1942: 104) wrote:

> The influence of the so-called state or *Katheder* socialists upon the ultimate development of National Socialist racism seems far more important. The writings of Friedrich List and Adolph Wagner clearly show the factors that contributed to the triumph of racial ideas. These men were attempting to counteract socialist theories of class struggle by repudiating liberal political thought and by setting up a state capitalist scheme that would "incorporate" the working classes and imbue the whole people with the spirit of their racial superiority. The aim was to organize society for imperialist adventures.

8 See Foreman-Peck (1999), O'Rourke and Williamson (2005).
9 See Ashley (1920 [1970]), Coats (1968), Backhouse (1985: ch. 19).
10 On the transition from liberalism to etatism in Germany in the second half of the nineteenth century, see also Hartwich (2009).
11 See Naumann (1918–1919), Bresciani-Turroni (1918), Meyer (1955), Droz (1960), Agnelli (1971 [2005]), Hayes (1994), Johnson (1996).

5

NEOLIBERALISM(S) AND CORPORATISM

A Europe of Sovereign Nations and Its Failure (1919–1943)

Introduction

On 11 November 1918, British Prime Minister David Lloyd George announced the signing of the armistice between the victorious Allied powers and the defeated Germany with these words: "I hope that we may say that thus, this fateful morning, come to an end all wars" (Kissinger 1995: 218).

Never has a prophecy been more resoundingly and dramatically proved wrong. A few years later, Germany and England found themselves fighting another, and even more bloody, world war. Yet at the Paris Peace Conference in 1919, an attempt was made to re-establish a just and stable European and world order. That order was founded primarily at the behest of the powerful American President, Woodrow Wilson, on the noble and democratic principle of the self-determination of peoples. According to Wilson, wars, including the latest one, were not caused by a lack of balance of power, but, on the contrary, by the obsessive pursuit of such a balance that led the great powers to trample on the legitimate rights of peoples to self-determination. In order to cut the roots of war once and for all, each nation had to be allowed to organise itself into a state.

John Maynard Keynes, Marshall's favourite pupil and a rising star in the firmament of British economic science, was also a member of the British delegation at the Paris conference. In the summer of 1919, Keynes controversially resigned from the British delegation and published a book, *The Economic Consequences of the Peace*, which brought him international notoriety. That same summer, Ludwig von Mises, Menger's intellectual heir, published a book on the same subject with a different kind of criticism of the peace treaties.

The "Paris Order" was established and the 1920s seemed to mark the beginning of a new era of peace and prosperity, so much so that they are remembered in history as the "Roaring Twenties". But the crisis was just around the corner

DOI: 10.4324/9781003188889-5

and exploded in the autumn of 1929 with the collapse of the New York Stock Exchange. The crisis caused the Paris Order to falter, and many wondered whether it was the controversial decision taken in the mid-1920s to reintroduce the gold standard, albeit in a more flexible version, that forced national governments to abide by the binding rules of the game. The issue directly concerned economists. These years between the wars are known in the history of economic thought as "years of high theory", during which decisive contributions were provided to understanding phenomena related to money, the business cycle and the functioning of imperfectly competitive markets. They were also years of "high economic policy". Economists participated directly and actively in the debate over major government decisions. The debate was dominated by the dispute between Hayek (a pupil of Mises) and Keynes (a pupil of Marshall), who offered opposing explanations of the business cycle, the great crisis and anti-crisis policies, and by an attempt at synthesis by Wilhelm Röpke, an exponent of ordoliberalism, a current of economic thought that originated in Germany. All three – Hayek, Keynes and Röpke – felt themselves, and were, liberals, or rather neoliberals, since they aimed to update or re-found the tradition of classical liberalism. Their attempts came to different, sometimes profoundly different conclusions. In the 1930s, a fierce battle of ideas was fought between a multiform neoliberalism and a variegated corporatism that fed on ideas from the medieval Catholic tradition, mercantilism and German historicism.

The year 1936 was in many ways a turning point. The last countries, including Italy, that had remained tenaciously anchored in a gold standard system, abandoned the "gold bloc", Germany intensified its rearmament plans, Keynes published his *General Theory*, a work that revolutionised economic science and culture, and neo-classical economists contributed to conceiving models of a regulated economy. Europe was preparing for war in a climate of apparent peace.

In this chapter, we ask what role economic ideas have played in the transition from a Europe of sovereign nations, eager to cooperate in an order of peace and democracy, to a Europe struggling for freedom threatened by totalitarian states bent on conquering a space vital to themselves and deadly to others.[1]

We shall examine, first, the Paris Order and the divergent critique of Keynes and Mises; second, the business cycles and great depression: Hayek *vs.* Keynes and Röpke's synthesis; and third, Europe towards the war between Keynesianism, Neoliberalism and Corporatism.

The Paris Order and the Divergent Critique of Keynes and Mises

On 11 November 1918, the armistice ending World War I was signed in the countryside of Compiègne. A few weeks later, on 18 January 1919, the Peace Conference solemnly opened in Paris. Bolshevik Russia did not take part in it and, having emerged from the European Concert, embarked on an arduous journey to build socialism in a single country. This path was marked by forced stages: "war communism" (1917–1921), the "new economic policy" or NEP (1921–1928), and the "five-year plans" (1928–1941).

The Conference, dominated by the four great victorious countries (the United States Great Britain, France, and Italy) lasted a full year: it began on 18 January 1919 and ended on 21 January 1920. The peace treaties signed during and after the Conference, and in particular the Treaty of Versailles of 28 June 1919, designed a new European order, which can be defined as follows: a Europe of sovereign nations embedded in a peaceful international community. According to Woodrow Wilson, the great winner of the war and architect of peace, the cause of the wars, including the last one, was not the lack of a sufficient balance of power, but, on the contrary, the insistent search for such a balance that ended up by disregarding and trampling on the legitimate aspirations of peoples for independence, unleashing an immense slaughter. In order to sever the roots of war once and for all, a new principle of democratic legitimacy had to be affirmed and implemented, that of the self-determination of peoples. It was necessary, with the peace treaties, to redraw the map of Europe to recognise the right of each nation to organise itself as a state. Wilson entrusted a new institution, the League of Nations, with the task of guaranteeing international security, that is, a fair peace. For the victors, and especially for the French, a just peace also had to be punitive towards Germany, considered solely or mainly responsible for the war.

In his speech to the American Congress on 8 January 1918, Wilson anticipated and summarised in "14 points" the characteristics of the new world order that America wanted to build with the Allies. The third point envisaged a gradual return to a free trade regime and thus, *de facto*, the adoption or restoration of a gold-based monetary system, which, in the opinion of the time, was a necessary condition for the smooth functioning of the world market. In 1919, America had reverted to the gold standard after the interruption of the war years, while in Europe the issue was a matter of widespread concern and was at the centre of public debate in the early 1920s.

Under the gold standard in force until World War I, the amount of gold contained in individual national currencies determined foreign exchange rates and the amount of domestic monetary circulation. For example, one pound sterling contained 113.0016 grains of gold and one US dollar contained 23.22 grains of gold. Consequently, in the foreign exchange market, one pound was exchanged for 4.86.6 dollars, that is, the exchange rate was the ratio between the amounts of gold contained in the respective currencies (113.0016 / 23.22 = 4.86.6). Both gold and paper currencies (banknotes and deposits) circulated in the domestic market. Paper money was convertible into gold, but the amount in circulation exceeded the gold reserves: the banks assumed that, to ensure convertibility, it would be sufficient to keep only part of the deposits collected as reserves.[2]

The countries adhering to the gold standard committed themselves to respecting three basic rules.

The first was to preserve a fixed exchange rate regime. Exchange rates could fluctuate within very narrow margins defined as gold points.[3]

The second was to adjust the money supply in proportion to changes in the gold reserve. In order to keep exchange rates fixed, central banks adjusted the amount of money in circulation according to gold flows (or gold reserves). In the case of a gold outflow, resulting from an excessive trade deficit, they contracted the money supply by increasing the discount rate. The effect of raising the discount rate was twofold. In the short run, it encouraged an inflow of foreign capital, attracted by the possibility of discounting bills of exchange and other debt securities. In the long run, it triggered a deflationary process that improved the trade balance. The double effect corrected the balance of payments imbalance and stopped the outflow of gold (and vice versa in the case of an inflow of gold following a trade surplus).

The third was to keep domestic prices flexible. The discount manoeuvre could only be effective in restoring external balance and keeping exchange rates fixed if domestic prices were flexible.

The fundamental rule was the first one, whereas the others were almost subordinate. It was in order to have a fixed exchange rate regime that the money supply had to be adjusted according to gold flows and domestic prices kept flexible. For if gold flows had been neutralised by compensatory monetary manoeuvres, or domestic prices had been rigid, the economic system would have slipped into a double imbalance, internal and external, which would have undermined exchange rate stability.

According to the gold standard proponents, fixed exchange rates were indispensable to ensure balanced and sustainable growth: they promoted an international division of labour in accordance with the principle of comparative advantage and guaranteed the monetary stability (internal and external) needed to build up savings to finance new investment. In other words, they preserved the two classic cornerstones of economic growth: the division of labour and capital accumulation. Moreover, they also ensured that economic growth was balanced and sustainable over time. A fixed or stable exchange rate signalled an internal and external equilibrium. If the exchange rate was stable, it meant that any trade deficit – resulting from domestic demand exceeding domestic output, that is, investment exceeding domestic savings – was financed by a stable inflow of foreign savings (and vice versa). Exchange rate fluctuations, on the other hand, signalled the existence of a double imbalance, internal and external. In particular, a gold outflow indicated an excess of domestic demand over production (and of investment over saving) that was not financed by a stable inflow of foreign savings.

Hence, fixed exchange rates ensured balanced and sustainable growth and were guaranteed by a money supply proportional to gold reserves and flexible domestic prices: three golden rules.

In the summer of 1919, Keynes contentiously left the Paris Conference and, within a few months, wrote *The Economic Consequences of the Peace*, the pamphlet that brought him international fame. Between the spring of 1922 and the winter of 1923, he edited 12 supplements to the *Manchester Guardian* on the subject of *Reconstruction in Europe*. The supplements, translated into the main European languages, provided the material for another successful book, also published in 1923: *A Tract on Monetary Reform*.

In these writings Keynes outlined a critique of the Paris Order and a radical solution to the post-war problems.[4] First, he considers the Versailles peace unjust (Carthaginian) and proposes to drastically reduce the sanctions against Germany in order not to jeopardise the chances of economic recovery for the whole of Europe. Second, he called for the abandonment of gold, a "barbarous relic", and for monetary policy to be decisively oriented towards the objective of domestic price stability rather than foreign exchange: the money supply should be managed in an expansive or restrictive direction so as to achieve and maintain price stability. For Keynes, in fact, both inflation and deflation are harmful and should be avoided: inflation leads to an unfair and involuntary redistribution of wealth to the detriment of savers and to the advantage of debtors, while deflation, that is, the fall in the general level of prices, in the presence of rigid downward costs, squeezes profits and harms the entire economy. Thus, writes Keynes (1923: 40), "Inflation is unjust and Deflation is inexpedient".

In that same summer of 1919, Mises published *State, Nation and Economy*, a book that implicitly critiques the peace treaties. The basic criticism is that in Central and Eastern Europe, due to the presence of scattered and strong national minorities, it is not possible to establish cohesive nation-states. For these minorities, democracy means subjection to the will of the majority belonging to other linguistic (and ethnic) groups. This is why they oppose democracy and prefer monarchical absolutism. The alternative solution outlined by Mises, and fully explained in later writings, is the full recognition of the three economic freedoms, namely the free movement of goods, persons, and capital. For Mises, Wilson's tragic mistake is not to have understood that, in order to ensure peace, in addition to democracy, economic liberalism is needed. In a world in which capital and people also circulate, Ricardo's hypothesis drops, free trade is no longer sufficient, and in order to ensure peace and development, it is necessary to guarantee complete economic freedom. Mises (1919 [2006]: 53) writes:

> If one drops that Ricardian assumption, then one sees a tendency prevail over the entire earth toward equalization of the rate of return on capital and of the wage of labor. Then, finally, there no longer are poorer and richer nations but only more densely and less densely settled and cultivated countries.

The proposals of Keynes and Mises were discussed but essentially rejected, and governments proceeded along the road mapped out in Paris: harsh sanctions were imposed on Germany, new national or multinational states were formed, and there was a return to a gold standard, albeit in the more flexible version of the gold exchange standard, a system that allowed dollars and pounds sterling to be held as gold reserves, gold removed from monetary circulation, and which gave the United States a role similar to that of an institution that helped countries in difficulty, starting with Germany. The system is more elastic, but the rules of the game remain those of the gold standard.

The equating of the dollar and the pound with gold gives the United States and Britain the enormous power to print paper as if it were gold. In reality, it is a relative power. The central banks of other countries would continue to hold dollars and pounds only as long as they were sure of their gold convertibility. To preserve the gold convertibility of their currencies, the United States and Britain would have had to follow the rules of the gold standard; that is, they could not have used monetary policy in a discretionary manner.

In the summer of 1924, the Dawes Plan was launched with which the United States loaned Germany 800 million *Reichsmarks* to phase out war reparations and return to gold.[5] Germany adhered to the gold exchange standard in August 1924. Between 1925 and 1928 England, Italy and France returned to gold. England re-established the old parity with the dollar by revaluing a depreciated pound. France stabilised the franc at its market value, effectively devaluing it, while Italy revalued the lira against the dollar and the pound.

In Europe, the two key countries were Great Britain and Germany. According to the rules of the game, Britain was supposed to trigger a domestic deflationary process to compensate, through lower wages and prices, for an exchange rate that had become prohibitive for exporting companies. Germany should have used foreign loans to restructure its domestic economy and generate the commercial surplus needed to obtain the currency to pay back the funds. But instead, Britain failed to deflate because of the harsh reaction of the trade union movement, which opposed wage restrictions, while Germany used foreign loans to finance unproductive expenditure as well. In 1926, the British general strike paralysed the country. In 1927, the Governor of the *Reichsbank*, Hjalmar Schacht, openly denounced those German public administrations using foreign funds to build "stadiums, swimming pools, squares and reception salons, conference halls, hotels, planetary offices, airports, theatres, museums, etc." (cited by Kindleberger 1986: 27).

The result was that in Britain and Germany there was more consumption (public and private) and fewer exports than there would have been had the rules of the game been applied. The European economy, from 1924 onwards, entered a phase of economic expansion fuelled by an excess of demand over domestic production and a resulting trade deficit financed by American loans, which had to be repaid.

In 1927, there was a widespread expectation of a corrective manoeuvre imposed by the rules of the game. England, which was losing gold, would have to reduce its money supply. France, worried about the state of the English economy, could have demanded the conversion of its sterling into gold and thus aggravated the debt situation of the Bank of England. Germany would have had to cut back on public spending. Lastly, the United States, which was experiencing gold inflows, would have had to expand its money supply. But American expansion was unlikely to compensate for European contraction, and the boom was likely to culminate – as at other times in the history of capitalism – in a salutary corrective crisis.

The first turning point occurred in 1927. The central banks of the major countries agreed on an expansionary policy. England did not contract the money supply (at least as much as it should have), France did not convert its sterling holdings into gold, and the United States expanded the money supply much more than it should have. The boom continued. The speculative bubble on the New York stock exchange burst: American savers, propelled by an irrational euphoria, continued to buy shares at rising prices on the simplistic assumption that prices would continue to rise. In the space of a few months, the value of the shares doubled without the balance sheets of the companies or the market outlook justifying such a performance.

In 1928, the Federal Reserve raised the discount rate, worried that stock market speculation would divert savings from productive investment. But yields on securities listed on the New York Stock Exchange remained higher than any other financial investment. Capital invested in Europe was beginning to return to America. For Europe, and first and foremost for England and Germany, the painful prospect of having to implement restrictive manoeuvres to drastically reduce foreign debt opened up.

The second turning point came in the summer of 1929 when the Fed tightened its monetary policy. In October, the Wall Street bubble burst: the expectations of speculators and savers were reversed and the downward sales of securities began in earnest.

In the autumn of 1929, the boom ended and the Great Depression began.

When the crisis erupted, the two main players in American economic policy had almost been there from the outset. President Herbert Hoover had been in office since 4 March 1929 and the Fed, founded in 1913, was facing its first crisis under the gold standard (the previous one having occurred in 1921).

According to the rules of the game, the gold exchange standard countries were supposed to preserve fixed exchange rates, money supply proportional to the gold reserve, and flexible prices. During a recession, prices and output contract, unemployment rises, and there is a danger of capital flight. In order to keep prices flexible (downwards), governments should have protected the freedom of companies to lay off workers and reduce wages. In order to prevent capital flight and the consequent devaluation of the exchange rate, central banks should have raised the discount rate: more precisely, they should have granted credit at increasing interest rates (the so-called Bagehot rule), thus lowering wages and raising the discount rate: that is the classic formula.

What did governments do? Did they follow the classical tradition or did they listen to the theories of the economic cycle and crisis developed by the new economists?

To answer this question, we must briefly examine the most influential theories.

Business Cycles and the Great Depression: Hayek vs. Keynes and Röpke's Synthesis

The 1930s were dominated by the dispute over the economic cycle and the related explanation of the great crisis of 1929. The protagonists were still Keynes and Mises, but now the old champion of Austrian liberalism was joined by his young pupil Hayek, while the German Röpke sought a difficult synthesis. In general, it can be said that economists point to two main and complementary causes of cycles: the real and monetary shocks that continually hit economic systems (wars, innovations and economic policy choices) and the difficulty of rapidly absorbing shocks due to the relative rigidity of wages, interest and prices.

In 1930, Keynes published *A Treatise on Money*, which was followed by a number of popular writings. In 1931, Hayek published *Prices and Production*, a small volume containing the texts of the lectures he gave at the London School of Economics at the invitation of Lionel Robbins, later expanded in a second edition in 1935.[6]

The great dispute between Keynes and Hayek revolves around the possibility of ensuring a balance between savings and investment.

Hayek and Keynes, starting from Wicksell, conceive of the economy as structured in two interconnected circuits. On the one hand, there are the income-earning households, which partly consume and partly save. On the other, there are the enterprises that produce consumer goods for households and capital goods (machines) for other enterprises. In the middle, there are the financial intermediaries – banks and stock exchanges – which collect household savings and transfer them to businesses to finance their investments. If household savings are equal to business investment, then demand for consumer goods is also equal to supply and the entire economic system is in equilibrium. On the other hand, if investment exceeds savings, the demand for consumer goods exceeds supply and the economic system shows an excess of consumption and investment over domestic production (and vice versa). The fundamental macroeconomic question therefore becomes the balance between savings and investment.

For Keynes (1930, 1931, 1934), there is no market or mechanism that can automatically balance saving and investment. Thus, the economic system is inherently unstable. The structural problem with capitalism is the excessive formation of savings compared to an unstable or volatile flow of investment. Households regularly save a constant fraction of their income, which tends to grow over time, while entrepreneurs are subject to animal spirits, that is, moods that easily shift from perhaps irrational euphoria to equally unjustified pessimism. Saving is a rising straight line while investment is a sine wave moving around it. Expansionary phases are triggered and characterised by an excess of investment over savings and a corresponding excess of domestic demand over production. That is, the expansion is driven by investment. Keynes sees no danger here. On the contrary, he thinks that, if it were possible to preserve a condition of over-investment, the economic system would continue to grow at the sole cost of gently rising prices. The assertion is implicitly revolutionary: it subverts the ancient classical wisdom that only previously accumulated savings can be invested. For Keynes, on the other hand, there is no trade-off between consumption and investment: on the contrary, an increase in consumption, and a consequent reduction in savings, increases cyclical profits and generates new investment. The expansionary phase is interrupted and reversed into a recessionary phase due to a fall in investment below the (ever increasing) savings line. This is the fragile soul of capitalism: investment volatility. Entrepreneurs invest when the expected rate of profit exceeds the interest rate required for financing, and vice versa. Investments fluctuate for one or a combination of both reasons. It may happen that, despite low interest rates, entrepreneurs decide to postpone investment decisions because they expect the economy to worsen in the medium term or because, although entrepreneurial expectations remain positive, banks raise interest rates above the expected rate of profit. For Keynes, the cause of the crisis is always a fall in the flow of investment below the growing flow of household savings. That is, the cause of the crisis is an excess of saving over investment.

In the specific case of the great crisis of 1929, the responsibility for the crisis, according to Keynes, lay with the major central banks which, fearing a rise in inflation and having to respect the rules of the gold exchange standard, from the spring of 1929, raised interest rates, causing a collapse in investments. The way out of crises is to invest more and, if necessary, consume more, that is, to create the over-investment necessary to trigger economic recovery and fuel a new expansionary phase. Keynes believes that it is preferable to support investment rather than consumption and clarifies how his theory differs from Hobson's sub-consumerist theory. For the sub-consumerists, savings, which are always invested, finance a production of consumer goods that is excessive compared to the purchasing power of consumers, and the imbalance and the crisis can only be resolved with income redistribution policies aimed at increasing consumption. For Keynes, on the contrary, the crisis stems from an excess of savings over investments, and thus the primary corrective action consists in stimulating investments. Stimulating consumption can only be a secondary and supplementary measure. In the specific case of the great crisis of 1929, Keynes suggested that the United Kingdom and the United States should abandon the gold exchange standard, devalue their currencies, and launch public spending plans to support investment and reverse the fall in prices. The formula for getting out of the labyrinth of the crisis is devaluation *plus* reflation. Countercyclical or macroeconomic stabilisation policies should instead consist of a managed currency policy geared to the objective of domestic price stability, not foreign exchange, and a public investment policy to help achieve macroeconomic equilibrium.

Hayek (1933, 1935), again based on Wicksell but also on the Austrian Böhm-Bawerk, developed an alternative theory of the business cycle from over-investment. Unlike Keynes, he believes that there is a mechanism to balance saving and investment. All that is needed is for banks to keep the "monetary" interest rate at the level of the "natural" interest rate (in the sense of Wicksell and Böhm-Bawerk), that is, to grant credit in proportion to existing savings. If household savings increase, the natural rate decreases and banks can and must reduce the monetary rate. Thus, the economic system is inherently stable. Expansionary phases are always triggered, as Keynes argued, by an increase in investment. But, according to Hayek, two fundamental cases must be distinguished, theoretically and factually. In the first case, the increase in investment follows the increase in savings. Households voluntarily increase savings and reduce consumption. Banks can then reduce the monetary interest rate by stimulating investment. In the second case, the increase in investment does not follow the increase in savings. The banks reduce the monetary interest rate without changing a household's consumption and saving choices, generating inflation and forced saving and triggering an unsustainable expansionary phase. The crisis highlights a double imbalance: an excess of investment over savings and a corresponding excess of demand for consumer goods over supply: that is, an excess of consumption and investment (of domestic demand) over savings and domestic production. Hayek speaks of "over and malinvestment": too many capital goods and too few consumer goods have been produced compared to what consumers demand. The blame lies with the banks, which reduced the monetary interest rate despite the fact that the natural interest rate had not changed. For Hayek, the fragile soul of capitalism is the temptation to accelerate the pace of growth by financing a volume of investment in excess of available savings.

But there is a constraint to be respected: in order to increase investment, it is first necessary to increase savings by containing present consumption with a view to greater future consumption. Crises can be averted but not cured. Crises can be overcome by doing nothing, with a do-nothing policy, that is, by waiting for the spontaneous rebalancing of the markets. What we absolutely must not have is a Keynesian policy to stimulate consumption or investment, which would only accentuate the double imbalance and delay recovery. If anything, what we need to do is to encourage, or at least not hinder, the spontaneous readjustment of the markets and let deflation, by increasing the purchasing power of incomes, encourage the formation of the savings needed to finance new investments. The countercyclical or macroeconomic stabilisation policy, on the other hand, requires a neutral monetary policy aimed at ensuring the flexibility (not stability) of domestic prices. Hayek refers to an expanding economy in which the volume of transactions increases. The monetary authorities, in order to preserve the balance between the two interest rates (natural and monetary), should leave money circulation unchanged and allow prices to fall.

Hayek (1932) used his own theory of the cycle to put forward an alternative explanation of the great crisis to that of Keynes. The crisis, for the Austrian economist, originated in an excess, and not a shortage, of investment. The responsibility is still with the banks (British and American), which, from 1927 onwards, implemented an expansive monetary policy aimed at stabilising the general level of prices – just as Keynes wanted. But for Hayek, this was a tragic mistake. Prices were falling thanks to the introduction of new technologies that lowered production costs. Deflation was thus a positive effect of development. The banks should have adopted a "neutral" monetary policy. In the terms of the quantitative equation $(MV = PQ)$ – although Hayek does not explicitly refer to it – they should have reacted to an increase in trade (Q) by keeping the money supply constant (M) and letting prices decline (P). Instead, the banks decided to increase M in order to stop P. The increase in money circulation required a reduction of the "monetary" interest rate below the "natural" rate: prices stabilised but firms invested more than they saved voluntarily. The crisis exploded when banks were forced to raise interest rates to limit the supply of credit. Hayek reverses Keynes's conclusions: the crisis is from over-investment and originates in an expansive and accommodative monetary policy. Keynesian policies only serve to delay economic recovery. The door that leads out of the labyrinth of the crisis opens by itself. There is no magic formula. All we have to do is wait.

In a 1933 essay, and later in the 1936 volume *Crises and Cycles*, Röpke attempted a synthesis.[7] For Röpke, economic cycles always originate in the financing of a flow of investment that exceeds existing savings. But a distinction must be made between normal cycles and prolonged cycles. In the former, Hayek is right and recovery occurs spontaneously at the end of a painful process of liquidation of inefficient firms and rebalancing between markets with excess demand or supply. In the case of prolonged cycles, on the other hand, despite the fact that the process of liquidating inefficient firms and readjusting unbalanced markets has been completed, economic recovery does not begin. The reason is the one given by Keynes. Businesses, due to the continuing climate of uncertainty and mistrust, do not invest their newly available savings. The economy spirals into a depression characterised by an excess of savings over stagnant investment. The primary and useful deflation is followed by a harmful secondary deflation or depression, which can and must be stopped by Keynesian policies to stimulate investment and/or consumption.

Interestingly, Röpke, while in favour of expansionary manoeuvres, criticised the New Deal. In his 1936 book, perhaps for the first time, the German economist distinguishes between "conformable" and "non-conformable" interventions to the market order. In general, the former preserve the market while the latter block it. For example, tariffs are compliant because they only represent a cost burden for consumers, whereas quotas are not compliant because they severely restrict consumers' freedom of choice. Röpke (1936: 171–172, 195) considers the New Deal to be a non-conformable intervention. The United States should have carried out an expansionary manoeuvre within the gold standard. It could and should have done so as a creditor country that had hitherto benefited from large inflows of gold: The American recovery would have driven the rest of the world. Instead, the United States chose an isolationist strategy, first by raising protective tariffs and then by devaluing the dollar to encourage an increase in the general level of prices (a reflation) considered as the necessary condition for economic recovery. Röpke's conclusion is that there is no alternative between internal and external stability. Both are only possible within a classical liberal order that requires a set of market-compliant interventions to be preserved.

A similar attempt at synthesis was made by Italian economists, who actively participated in the international debate on the business cycle and the great crisis (see Magliulo 2012). In Italy, the economic debate was conditioned by the attempt, desired or imposed by the Fascist regime, to elaborate a model of corporate economy. In general, we can say that Italian economists, by a large majority, accepted or shared the conditions of balanced growth indicated by neoclassical theory: flexible prices, stable exchange rates, balance between savings and investment. The significant and characteristic aspect is that they do not believe that these conditions can be guaranteed or entrusted to a free market. What is needed is a strong state that intervenes, with coercive actions, to ensure price flexibility, exchange rate stability and the balance between savings and investment. In Italy, the neoclassical theory inspired two alternative strategies of economic policy: a liberal one, authoritatively expressed by Luigi Einaudi, and an interventionist one, shared by many economists who were only formally close to the Fascist regime. The Italian anomaly is that a neoclassical, not Keynesian, interventionist economic culture prevails.

In brief, Keynes and Hayek propose two alternative explanations of the cycle, of the great crisis and of anti-crisis and anti-cyclical economic policies. For Keynes, the cycle is always a negative phenomenon resulting from real and monetary factors; the crisis highlights an excess of savings over investments; the anti-crisis policy should re-establish, directly (more investments) or indirectly (fewer savings), a favourable investment gap; the counter-cyclical policy should keep the economic system in a phase of high expansion with a public control of investments and an active monetary policy of domestic price stabilisation. For Hayek, on the other hand, the cycle is a negative phenomenon only if it is caused by monetary policy errors (money cannot accelerate the pace of economic growth); the crisis derives from an excess of investments (and consumption) over savings; the anti-crisis policy should limit itself to encouraging the spontaneous readjustment of the markets and the formation of new savings; the anti-cyclical policy should ensure the flexibility (and not the stability) of domestic prices with a neutral (and not manoeuvred) monetary policy. Röpke attempts a synthesis by considering the Keynesian analysis to be valid only in the particular case of large or prolonged depressions when, due to continuing negative expectations, a situation of investment stagnation arises that requires extraordinary public intervention.

In short, for Hayek, the way out of the great crisis was to rely on the market; for Keynes and Röpke, it was government action. For Keynes, monetary stability, which ensures macroeconomic equilibrium, is the stability of domestic prices, while for Hayek, as in 1927–1929, there can be price stability that hides latent inflation (because prices should fall), and this is a harbinger of serious imbalances: for Hayek and the neoclassics, monetary stability continues to be guaranteed by the stability of foreign exchange rates (and the related flexibility of domestic prices).

We have just seen that, under the current gold exchange standard rules, the political authorities were supposed to promote or encourage a deflationary tightening, including wage cuts and selective increases in the cost of money. Let us see what actually happened.[8]

In the United States, the Fed, contravening the Bagehot rule, lowered the discount rate and injected liquidity into the economy: its securities doubled between October and November and rose by the same amount between November and December 1929. Instead of encouraging or allowing wages and prices to fall, Hoover tried to stop deflation: he launched a public works programme, created the Federal Farm Board, to buy up agricultural surpluses and grant loans to ailing businesses, acted as a moral suasion to persuade the major industrial groups not to cut wages, and did not veto the Smooth-Hawley protectionist law. The 1929–1930 financial year ended with a surplus, but the following year saw a large deficit. The

United States implemented an expansionary economic policy to support domestic demand and halt the fall in prices and output. They violated the third rule of the game: instead of supporting downward flexibility in wages and prices, they implemented a reflationary policy. In December 1930, the Bank of the United States went bankrupt and panic set in.

The crisis hit Europe, with Germany and England at the forefront. In 1928, the withdrawal of American capital opened up the painful prospect of a restrictive policy. The prospect had become more acute. Germany and the United Kingdom had to reduce domestic demand in order to reduce their trade deficits and stop the outflow of gold. Contracting demand means lowering private consumption and public spending, that is, cutting wages and benefits, a restrictive policy that, from an economic and social point of view, is tearing the European political world apart.

In Germany, the coalition government led by Social Democrat Müller, who was against reducing public spending, collapsed.

In March 1930, a new government was formed, without the Social Democrats and headed by the leader of the Centre Party, Brüning. The new government prepared an austerity policy and placed it before the people in the general election of September 1930. The election saw the clamorous and unexpected success of Hitler's party, which increased its votes from 2.5% to 18.3%. Germany began to lose its gold reserves: the general uncertainty was compounded by the political concern aroused by the Nazi victory.

The crisis came to a head in May 1931. The French, opposed to the establishment of the planned Austro-German customs union, suddenly withdrew their deposits from the Credit-Anstalt. The collapse of the Austrian bank caused a domino effect and accelerated the flight of capital from Germany and England.

Germany applied the classical recipe. The *Reichsbank* raised its discount rate and ruled out any devaluation of the mark. On 5 June, the government approved a package of measures aimed at reducing the public deficit, that is, cutting domestic demand and the trade deficit. The package included lower expenditure and higher government revenue. Subsidies to the unemployed and to companies in crisis were cut by 6%, civil servants' salaries by 4 to 8% and war pensions by 6%. Taxes on sugar and petrol were increased and an income surcharge introduced.

A few weeks earlier, the government had appointed a special commission to propose measures to stem the rising unemployment. One of the most influential members of the Commission – called the Brauns Kommission after its chairman – was Wilhelm Röpke.

The restrictive measures did not stop the flight of capital. On 20 June 1931, President Hoover announced a one-year moratorium on all war debts, especially German debts. But Germany needed new foreign loans, which it did not hesitate to ask for. At the same time, the Brauns Kommission published a report, written mainly by Röpke, suggesting that part of the new loans should be used to finance a public works plan to reduce unemployment. The idea of financing public works with foreign loans, that is, with real savings, would make the expansionary manoeuvre for employment purposes compatible with Brüning's more general deflationary policy.

In this period, there occurred a little-known episode of great scientific and political value. Hayek sent Röpke an article critical of the proposals put forward by the government commission. The arguments are familiar. According to Hayek, the crisis arose from a macroeconomic imbalance, generated by the central banks, between the production of consumer goods (deficient) and the production of capital goods (excessive). If prices and wages were flexible, the traditional process of adjustment would be activated spontaneously with the shift of inputs from the hypertrophic capital goods sector to the hypotrophic consumer goods sector. But wages are rigid and the imbalance remains. Prolonged deflation is for Hayek a painful process that eventually forces firms to reduce nominal wages, restoring the desired and necessary flexibility of all prices. An expansive economic policy aimed at stopping "secondary deflation" could only be justified by "political considerations", namely to temporarily reduce the mass unemployment that was preparing Hitler's rise in Weimar Germany. In his accompanying letter, Hayek suggests to Röpke that the article should not be published if these fears were to prevail. "Apart from political considerations", he writes,

> I think you should not – not yet at least – start expanding credit. But if the political situation is so serious that continuing unemployment would lead to a political revolution, please, do not publish my article. That is a political consideration, however, which I cannot judge from outside Germany, but which you will be able to judge.
>
> *see Magliulo 2016: 42 and Magliulo 2018*

The article, which remained unpublished for decades, has only recently been published, and in the 1970s, after receiving the Nobel Prize for Economics, Hayek would reflect on that episode (cf. Magliulo 2016: 44 ff.).

On 15 July 1931, German reserves fell below the 40% safety threshold. Germany was virtually out of the gold exchange standard. The new *Reichsbank* governor, Luther, requested a huge foreign loan. Negotiations dragged on without success. In August, Germany took an extreme decision: it introduced exchange rate control. Exchange rates remained fixed thanks to government control of the main items in the balance of payments. The first measure was to freeze foreign deposits. This measure effectively prevented Germany from obtaining further foreign loans.

On 15 September 1931, a new employment plan, the so-called Lautenbach Plan, was presented at the *Reichsbank*, with Röpke, among others, in attendance. The plan proposed that, once the possibility of new foreign loans had disappeared, the public works programme to absorb unemployment be financed with domestic credits. But the German monetary authorities considered credit expansion incompatible with the overriding objective of exchange rate stability.

Thus, between June and September, the crisis precipitated. Germany implemented a restrictive, deflationary economic policy to reduce external debt and stop the outflow of reserves. The manoeuvre failed and the outflow continued. But Germany did not change its economic policy objectives: fixed exchange rates and deflation, that is, downwardly flexible prices. In order to comply with the first rule, it violated the second: gold flows no longer depended on free economic transactions but were regulated centrally by a political authority.

In the summer of 1931, the crisis also precipitated in England, which implemented the same restrictive policy and encountered the same difficulties as Germany. A government of national unity led by Labour leader Ramsay MacDonald succeeded in a few days in drastically reducing the public deficit and obtaining substantial foreign loans. But by now England was suffering from a crisis of confidence and capital was flowing out of the country. On 21 September 1931, the pound sterling broke away from gold and depreciated against the major currencies. The *Economist* headlined: *The end of an epoch.*

In the first two years of the crisis, from October 1929 to September 1931, the major countries experimented with various strategies to extricate themselves from the crisis. However, sooner or later and more or less voluntarily, they all broke the rules of the game. Hoover's America broke the third rule: combat deflation. Brüning's Germany broke the second rule: keep the exchange rate stable. And MacDonald's England broke the first and fundamental rule because it failed to deflate.

The Paris Order began to crumble.

On 21 September 1931 began the third and final turning point in the economic cycle in which the 1929 crisis was embedded.

The crisis was rebounding from Europe to America. The dollar was still the only currency that could be converted into gold, and it was the focus of attention of traders worldwide: what would have happened if, as confidence in the US economy had waned, bankers and savers had begun to convert their dollars into gold?

Uncertainty was emerging in US economic policy. Between August and November, the money supply collapsed: savers converted their deposits into notes and the notes into gold. The monetary multiplier worked in the opposite direction, accentuating the fall in the money supply. According to Eichengreen, the Fed refused to carry out any further expansionary open market operations. Instead, according to Rothbard, it injected new liquidity into the economic system. Hoover set up a government agency to assist and rescue banks in difficulty. In any case, any expansionary manoeuvre does not compensate for the spontaneous contraction and the money supply is reduced. The Hoover administration continued to increase public spending, but in the 1932–1933 financial year attempted to reduce the public deficit by increasing the tax burden even more. The US authorities then implemented only partially expansionary monetary and fiscal policies.

The uncertainty vanished with Roosevelt, who took office as US president in March 1933. Monetary and fiscal policies became fully expansionary. In April 1933, Roosevelt made the historic decision to suspend the gold convertibility of the dollar. At the same time, he implemented the new deal policy aimed at stimulating domestic demand and curbing the fall in the general level of prices with codes of productive discipline, subsidies for farmers, major public works and unemployment benefits.

After the collapse of the pound, the United States could no longer guarantee the gold convertibility of the dollar. At the same time, they did not want to abandon the reflationary policy initiated by Hoover and intensified by Roosevelt. A trade-off arose between exchange rate stability and reflation. Roosevelt dissolved it by abandoning the gold standard of fixed exchange rates and devaluing the dollar. He loosened the external constraint to be able to carry out fully expansionary policies. In the spring of 1933, the United States came up with an anti-crisis strategy similar to the British one: devaluation and reflation.

In the early 1930s, Britain and the United States implemented Keynesian-oriented policies, with public works plans to support domestic prices and devaluation of their currencies. Italy, on the other hand, adopted an active economic policy that was "conformable" to the neoclassical theory of economic equilibrium and development. In November 1930, the government, through the Fascist trade unions, decreed an 8% reduction in wages and salaries. Private deflation was followed by an increase in public spending. The government financed a multi-year programme of "integral land reclamation", that is, public works. In 1932, the Fascist government introduced compulsory consortia between companies to operate a public control on prices and production. In January 1933, the Institute for Industrial Reconstruction (IRI) was created, a public holding company charged with saving banks and companies on the verge of bankruptcy by nationalising them. That same month, Parliament passed a law obliging private companies to ask the state for permission to build new plants or expand existing ones. The aim was to finance an investment volume that did not exceed the available savings. Government intervention increased the public deficit and aggravated the external imbalance. In July 1933, Italy joined the so-called gold bloc along with France, Belgium and other countries. In April 1934, the government decreed a further reduction in wages and salaries, but this did not correct the external imbalance. On 8 December 1934, following Germany's example, Italy adopted political exchange controls to keep the external value of the lira stable even after the devaluation of the dollar and the pound. In short, it used atypical instruments to achieve typical objectives: flexibility of internal prices, exchange rate stability, and a balance between savings and investment.

Germany, meanwhile, blocked the exchange rate and reinforced its deflationary policy. On 8 December 1931, the Brüning government decreed a further reduction in wages. But unemployment was rampant and exceeded the alarm level by six million. In May 1932, Brüning was forced to resign, in his own words, "in the last hundred metres before the finish line". The international conference in Lausanne the following June–July significantly reduced the amount of reparations and suspended payments for three years (after which they would not be resumed). At the end of 1932, the new Chancellor, von Papen, experimented with the policy of public works financed by domestic credit as outlined in the Lautenbach Plan. But this was a timid attempt that did not make a dent in unemployment and did not halt the joint rise of the National Socialist movement.

On 30 January 1933, Hitler was appointed Reich Chancellor and immediately embarked on a fully expansive economic policy based on a programme of public works financed by domestic credit. Hitler established a command economy, including public control of credit, exchange rates, production and labour (with the creation of the "German Labour Front"). Under Hitler, Germany's anti-crisis strategy was the following: controlled fixed exchange rates and reflation. At the same time, the principle of self-determination of peoples was instrumentally invoked to annex countries with German populations.

In Europe, some states, including France and Italy, were sticking to gold and a fixed exchange rate regime (the so-called gold bloc). England, on the other hand, followed a different strategy. At the Ottawa conference in July 1932, it approved a system of preferential tariffs that favoured trade with the Commonwealth countries. In other words, Britain sought recovery in its own domains.

During 1933, the United States, following England's example, devalued the dollar. Other countries, including Germany, Italy, and France, retained fixed exchange rates. In the alternative between fixed and flexible exchange rates, all implemented expansionary policies.

In 1934, a weak recovery began that is still shrouded in mystery. Was it a real recovery? And was it due to the expansionary policies undertaken in 1932–1933? In 1937, the world economy fell into a new recession – the "depression within the depression" – which only ended with the first signs of war. In 1936, the gold bloc also broke up and all countries adopted a common anti-crisis strategy: devaluation and reflation.

The economic cycle between 1924 and 1936 was, therefore, characterised by three main phases: boom (1924–1929), great crisis (1929–1933), and weak recovery (1934–1936). But the cycle was also marked by three crucial policy decisions. The first was taken in 1927, when the major central banks agreed on an expansionary monetary policy that prolonged the boom. The second came in the summer of 1929, when the Fed tightened its monetary policy, leading to (causing?) the Wall Street crash. The last was again the Fed's choice, which in the autumn of 1931, after the devaluation of sterling, implemented a partially expansive monetary policy that did not compensate for the spontaneous contraction of the money supply.

There are three phases and three choices that the great economists, taking divergent paths, attempt to explain and that, at least in part, they contribute to addressing. In the course of the prolonged and acute crisis of 1929, the Paris Order, based on the idea of a Europe of sovereign nations within the framework of an open and cooperative international community, dissolved. In the face of this crisis, nationalism prevailed over supranational cooperation. The United States was the first to return to protectionism in 1930. In 1931, England broke away from gold, devalued the pound, and took refuge in the Empire. In 1936, the gold bloc also dissolved and each state tried to save itself. During the crisis, political short-sightedness also seemed to emerge: Brüning rejected the expansionary programmes drawn up by the

Brauns Kommission and continued undaunted with the austerity policy, underestimating the economic consequences of prolonged deflation (a secondary deflation) and the political consequences of widespread unemployment – the unemployment that would bring Hitler to power.

In 1936, the two pillars of the Paris Order – national democracy and an open market economy – wavered frighteningly.

Europe Towards the War Between Neoliberalism, Keynesianism and Corporatism

The great crisis of capitalism discredited classical liberalism and fuelled a series of attempts both to renew the old liberalism and to replace it with a radical corporatist alternative.

In 1936, Hitler's Germany launched a four-year plan to prepare the country for war. In the same year, Keynes published *The General Theory of Employment, Interest and Money*, the work that founded modern macroeconomics and revolutionised economic culture. Keynes, along with Beveridge, was the leading exponent of an early-twentieth-century movement of ideas called "New Liberalism". Four years later, in 1940, Keynes extended the scheme of his *General Theory*, designed for an economy plagued by widespread unemployment, to the war economy, characterised by the opposite problem of managing a situation of full employment of available resources. In 1938, the Lippmann Colloquium was held in Paris, where the Austrian neoliberals, led by Hayek and Mises, and the German ordoliberals, led by Röpke and Rüstow, began a close confrontation.[9] In 1939, Benito Mussolini transformed the Chamber of Deputies into the Chamber of Fasces and Corporations, thus realising a plan conceived at the beginning of the regime.

In his *General Theory*, Keynes poses and deals with a new historical–analytical problem: the underemployment equilibrium. Until then, as we have seen, the business cycle had been discussed. But the cycle suggested that after the recession, sooner or later, economic recovery and a new expansionary phase would ensue. Keynes, on the other hand, as a result of the experience of the prolonged depression of 1929, was convinced that the economic system could be stuck, for years, in a situation where there was equilibrium (between production and demand), while at the same time vast, involuntary unemployment would remain.

In Keynes's work, we can distinguish, simplifying and schematising, a *pars destruens* and a *pars construens*. We begin with the first.

For the neoclassics, as we know, the economic system tends towards equilibrium if markets are competitive and prices flexible. In particular, wage flexibility ensures labour market equilibrium and interest rate neoclassicists flexibility ensures capital market equilibrium. Keynes criticises both mechanisms.

First, the (real) wage cannot ensure labour market equilibrium because bargaining takes place on the nominal wage, the only one that workers know and value and, thanks to or because of trade unions, there is an obvious downward stickiness of wages, so that unemployment cannot be absorbed by reducing nominal wages.

Moreover, a reduction in nominal wages, if it is possible at all, could lead to a worsening of expectations of consumption growth on the part of businesses, with a consequent reduction in employment levels. In short, wage movements do not ensure full employment of the labour force.

Second, the flexibility of the interest rate cannot ensure the equilibrium between saving and investment for the simple reason that it is not, as neoclassical economists think, the price for foregoing present consumption but the premium for foregoing liquidity. Keynes (1936: 167) writes:

> The rate of interest is not the "price" which brings into equilibrium the demand for resources to invest with the readiness to abstain from present consumption. It is the "price" which equilibrates the desire to hold wealth in the form of cash with the available quantity of cash.

The interest rate is the equilibrium price of the money market where liquidity is offered and demanded; it is not the equilibrium price of the capital market.

Thus, the economic system does not spontaneously tend towards the equilibrium of full employment.

In the *pars construens*, Keynes overturns Say's law and introduces the principle of effective demand or, as we are used to calling it today, aggregate demand, the sum of household consumption, business investment, public spending, and net exports, the difference between exports and imports. In the short run, what Keynes considers – because "in the long run" (as he loved to repeat) "we are all dead" – is the aggregate demand that determines the level of output, employment, and inflation. Keynes wants to explain what he called the "paradox of poverty in the midst of plenty" into which Western countries had fallen. Rich but poor: rich in resources but poor in goods and labour. The explanation lies in the principle of effective demand. In neoclassical theory, a reduction in consumption corresponds to an increase in savings and thus in investment. In other words, the reduction in consumption is offset by the increase in investment and there is no fall in total demand. For Keynes, on the other hand, it can, and frequently does, happen that a fall in consumption is followed by a fall in investment and thus a fall in total demand. When uncertainty grows or negative expectations about the future of the economy spread, the preference for liquidity grows. In addition to its traditional function as an intermediary in trade, money also performs the delicate function of a "store of value". It then happens that money is taken out of the expenditure circuit: neither consumed nor invested, but simply hoarded, for example in sight deposits that banks cannot use to finance investments. In the economy of uncertainty, consumption and investment fall together, dragging production and employment down. In other words, it is aggregate demand that determines output and employment.

In a situation of uncertainty, according to Keynes, traditional economic policy measures become ineffective. A reduction in wages could, and usually does, cause a further contraction in aggregate demand, just as a decrease in interest rates may not be enough to reverse the pessimistic expectations of entrepreneurs. The effective economic policy to get out of the crisis and reach full employment equilibrium is an expansionary manoeuvre in the framework of a flexible or adjustable exchange rate regime. In particular, Keynes proposed a programme of public spending, to be financed in deficit, which would have the immediate effect of bringing about a multiple increase in aggregate demand, a consequent increase in output and national income, and a final increase in savings.

In Keynes's view, the classical and neoclassical sequence is reversed: it is investment that, by leading to a multiple increase in income, generates the savings needed to redress the macroeconomic imbalance.

On 1 September 1939, Germany invaded Poland, sparking World War II. We move from an economy of peace to an economy of war. For Keynes, from the "general case" in which, in order to reach the equilibrium of full employment, it is necessary to raise, with government intervention, the level of aggregate demand, we pass to the "particular case" in which the level of full employment is forcibly reached. It thus becomes a question, if anything, of changing, again with government intervention, the composition of aggregate demand by raising war consumption and reducing civilian consumption. In 1940, Keynes addressed this issue in a pamphlet entitled *How to Pay for the War*. If, before the war, the problem was to raise the level of aggregate demand until full employment was reached, with the war it was necessary to prevent global demand – increased in the war consumption component – from exceeding production capacity and generating inflationary tensions. It was therefore a question of changing the composition of demand while leaving its level unchanged. More precisely, it was a question of reducing civilian consumption to allow an increase in military production. To this end, Keynes proposed a form of compulsory savings. The government was to withdraw part of the national income by forcing the sums taken from savers into special current accounts and undertaking to return them at the end of the conflict. The reduced purchasing power of the consumer goods sector would be used to increase military production, thus avoiding imbalances and inflationary flare-ups. Keynes's plan was also applauded by Hayek and attracted the attention of Italian economists, who were equally busy formulating programmes to finance the war.

The meaning of the Keynesian revolution can be summarised as follows: market economies, in addition to cyclical instability, risk getting stuck in an equilibrium of underemployment caused by an insufficient level of effective or aggregate demand. The modern economy must be governed from the demand side by raising the level of aggregate expenditure to reach full employment equilibrium and by changing, if necessary, the composition of demand between civilian and war consumption or between public and private consumption or between public expenditure and private investment. The principle of effective demand modifies two fundamental assertions of neoclassical theory: first, investment determines savings (and not vice versa); second, there is no dichotomy between the real and monetary sectors but, on the contrary, money, by determining the rate of interest, influences investment and therefore production and employment.

For Keynes, the old *laissez faire* liberalism cannot overcome the uncertainty that periodically depresses the market economy because it does not allow for policies of deficit spending and manoeuvred money to support aggregate demand. Keynes envisages a new European and world economic order in which national governments are placed in a position to implement policies to manage aggregate demand (in an expansive or restrictive sense) in order to achieve the priority domestic balance of full employment. For Keynes, sovereignty, that is, the legitimate power to direct the economy towards desired social objectives, starting from full or maximum employment, belongs to national and supranational institutions that can and must govern the market. Keynes prefigured a regime of flexible or adjustable exchange rates that would allow national governments to implement the necessary policies of deficit spending and managed currency. This proposal, as we shall see in Chapter 6, would be put forward at the Bretton Woods International Conference.[10]

In August 1938, the French philosopher Louis Rougier summoned a small but influential group of scholars to Paris for a "Colloquium" on the American Walter Lippmann's book *The Good Society*. Among the few others present in Paris were the Austrians Mises and Hayek and the German ordoliberals Röpke and Rüstow. It was here that the term neoliberalism was coined by Rüstow. Keynes was absent: he had not been invited. At the heart of the Colloquium was a major theme: causes of and remedies to the crisis of classical liberalism. The participants agreed that the crisis consisted essentially in the progressive degeneration of competition into monopoly and oligopoly. Around this theme consensus and disagreement emerged between German ordoliberals and Austrian liberals. The decisive day was perhaps 27 August, when the key question was posed: "Is the decline of liberalism due to endogenous causes?" Both Austrians and Germans answered in the negative, but using different and almost opposing arguments.

For Rüstow, the substantial cause was the presence of a "weak State", which limits itself to watching, refusing to oppose, with appropriate antitrust action, those industrial concentrations not justified by economic reasons that result in a monopoly power to the detriment of consumers. In the modern economy, there is a natural and positive tendency towards industrial concentration due to organisational and technological factors, although companies often go beyond the optimal size in order to acquire the market power that allows them to escape competition from rivals. Rüstow (1938 [2018]: 124) declares:

> No doubt, there is a trend toward concentration which is of a purely economic type, due to technical and organizational progress, therefore inherent to and legitimate in the competitive system. This economic tendency does not incline toward the maximum but only toward the optimum of concentration. In most cases, however, the purely economic optimum concentration is significantly lower than the maximum. The tendency to exceed the economic optimum of concentration can obviously not be a trend of an economic kind, in the sense of the competitive system. It is rather a monopolizing trend, a

neo-feudal, predatory, trend that cannot succeed without the support of the State, laws, tribunals, judges, public opinion.

Firms can only acquire an unjustified monopoly position because the State refrains from intervening in accordance with the ancient principle of *laissez faire*. The remedy for the crisis of liberalism, according to Rüstow, is a "strong State" that works to defend competition:

> Thus, it is not competition that kills competition. It is rather the intellectual and moral weakness of the State that, at first ignorant of and negligent in its duties as policeman of the market, lets competition degenerate, then lets its rights be abused by robber knights [*chevaliers pillards*] to deal the fatal blow to this degenerate competition.

Immediately afterwards, Mises took the floor, introducing another crucial distinction between production and sales monopoly and price monopoly. The true and dangerous monopoly is one in which a single firm, which satisfies the entire market demand, can increase profit by raising the price and reducing output. When, on the other hand, the only firm operating in the market does not have this power (because by raising the price it fears the entry of potential rivals), then the market only formally takes the form of a monopoly but in reality ensures the best allocation of resources (today we would say it is contestable). Mises (1938 [2018]: 124) states:

> The fact that a given business is the only one to produce and sell a given good is, from an economic viewpoint, without significance. The key factor here is knowing if this business is in a position to grow its profits by reducing the volume of its sales. It is not the monopoly of production and sale, but the existence of a monopoly price that constitutes the key factor.

For the Austrian economist, the formation of true (and harmful) monopolies is mainly due to the formation of cartels and trusts, favoured or permitted by governments, which sheltered firms from potential competitors. The real cause of the degeneration of the market and the related decline of liberalism is an "Omnipotent Government" (the title of his famous 1944 book): "It is legislation, it is policy, that have created the tendency toward monopoly" (Mises 1938 [2018]: 121).

The most evident (and profound) division between Austrians and Germans was over the role of the State in defending competition: the ordoliberals were in favour of a strong State which, by means of appropriate antitrust legislation, would discriminate between natural and positive agglomerations and between artificial and harmful (for consumers) cartels, while the Austrians feared a strong State and wanted legislation which would simply break down all barriers, including those erected by the government itself, which, by limiting the entry of potential new firms into markets, restricted competition. The division tended to widen on the related issue of the so-called conformable and non-conformable interventions which, after the tragic pause of the war, would be taken up again within the Mont Pèlerin Society. Divided over the means, Austrians and Germans are united in the end. Austro-German neoliberalism is characterised by the end it pursues: to give back to the market its lost sovereignty, namely the power to determine, through the invisible mechanism of competition, the allocation of the scarce resources available to men.

Corporatism presented itself as a radical alternative to both classical liberalism and Marxist socialism. The great fault of classical liberalism would have been that it separated and contrasted the individual, society and the State. The individual was urged to pursue his or her own self-interest, separated from the general interest, in the belief that the invisible hand of the market would recompose the many particular interests into a single and superior common good, while the State was assigned the residual task of overseeing order and security. The economic crisis of 1929 showed the irreversible failure of liberalism.

Corporatism took on the historical task of healing the rift between the individual, society and the State by creating a social order that made it possible for the individual to identify with the State. The individual would be fulfilled by becoming a citizen participating in the life of the State. A slogan coined by Mussolini sums up the philosophy of Fascist corporatism: "Everything in the State, nothing outside or against the State".

In the Fascist version, the individual becomes the State through the mediation of society. Society is in fact organised into intermediate bodies, the corporations, which facilitate the integration of the individual into the State. An Italian philosopher and economist very close to the regime, Ugo Spirito, compares the corporation to a pedestal by means of which the individual ascends towards the State and the State descends towards the individual. The bottom line is that the regime conceives corporations as organs of the State and not as free and voluntary associations of social groups. The *Charter of Labour* of 1927 had already outlined the guiding ideas of Fascist corporatism, which were then taken up and developed for over a decade. It prefigured the recomposition that the regime wanted to implement: private initiative was functional to the national interest, work was primarily a social duty, civil society was organised into corporations, and the national interest was expressed and implemented by the State:

> The Corporative State considers private initiative, in the field of production, as the most effective and useful instrument in the interests of the Nation … Work in all its forms – intellectual, technical, and manual – however organized or carried out, is a social duty. On these grounds, and on these grounds alone, it is safeguarded by the State … The Guilds constitute the unitary organization of the forces of production and integrally represent their interests … the law recognizes the Guilds as State organizations … The Italian Nation is an organism endowed with a purpose, a life, and means of action transcending

those of the individuals composing it. It is a moral, political, and economic unity which finds its integral realization in the Fascist State.

see Pasetti 2017

In the Nazi version, the identification of the individual with the State is more immediate or direct and takes place through the members of the national community (*Volksgemeinschaft*) following the Führer. According to scholars, Nazi ideology was not corporatist both because the Nazis wanted the individual to identify only with the national community and not also with the professional bodies, and because companies and mixed associations (including the German Labour Front) were directed by leaders who acted according to a top-down logic. Moreover, the mixed associations were public law bodies and not expressions of civil society. In his classic work, *Behemoth*, Franz Neumann (1942: 233) wrote:

> The economic organization of Germany has, indeed, no resemblance to corporative or estate theories. Even the food estate and the chamber of culture, which are both officially called estates, do not have that character. They are not autonomous, but are organs of the state. They do not operate from the bottom to the top, but inversely. They do not regulate wages and labour conditions. They are organizations of businessmen, excluding labor, controlled by the state and performing certain administrative functions.

Klaus Neumann (2017: 136) adds recently: "In 1934, a Nazi expert in constitutional law added that the German people were not a static organism in the sense of corporatist philosophy, but were 'followers of the Führer on the road to the *Volksgemeinschaft*'".

However, in my opinion, one can also speak of corporatism in the Nazi variant, since society is organised into corporations and mixed associations which, as in Italy, are controlled and directed by the State.

Corporatism, in its twofold Italian–German version, which spread to various parts of Europe, was characterised by the end it pursued and the instruments it used. The aim was the defence of the national community, a goal that could require, as historically occurred, the search for a living space in Germany, with the forced annexation of non-Aryan peoples, and a large self-sufficient space in Italy, with the irrational exploitation of internal resources. The instruments included a series of direct government interventions on prices, production, savings and investments, according to a command economy model. Corporatism in fact represented a third way between socialism and liberalism. It was separated from socialism by the recognition and protection of the right to private property and the market, whereas it was separated from ordoliberalism, which emerged in Paris in 1938, by the justification (and implementation) of interventions on prices and quantities that the ordoliberals considered non-conformable to the market order. Corporatism also differed from the new Keynesian liberalism because the theoretical frame of reference remained the neoclassical one, focusing on price flexibility, exchange rate stability and the balance between savings and investment. The Keynesian policies implemented by Schacht were, if anything, a special case.[11]

In Short

At the Paris Peace Conference, a Europe of sovereign nations was envisaged within the framework of an open international community based on free trade and the gold standard. Keynes considered a return to gold harmful, while Mises considered the formation of nation-states in Central and Eastern Europe, with its scattered national minorities, impossible. Their voices went unheard, and Europe took the path mapped out in Paris.

The great crisis, which erupted in October 1929, confronted governments with the alternative of violating or respecting the common rules of the gold exchange standard. Between 1930 and 1936, all countries abandoned gold and adopted expansionary measures to protect their national economies. The economic debate was dominated by the dispute over the cycle between Hayek and Keynes and Röpke's attempt at a synthesis. In 1936, with the end of the gold bloc and the launch of the four-year plan to prepare for war, the two pillars of the Paris Order – national democracy and the global market – were shaken. In the four-year period from 1936 to 1939, just prior to the war, the major responses to the great crisis of capitalism and classical liberalism were fully outlined: Keynes's new liberalism, which aimed to build a European (and world) order that would allow national governments to implement the management policies of aggregate demand necessary to achieve the equilibrium of full employment; Austrian–German neo-liberalism, which, albeit by different means, pursued the objective of restoring the sovereignty of the market; and Italian–German corporatism, which intended to build a command economy capable of ensuring the living space or the great autarkic space for national communities.

What influence, then, did the great economic ideas have on the transition from a Europe of sovereign nations bound by common rules to a Europe struggling to defend its freedom threatened by totalitarian States determined to conquer their living space? Perhaps we can say that they contributed, first, to reinforcing the conviction that loyal cooperation among sovereign nation-states was possible by respecting the informal rules of free trade and the gold exchange standard, and then, with the outbreak of the great crisis, by spreading the opposite conviction that those rigid rules, forcing national governments to implement restrictive manoeuvres even in times of crisis, could no longer safeguard the legitimate national interest, and that it was therefore necessary to escape external constraints by regaining full economic sovereignty. The spirit of cooperation was replaced by a nationalism that led to war.

Amidst the rubble of the war, the constituent values of Europe are still to be found, albeit profoundly deformed: the extension of positive freedom leads to the paradoxical result of democratically electing dictators who will compress negative freedom; full employment becomes a priority objective of economic policy but also the tragic effigy of concentration camps (*Arbeit macht frei*; "work makes you free"); the community to which everything is subordinated, including individual freedom, becomes the national community created and defended by totalitarian States.

The lesson of this story is that nations exist and do not accept being subjected to mechanisms that force governments to automatically adapt their domestic economies to world market trends. The abandonment of the gold-exchange standard highlights the problem of reconciling the internal equilibrium (of income and employment) with the external equilibrium (of the balance of payments). In other words, it highlights the major problem of reconciling national interest with international order.

Notes

1 On the history of Europe in the interwar years, see Seton-Watson (1967), Kindleberger (1986), Eichengreen (1992), Macmillan (2003), Tooze (2007) and Kershaw (2016). On the history of economic thought during the same years, see Haberler (1963), Hagemann (2002), Screpanti and Zamagni (2005: chaps. 7–8).

2 Two systems were devised to ensure gold convertibility. England, already with the Bank Charter Act of 1844, imposed a "ceiling" on the issue of non-gold banknotes. Other continental European countries, including Germany and Italy, in addition to the "ceiling", required their central banks to maintain a "minimum reserve" of gold to cover the banknotes issued. In both cases, convertibility was guaranteed by an optimal ratio of gold reserves to money circulation. English legislation aimed at directly controlling the monetary aggregate (the denominator) while continental legislation aimed at regulating the gold reserves (the numerator). The minimum reserve requirement ratio was set at around 40%.

3 Before the war, as we have noted, one pound was worth 4.86.6 dollars (4.87 for simplicity). The gold convertibility of the two currencies made it possible for the exchange rate to fluctuate within margins corresponding to the cost of transporting gold from New York to London (which at the time amounted to 3 cents per pound of gold). The exchange rate could have fluctuated between a minimum of $4.84 and a maximum of $4.90 per pound. An American debtor would never have agreed to pay more than $4.90 per pound: he could have bought the gold in New York, transported it to London for 3 cents, and sold it for $4.87 per pound. Similarly, an English creditor would never have agreed to receive less than $4.84 per pound if he could demand to be paid in gold.

4 On J.M. Keynes (1883–1946), see Skidelsky (1998) and Crotty (2019).

5 On business cycles and the great depression (and for the abundant literature on the topic), see Magliulo (2016, 2018).

6 See Ebenstein (2001) and Wapshott (2012).

7 On Wilhelm Röpke (1899–1966), see Gregg (2010).

8 On 17 May 1930, the French foreign minister, Aristide Briand, presented a memorial to the governments of the European states in which he outlined a European federal union with mainly economic tasks. In September that year, Briand presented the plan to the sixtieth session of the League of Nations Council. The Council approved a "European Manifesto" but went no further than a general wish. The leading players on the European and world stages remain the nation-states.

9 On neoliberalism, see Hartwich (2009), Mirowski and Plehwe (2015), Masala (2017), Reinhoudt and Audier (2018).
10 On the spread of the Keynesian Revolution, see Hall (1989), Pasinetti and Schefold (1999).
11 On corporatism, see Mancini, Perillo and Zagari (1982), Overy (1996), Tooze (2007). On the spread of corporatism in Europe, see Pinto (2017). On the difference between *Großraum* (great space) and *Lebensraum* (living space), see Fonzi (2015).

6

THE INVENTION OF FUNCTIONALISM AND THE "SEPARATED UNIFICATION" OF EUROPE (1944–1973)

Introduction

On 5 March 1946, Winston Churchill uttered these famous words:

> From Stettin in the Baltic to Trieste in the Adriatic an "iron curtain" has descended across the continent. Behind that line lie all the capitals of the ancient states of Central and Eastern Europe. Warsaw, Berlin, Prague, Vienna, Budapest, Belgrade, Bucharest and Sofia; all these famous cities and the populations around them lie in what I must call the Soviet sphere, and all are subject, in one form or another, not only to Soviet influence but to a very high and in some cases increasing measure of control from Moscow.

Europe unites and separates. For the first time in history, a process of real political unification begins. But it is a unity that divides, it is the "separate unification" of Yalta: on the one hand, Western Europe, which falls within the American sphere of influence, on the other Eastern Europe, which enters the Soviet orbit, while Central Europe disappears.

In the post–World War II period, the post–World War I debate about whether an effective international community could be reconstituted by returning to a free trade regime and a gold-based monetary system was repeated. By the end of the war, in August 1944, the Bretton Woods Monetary Agreements had already been signed, marking a substantial return to gold. In 1947, the General Agreement on Tariffs and Trade (GATT) was signed, outlining a process of gradual but progressive liberalisation of international trade.

In the immediate aftermath of World War II, the countries of the two Europes were called upon to decide whether or not to join the new international institutions, but also to consider a further option: whether, how and why to initiate a parallel

DOI: 10.4324/9781003188889-6

process of European unification. This choice would become decisive in 1948 with the American offer of an aid programme, the Marshall Plan, for the reconstruction of Europe.

In Eastern Europe, Marxism–Leninism became the official doctrine, taught in schools and universities and adopted as a political guide by governments.

In Western Europe, the challenge between the different neoliberalisms was renewed, while corporatism, almost clandestinely, flowed into various models of mixed economy adopted by some countries. Pure Keynesianism was mitigated by Hicks in the IS-LM model, which represented a new neoclassical synthesis; the pure neoliberalism of Hayek and Mises was shared only by a minority of economists who consciously chose to assume the role of critical soul; and ordoliberalism inspired Germany's model of social market economy, which was adopted, at least in part, by Europe with the 1957 Treaties of Rome.

In this chapter, we attempt to understand the influence of economic ideas on the process of "separate unification" in Europe between 1944 and 1973.[1]

We shall examine, first, the two Europes in the Yalta and Bretton Woods Order; second, the spread of Keynesianism in the West and Marxism–Leninism in the East; and third, the Marshall Plan and the beginning of the political unification of Europe.

The Two Europes in the Yalta and Bretton Woods Order

The great victors of World War II – Roosevelt's America, Churchill's Britain, and Stalin's Soviet Union – met in Yalta, Crimea, from 4 to 11 February 1945, to define a new European and world order. Twenty years earlier in Paris, President Woodrow Wilson had strongly advocated an order based on democratic legitimacy, even at the cost of giving up the balance of power. At Yalta, the pendulum of history seemed to be swinging in the opposite direction. The Great Powers felt they had to play a role, to exercise direct control over the main geopolitical areas, to ensure peace in the world. "Was this not", asked Fejtö, "incompatible with the 'free disposition' of all peoples?" (1955: 54, my translation from the Italian edition)

One of the Yalta objectives was to "establish in Eastern Europe governments that were *genuinely democratic* and at the same time pro-Soviet". It was a difficult goal to achieve. "The atmosphere in Potsdam", writes Fejtö (1955: 150, my translation),

> where the Great Powers met in July 1945, already bore the sign of a growing disagreement between East and West. The spirit of cooperation that existed at Yalta had been succeeded by a new spirit, that of "competition between the United States and Russia".

The new political order of Yalta and Potsdam was accompanied by the new economic order of the Bretton Woods Monetary Agreements and the GATT trade agreements.

The Bretton Woods Conference was convened to define a new international monetary system. At the heart of the debate is the ancient and fundamental question of the relationship between national sovereignty and international order. In the gold-based monetary systems, as we have seen in both the gold standard of the decades around the turn of the nineteenth century and the gold exchange standard of the inter-war years, there is a fixed exchange rate regime that obliges national governments to subordinate, in a sense, the internal balance of income and employment to the external balance of payments. This subordination consists in the fact that the political authorities, in order to maintain the balance of payments equilibrium needed to preserve the agreed parity of exchange rates, refrain from implementing inflationary policies that could lead to a trade deficit and a consequent depreciation of the currency. In other words, they refrain from implementing excessively expansionary monetary and fiscal policies. Governments agree to respect the external constraint of exchange rate stability because they consider it to be a fundamental condition for economic development. In this sense, it is a subordination of the internal balance of income and employment to the external balance of payments. The primary objective always remains internal or national economic development. Problems arise when imbalances result from exogenous shocks and not from wrong economic policy choices. In those situations, it is more difficult for a government to accept that it must implement austerity policies to redress imbalances for which it does not feel responsible.

The conference at Bretton Woods, New Hampshire, was carefully prepared in good time. The protagonists were Britain's Keynes and America's White, authors of two alternative plans, although Hayek would also intervene in this long-distance debate.

There were essentially three issues to be resolved: whether or not a fixed exchange rate regime should be reintroduced, how it should operate (based on strict rules or on discretionary cooperation among participating countries) and the question of the burden of adjustment: whether it should fall, as in the past, only on debtor countries or also involve creditor countries.

Keynes advocated a system of adjustable exchange rates (i.e., stable but not rigidly fixed) that would give national governments sufficient leeway to implement the aggregate demand management policies needed to achieve the domestic balance of full employment. The system would have to be governed by a logic of international cooperation, and the burden of adjustment would also have to fall on creditor countries. The latter is perhaps the most revolutionary proposal and the most consistent with Keynesian thinking. In fact, a fair distribution mechanism was envisaged in the traditional gold standard system: debtor countries would have to adopt a deflationary policy in order to stop the outflow of capital and the devaluation of the exchange rate, while creditor countries would have to implement a parallel expansionary policy to arrest the inflow of capital and the revaluation of the exchange rate. However, it was an asymmetric process, as Keynes noted in 1941: "The process of adjustment is *compulsory* for the debtor and *voluntary* for the creditor ... For whilst a country's reserve cannot fall below zero, there is no ceiling which sets an upper limit" (quoted by Steil 2013: 138).

At Bretton Woods, Keynes proposed the creation of an International Clearing Union, a clearing house for international credits and debits, whose function was to discourage the formation of large trade surpluses in a kind of anti-mercantilist policy. The proposal was that, above a certain amount, not only debts but also credits would be subject to interest. The underlying idea was that both creditors and debtors, in a logic of mutual cooperation, would be responsible for restoring a substantial balance in international economic relations. However, perhaps a further underlying factor was the typically Keynesian idea that the creditor was even more culpable than the debtor. In Keynesian economics, the sin of avarice (committed by the hoarder) is more serious than the sin of sloth (committed by the one who indulges in idleness and error). For while the international debtor is the one who, regardless of his errors, produces less than he spends and, consequently, invests more than he saves, and imports more than he exports, the creditor is the one who spends less than he produces, invests less than he saves, and imports less than he exports. In short, he is the one who, by burying his talent (savings), pushes his own and other people's economies towards the perverse equilibrium of underemployment, towards the cruel paradox of poverty in abundance, from which escape is possible only via "generous" expansionary measures.

Hayek, while recognising the limitations of the traditional gold standard, defended its advantages, which consisted essentially in allowing a form of monetary union and therefore of economic integration between national states that maintained their sovereignty while respecting common rules and obliging each other not to implement destructive inflationary policies. Hayek (1943 [1999]: 106) writes:

> The gold standard as we knew it undoubtedly had some grave defects … Compared, however, with the various schemes for monetary management on a national scale, the gold standard had three very important advantages: It created in effect an international currency without submitting national monetary policy to the decisions of an international authority; it made monetary policy in a great measure automatic and thereby predictable; and the changes in the supply of basic money which its mechanism secured were on the whole in the right direction.

The United States, as the world's largest creditor, found it hard to feel guilty or otherwise accept punitive measures against them. Eventually, however, they accepted the idea that creditor countries should also contribute to restoring international economic equilibrium. The solution they proposed was called the "scarce currency clause": debtor countries would be able to apply protectionist measures (tariffs and quotas) against countries with excessive trade surpluses that tended not to spend their currency, which became relatively scarce in the world market.

Roy Harrod (1951 [1963]: 544–545), a friend, colleague, and biographer of Keynes, recounts the moment he heard the news that the Americans had accepted the principle of common responsibility in the management of international economic relations. The scarce currency clause had been included in a US Treasury document of 16 December 1942 regarding the establishment of a special Currency Stabilisation Fund:

> I could not believe my eyes or my brain. I read it again and again. I studied some notes by Keynes which I had with me. They did not seem helpful. I was transfixed. This, then, was the big thing. For years we had complained of the United States' attitude as creditor. For months we had struggled in vain to find some formula which would pin them down to a share of responsibility. Now they had come forward and offered a solution of their own, gratuitously. This was certainly a great event. For it was the first time that they had said in a document, unofficial, it was true, and not committal, but still in a considered Treasury document, that they would come in and accept their full share of responsibility when there was a fundamental disequilibrium of trade.

In the end, a noble compromise was reached. The body of rules comprised a regime of adjustable exchange rates pegged to the dollar (the only currency convertible in gold) while national governments retained a margin of flexibility and could count on the help of the new international institutions in order to attain external equilibrium. In particular, they could change their par value by less than 10% without International Monetary Fund (IMF) approval and could adopt temporary capital controls and other restrictive measures to reduce the balance of payments deficit. If the disequilibrium remained, they had to trigger the classic deflationary process. The spirit of the agreements was perhaps more significant. The member states, together with the twin international institutions (IMF and World Bank), were willing to seek a shared management of the global imbalances. The symbol of this willingness was the "scarce currency clause" introduced in article 7 of the agreements. It allowed debtor countries to adopt restrictive measures against creditor countries that, by maintaining a trade surplus, tended not to spend their own currency, which became quite scarce. Even if it was never applied, it showed that the spirit of cooperation in the management of global imbalances had ultimately prevailed in Bretton Woods.

It may be useful to mention how the agreements was interpreted, and then ratified, by Italy.

At the end of 1945, the Ministry for the Constituent Assembly set up an Economic Commission to draw up a series of reports on the country's main economic issues. Operators and experts were heard. The first crucial economic policy choice was Italy's participation in the Bretton Woods monetary agreements. Doubts arise over the nature of the agreements. What was Bretton Woods? Was it a substantial return to the gold standard or the beginning of a policy of international cooperation? Will national governments have to submit to the external constraint of price flexibility to preserve exchange rate stability, or will they be able to implement an active economic policy geared towards the stability of their domestic economies? Will they have to adapt the domestic market to changing world market conditions or will they be able, with the help of the World Bank and the IMF, to pursue domestic growth objectives by relaxing the external constraint?

Around these questions, the Commission is divided. The liberals interpret the monetary agreements as a substantial return to gold, a gold regime that is only slightly more flexible than those of the past. Countries with trade deficits can obtain financial aid from supranational bodies, they can devalue their currency at their discretion up to 10% and, in the presence of undefined fundamental imbalances, can also modify (adjust) the exchange rate parity with other partners. But if all this were not enough, they would have to activate the classic deflationary process that, through a reduction in wages and prices, restores the external balance of payments. Catholics interpret monetary agreements as the start of a new policy of international cooperation. Francesco Vito, an authoritative economist at the Catholic University of Milan, believes that the function of supranational bodies is to assist national governments in the difficult task of achieving a position of external balance without interrupting expansive processes geared towards internal balance. Costantino Bresciani Turroni, an influential neoclassical economist, questioned as President of Banco di Roma, offers an original interpretation. In the long run, price stability and exchange rate stability are irreconcilable objectives. One can have either one or the other. Bretton Woods opts for exchange rate stability, that is, the stability of the currency's external purchasing power. However, in the short term, the two objectives may be compatible. Italy, by accumulating a fund of foreign exchange reserves to finance temporary trade deficits, without having to resort to devaluation or deflation, could make the two objectives of price stability and exchange rate stability compatible. Bresciani states:

> In the short term they can be achieved simultaneously; by using the expedient of accumulating reserves we can overcome certain temporary periods of disruption in the balance of payments by drawing on reserves, leaving exchange rates stable while domestic prices remain stable.
>
> *my translation from Italian, see Magliulo 2007: 80*

The Economic Commission, in the final report presented to the Constituent Assembly, recognised that Bretton Woods established an elastic monetary regime, which did not exclude the deflationary process of adjustment of the domestic economies to the world market trend, and that it was convenient for Italy to sign the monetary agreements because the advantage of breaking the isolation outweighed the disadvantage of submitting to the external constraint. In March 1947, the Constituent Assembly ratified Italy's participation in the Bretton Woods monetary agreements. It was the last decision shared by the political forces of liberation and the first major economic policy choice of Republican Italy. That choice opened a decision-making process: Italy joined the international economic community and committed itself to respecting its rules.

The General Agreement on Tariffs and Trade (GATT) is an international organisation created in 1947 with the aim of promoting the liberalisation of trade through a series of multilateral negotiations and in compliance with certain fundamental principles, such as non-discrimination among countries, that is, the application of the most-favoured-nation clause with the extension of bilateral tariff reductions to all member countries, the progressive elimination of non-tariff barriers, and consultation as a method for resolving trade disputes.

In the post-war peace and economic conferences, a new European and world order was drawn up in a more or less organic manner, with only a partial renunciation of the economic and political sovereignty of the nation-states. From a political point of view, the principle of national sovereignty was reaffirmed, both in the East and in the West, but the two Europes fell within the sphere of influence of the great victors of World War II: the United States in the West and the Soviet Union in the East. From an economic standpoint, participation in the new international institutions (GATT, IMF and World Bank) implies compliance with a series of common rules, which in turn result in compliance with the external constraint of the balance of payments but, within certain limits, leave the traditional instruments of economic policy available to national governments: currency, duties and taxation.

In the post-war period, the major European countries, in both East and West, were faced with the question of whether or not to join the new institutions of the international community. At the same historical juncture, they wondered whether it was appropriate to set up a European community. This is a topic that preoccupies economists.

The Rise of Keynesianism and Marxism and the Invention of Functionalism

On 21 April 1946, J. M. Keynes died. A year later, in April 1947, Hayek gathered a small group of surviving neoliberal economists at Mont Pèlerin, a Swiss mountain resort. Keynes died, yes, but his ideas spread around the world. Hayek, on the other hand, knew he had (temporarily) lost the battle of ideas with his great rival and hence prepared for a long resistance.

Keynes's ideas were taken on board and adapted, but perhaps the original revolutionary message was somewhat weakened. In 1937, Hicks presented the IS-LM model, still at the core of macroeconomic textbooks and analyses. The IS (investment and saving) is the set of combinations between interest rate and income level that ensures the balance between saving and investment and therefore the balance of the goods market. LM (liquidity preference and money supply) is the set of combinations, again between interest rate and income level, which ensures the equilibrium of the money market. At the point of intersection of IS and LM, there is simultaneous equilibrium in the goods and money markets, that is, macroeconomic equilibrium.

Hicks's 1937 article is entitled "Mr. Keynes and the 'classics'" (meaning those who identify with the pre-Keynesian tradition). The explicit objective is to present Keynes's theory in a concise way, but the ultimate aim is to present a general macroeconomic model that allows one to reconcile Keynesians and neoclassics, that is, to determine when one is right and when the other is right.

Hicks's solution is that in general the neoclassics are right and only in a particular case is Keynes right. In a general case, which can be represented by an average slope of the IS-LM curves, full employment equilibrium can be achieved using a mix of economic policy instruments (monetary and fiscal). In a special case, which can be represented by assuming an almost vertical IS (investments are not very sensitive to interest rate changes) and an almost horizontal LM (individuals show a high preference for liquidity), fiscal policy is very effective (IS can be shifted to the right with an increase in public spending) while monetary policy is ineffective (any increase in the money supply is hoarded). But this is a special case because the two conditions rarely occur. They occurred, for example, during the great crisis of 1929. So, Hicks's answer is that the neoclassical theory, represented through the IS-LM model, is valid in interpreting the normal course of market economies, while the Keynesian theory is valid as a description and explanation of an economy in severe recession.

In the IS-LM model, the adjustment process from a (Keynesian) equilibrium of underemployment to a (neoclassical) equilibrium of full employment can be interrupted in the presence of three hypothetical rigidities of wages, which do not fall when there is unemployment; of the interest rate on securities, which do not fall even if the money supply increases because individuals, anticipating a fall in prices, do not buy securities and prefer to hold their assets in liquid form (horizontal LM); and of investment, which does not rise even if interest rates fall because negative expectations about future profit rates prevail (vertical IS).

In a 1956 book, the Israeli economist Patinkin argues that, thanks to the real balance effect (i.e. the increase in purchasing power of incomes resulting from a reduction in general price level), the three rigidities can be reduced to a single one: the first one, which prevents wages from falling when there is unemployment. The macroeconomic debate of the 1960s and 1970s, led by the neo-Keynesian Franco Modigliani and the neoclassical Milton Friedman, revolved around the relative slope of the IS-LM curves and the wage rigidity hypothesis.

In the post-war period, an impure or "bastard" Keynesianism, as Joan Robinson called it, spread throughout Europe and the world, inspiring the work of economists and the choices of governments. What prevails is the idea that it is necessary "to manage the economy" by abandoning the myth of the invisible hand of the market that transforms private interest into the common good. In Eastern Europe, Marxism–Leninism became the official doctrine adopted by governments to direct national economies towards socialism with State intervention.[2]

In this cultural and political climate, both in the East and in the West, the twofold question of why and how to unite Europe emerges.

Eastern Europe was never a true supranational community, but neither was it a simple sum of national states. At the end of the war, borders did not change but people were forcibly displaced: from 1939 to 1950 approximately 30 million Eastern Europeans were victims of multiple forms of "ethnic cleansing": from population exchange to forced relocation, from deportation to labour camps to physical anni-hilation as a result of massacres (Bottoni 2011: 101).

The fundamental economic problem, common to the entire area and similar to that experienced in Soviet Russia, was the structural imbalance between agriculture and industry. Too many people were employed in agriculture, dispersed in a multi-tude of small and inefficient farms, and too few were employed in a technologically backward industry. The result of this combination was low productivity of human labour and a consequently low standard of living for the entire population.

Stalin's Russia, following and adapting the doctrine of Marxism–Leninism to the conditions of the country, had experimented with a radical solution, which envisaged a broad nationalisation of farms, a planned and forced industrialisation of the country, both to absorb the excess agricultural population and to supply the agricultural sector with machinery and fertilisers at competitive prices and, lastly, the reorganisation of agriculture with the destruction of large landed estates and the formation of efficient collective farms. The expected, and in part proven, result was a higher productivity of human labour and thus a rise in the standard of living of the population. Fejtö (1955: 192, my translation from Italian) writes:

> By inviting the peasants of Eastern Europe to divide up the large estates, to occupy the possessions abandoned by the expelled Germans, the communists (and the occupying Soviet authorities who supported them) were merely applying a strategy worked out by Lenin towards a type of society closely resembling the agrarian countries of Eastern Europe. The agrarian revolution, according to their doctrine, was to take place in two stages: the first involved the destruction of feudalism and the breaking up of the land; the second, which they were careful not to talk about in 1944–1945, was collectivist concentration. The aim was not initially economic but social and political: to destroy the former ruling class and neutralise the peasants while the struggle for political power took place in the cities.

The aim of Yalta had been to transform Eastern Europe into a group of coun-tries that were both genuinely democratic and friendly to Soviet Russia. At first, attempts were made to remain faithful to the good intention. On 24 October 1945, the Czechoslovak Assembly passed a law nationalising all workshops with over four hundred workers and leaving the others in private hands. In Czechoslovakia and other Eastern European countries, a public system of nationalised companies and a private system of free capitalist enterprises coexisted, while in Yugoslavia General Tito was free to experiment with a new economic model comprising cooperative enterprises run by the workers themselves. Trade relations between the two Europes were not interrupted, and indeed the East supplied the West with raw materials and capital. Democratic governments were formed, under vigilant Soviet control.[3]

In brief, until the spring of 1948, Eastern Europe lived in a precarious balance, suspended between a new and ideal model of "popular democracy" and a consolidated system of real socialism. This was a precarious balance, destined to break down.

In the West, the debate over Europe reached the highest peaks of social-economic thought, involving writers of the calibre of Lionel Robbins, Friedrich von Hayek, Ludwig von Mises, Wilhelm Röpke, Altiero Spinelli, David Mitrany and many others. The reflection began during the war years, in the case of Robbins as early as 1937, and continued uninterrupted during the reconstruction period. Deep divergences but also common orientations emerge.

The common underlying orientation is the realisation that the social disorder, from which war springs, stems from a split between the space of the economy and that of politics. The economy is increasingly global while politics is increasingly national. In the old economy, where there was little mobility of productive factors (labour and capital), it was enough for national governments to respect the (informal) rules of free trade and the gold standard to allow even less efficient countries to access the benefits of international trade. In the new economy, which emerged during the *belle époque* and was destined to re-emerge after the catastrophe of World War II, productive factors also circulate, and less efficient countries undergo processes of depopulation and/or impoverishment that lead national governments to intervene with restrictive measures which, by triggering the reaction of partner countries, generate economic and political conflicts. The other common basic orientation is that in order to re-establish an economic, world and European order, informal institutions, such as a free trade regime and a gold-based monetary system, are necessary but insufficient. Formal international and European institutions are also needed to govern the new global economy. In other words, Europe must become a political entity.

This dual orientation embraces the entire debate on Europe but does not stifle diversity. Three great and multiform currents of Europeanist thought emerge: federalism, internationalism and functionalism.

The federalists have one idea in common: the first step in the process of building a united Europe should be the establishment of a political union on a federal basis. Only a European government could manage the difficult phase of opening up the markets: first political unification, then economic integration. However, it would be a mistake to consider the federalists as a compact political movement. United at the start, they moved in parallel directions, imagining distinct models of European federation: socialist, liberal and Christian-inspired.

In the summer of 1941, Ernesto Rossi and Altiero Spinelli wrote a pamphlet entitled *Per una Europa libera e unita* (*For a Free and United Europe*), which later became known as the Ventotene Manifesto, named after the small island where they had been confined for opposing the fascist regime. The war had been going on for two years and was soon to become worldwide. At the heart of Spinelli and Rossi's reflection was the theme of war, its origins and possible remedies. According to the authors of the Manifesto, the cause of the disorder at the origin of the war is the deep-rooted presence of nation-states that are victims of a process of a heterogenesis of ends. The modern state, in fact, born to quell internal civil wars by recognising as legitimate only external conflicts regulated by international law, had ended up becoming an instrument of territorial conquest, trampling on and disregarding the value of international law. The "war without rules" of 1939 marked a point of no return, showing, on the one hand, the strength of a nationalism that had exalted the nation as "a divine entity" and, on the other, the weakness of international law lacking powers of sanction.

The solution proposed by Spinelli and Rossi is not a return to impotent international law but the transformation of powerful nation-states into member states of a supranational European Federation. For the authors of the Manifesto, what Hedley Bull would later call "domestic analogy" applies. Just as in domestic relations, a Leviathan is needed to repress interpersonal conflicts, so in external relations, a higher authority with coercive powers is needed to ensure peace. With federation, the only possible wars become those of secession, which, as the American experience shows, are rare and unlikely. Spinelli and Rossi outlined a socialist federation in its aims and instruments, albeit a tempered socialism with liberal overtones introduced by Ernesto Rossi. The aim is to subject market forces to public control in order to guarantee the emancipation of the working classes and the recognition of fundamental social rights, while the instruments include the regulation of private property rights, the nationalisation of monopolies, the abolition of corporate institutions, agrarian and industrial reform, and a policy of wealth redistribution:

> To meet our needs, the European revolution must be socialist in nature; in other words, its goal must be the emancipation of the working classes and the guarantee of a decent quality of life for them … The truly fundamental principle of socialism (and not its hurried and erroneous interpretation as general collectivization) is that economic forces, rather than dominating man, should be ruled over by him, like the forces of nature, guided and controlled by him as rationally as possible, so that the general population does not fall victim to them.
>
> *Spinelli and Rossi 1941 [2011]: 107*

At the antipodes of the socialist federalism of Ventotene, we find the liberal federalism elaborated by Robbins, Hayek and Einaudi, which also inspired the authors of the Manifesto. The problem is always the absence of a supranational authority able to curb and order the presence of nation-states. The domestic analogy also applies to liberals. The mistake of the classical economists – according to Robbins – was to believe that economic reason was enough to demonstrate the irrationality of state interventionism and to dissuade national governments from implementing those restrictive measures that would then prove harmful to national interests. But reason is not enough. The force of law is also needed to harmonise legitimate national interests. Without force, there is no order, and without order, there is no harmonious development. Robbins (1937: 240–241) writes:

> They thought that if they demonstrated the wastefulness and futility of economic and political warfare it was enough. If each national state were limited

to the performance of the functions proper to a liberal government there would be no occasion for international conflict. There would be no need for a super-national authority. But this was a grave error. The harmony of interests which they perceived to be established by the institutions of property and the market necessitated, as they had demonstrated, an apparatus for maintaining law and order. But whereas *within* national areas such apparatus, however imperfect, existed, *between* national areas there was no apparatus at all. Within the national areas they relied upon the coercive power of the state to provide the restraints which harmonized the interests of the different individuals. Between the areas they relied only upon demonstration of common interest and the futility of violence: their outlook here, that is to say, was implicitly not liberal but anarchist. But the anarchist position is untenable. It is true that, for the citizen who does not love war as such, abstention from violence is an obvious matter of self-interest. It is true that, in the long run, aggression seldom pays the aggressor, and that even victory is associated with impoverishment. But if we are not content to rely on such arguments for the preservation of order within the nation, we have no reason to believe that such reliance would be effective in preserving international order.

The solution is a liberal federation that takes economic powers away from the nation-states and transfers them to a European supranational authority capable of recreating and preserving a large, single market in which goods, services, people, and capital can circulate freely. If an area or region loses value, it is inevitable that it will undergo a process of depopulation and/or impoverishment. Robbins (1937: 312) further writes:

> To maintain an industry, as such, regardless of whether the factors of production thus employed are as productive there as they would be if devoted to other uses, is as fruitless from the point of view of the majority of the inhabitants of the national area as it is from the point of view of the majority of the inhabitants of the world as a whole.[4]

The purpose of a federation is to contain the power of interference of nation-states in the economy and certainly not, as the Ventotene Manifesto called for, to subject natural market forces to the control of a European government. Hayek (1944: 172) writes:

> But this does not mean that a new super-state must be given powers which we have not learnt to use intelligently even on a national scale, that an international authority ought to be given power to direct individual nations how to use their resources. It means merely that there must be a power which can restrain the different nations from action harmful to their neighbours, a set of rules which defines what a state may do, and an authority capable of enforcing these rules. The powers which such an authority would need are

mainly of a negative kind: it must above all be able to say "no" to all sorts of restrictive measures.

see also Hayek 1939 [1948]

In an intermediate position between socialist and liberal federalism is the federalism of Christian inspiration, outlined by Pius XII in his radio messages of the war years, commented on and disseminated by Guido Gonella, interpreted at the economic level by Francesco Vito, and translated at the political level by Alcide De Gasperi, one of the founding fathers of Europe.

The problem, for Catholics, is not the nation-state. The problem is etatism, that is, an absolutist conception, without limits, of national sovereignty that has asserted itself due to the pervasive influence of legal positivism that has severed every link between natural law and positive law, affirming the principle according to which the exclusive source of legitimacy of power is in the people and therefore in the legislator. The great crisis of 1929 marked, for a Catholic economist like Vito, an epochal turning point in which the national states refused to submit to the rules of an automatic mechanism such as the golden one in order to exercise their right and duty to protect the national interest. The refusal to submit to an impersonal mechanism, however, turns into the claim to solve the problem of adapting the domestic economy to changes in the world market by pursuing an improbable and harmful economic self-sufficiency, for themselves and for others.

The solution, for Catholics, is neither a socialist federation establishing a strong supranational government of the European economy, nor a liberal federation restoring a traditional minimal government. The solution is the construction of a European and global community of nation-states. There is no "domestic analogy" to fear. States are not like wolves to be tamed, and there is no need for a Leviathan to ensure peace. International relations can once again be governed by the principles of natural law. Of course, as in every community, even in supranational ones, some authority with coercive powers is needed to guarantee order. Catholics are gradually moving from a preference for the Confederal model (or Community of States) to one for the Federal model. This federalism is based on the principle of subsidiarity, which considers the national economy – in the words of Pius XII – as a "natural unit", and therefore indestructible and worthy of protection. At the centre, there also remain the nation-states, whose task it is to ensure the balanced development of their economies. The principle of subsidiarity justifies transfers of power from the bottom up – from the member states to the supranational government – only to perform functions that can no longer be exercised at a lower level. The aim is to build a federation that contributes, together with the nation-states, to ensuring the harmonious development of the nations that comprise the "European community". Vito (1949: 189, my translation) writes:

> The European organisation, whether in the form of a federation or confederation or simply a union [should] ... be implemented in such a way that individual countries are not impeded by external relations in the task of

making all social classes and all their members share in the benefits of economic progress.[5]

Alongside federalism, a second current of Europeanist thought emerges: internationalism. The internationalists or globalists or universalists have in common the idea that the cause of social unrest, which is at the root of war, lies in an interventionism that is "non-conformable" (in the broadest sense) to the market. They propose a solution that involves the recognition of the three freedoms and, alongside the traditional rules of free trade in goods and a gold-based monetary system, the introduction of new formal institutions that differ from those of classical federalism. The most authoritative and influential exponents of European internationalism are the neoliberals Wilhelm Röpke and Ludwig von Mises (see also Slobodian 2018). During the war years, the former published in German the trilogy that made him world-famous: *The Social Crisis of Our Time* (1942), *Civitas Humana* (1944), and *The International Order* (1945). The latter, also during the war years, composed two treatises in which his economic and political thought is masterfully summarised: *Human Action* (first published in German in 1940) and *Omnipotent Government* (1944).

At the heart of Röpke's analysis is the distinction, already introduced in his 1936 volume on business cycles, between conformable interventions (which preserve and strengthen the market) and non-conformable interventions (which violate and over time destroy the market order).

A free world economy – according to Röpke – flourished in the mid-nineteenth century. People were free to travel, emigrate, trade and invest anywhere. Nation-states existed or were, as in the case of Germany and Italy, in the process of being formed, but they felt no need to conquer and annex new territories in order to obtain raw materials, for the simple reason that they could obtain everything they needed, at reasonable prices, on the free international market. The existence of a world economy made it possible to separate *imperium* (national political sovereignty) from *dominium* (ownership of goods); that is, it cut off all forms of imperialism and ensured a long period of peace and development. The destruction of the world economy began in the late nineteenth century and, after the war, resumed its devastating course in the 1930s. The destruction came about through a combination of "interventionist nationalism" and "absentee liberalism".

At the end of the nineteenth century, nationalism steeped in historicist ideas tolerated or promoted the formation of monopolies and trusts which, by artificially raising domestic production costs, made it necessary to adopt measures to protect the national economy and to seek vital spaces for the supply of raw materials and the sale of finished products. The world economy broke up into many more or less closed markets, the distinction between *imperium* and *dominium* fell away, and the resurgent nationalism generated an imperialism that was a harbinger of war.

In the early 1930s, after the difficult reconstruction and the precarious return to a liberal order based on free trade and gold money, the wind of nationalism blew again. According to Röpke, the whirlwind that swept away any remaining traces of liberal order was Roosevelt's New Deal. Röpke, as we have seen, studied the case of the great crisis as part of a more general theory of the business cycle. In his model, the great crisis was an exceptional case of a normal recession degenerating into secondary deflation, which required an expansive public intervention to support consumption and investment. The point is that, for Röpke, this manoeuvre had to be adopted within the framework of, and in compliance with, the rules of the gold exchange standard.

In the trilogy conceived during the war years, Röpke indicated a third way to rebuild a free world and European economy. Reconstruction could be entrusted neither to nationalism, which was at the root of the destruction, nor to classical liberalism which, in the name of *laissez faire*, had merely observed the catastrophe and refrained from any intervention. Röpke outlined a complex and articulated economic policy strategy in defense of the market. Here, it is sufficient to briefly recall two aspects. First is the protection of competition: without an adequate legal framework and effective antitrust action, competition degenerates into monopoly and oligopoly. An active competition policy is therefore needed. The second aspect of the complex strategy is an intervention to "adjust" to the new equilibrium towards which the market is tending rather than to "preserve" the old one. This is a crucial step, which marks a further element of affinity and diversity between Austrian neoliberals and German ordoliberals. Röpke, like the Austrians, thinks that the international division of labour, from which the wealth of nations derives, is constantly evolving: the structure of comparative advantages is constantly changing, forcing nations, like Swiss cantons or the cities and provinces of any country, to adapt their patterns of specialisation. Adjustment can be spontaneous or imposed by a central authority. In the classical (and Austrian) view, the process is spontaneous. It is only the market which, by selecting comparative advantages, can determine the best territorial division of labour, and it is only the enlightened entrepreneur (innovator) who can know in advance what consumers will demand in the future. In 1920, Mises wrote: "Mankind does not drink alcohol because there are breweries, distilleries and vineyards; men brew beer, distil alcohol and grow grapes because there is a demand for alcoholic beverages" (Mises 1922 [1951]: 492). So, if mankind no longer drinks alcohol, brewers must resign themselves to producing more by trying to anticipate new or latent consumer needs.

Röpke emphasises that adaptation is inevitable, requires a sacrifice, and can lead to an impoverishment, even a permanent one, of the area affected by the change. If consumers no longer drink beer, it is inevitable that producers will take note and move on to other productions. If England, after the war, lost its position as a creditor country, it is inevitable that it would adopt policies to rebalance the balance of payments by reducing imports (consumption) and/or increasing exports. Röpke excludes adjustment imposed by a central authority, which he considers a form of interventionist nationalism incompatible with the market order and therefore doomed to failure. But he also excludes spontaneous market adjustment because the economic and social costs of adjusting to the new equilibrium are neglected. In the classical Austrian view, the government cannot intervene in the process of market transformation. Röpke outlines a course of action instead. Rather than preserve the old equilibrium (subsidies to brewers), the intervention should aim to favour the adjustment to the new equilibrium, that is, in concrete terms to assist and direct the "losers" of innovation towards new production. This is, of course, a very delicate step, not so much because of the welfare measures (which Hayek also contemplates), but because of the implicit assumption that the government will be able to know in advance which products and sectors will be successful in the future. Röpke believes that the alternative strategies would, in any case, be more harmful: the nationalist one because, by restricting the international division of labour, it would destroy the common wealth, and the liberalist one because, by abandoning the losers to their fate, it would incur huge economic and social costs. Röpke (1942 [1950]: 187–188) writes:

> Here, as everywhere else, the solution of the problem is to be found in a "third" direction: neither in laissez-faire nor in intervention for preservation (obstructive intervention) but in intervention for adjustment (constructive intervention). Instead of counteracting the tendency to establish a new balance by subsidies, &c., as would intervention for preservation, adjustment intervention accelerates and facilitates the attainment of such a balance in order to avoid losses and hardship, or at least reduce them to a minimum ... Instead of the production branch which is forced to make a change being left to find new ways by itself, as was usual under the old form of liberalism, adjustment intervention will actively promote this process by constructive reorganization plans, credits, re-training courses and publicity campaigns. It neither wants to dam the natural course of development by the concrete walls of intervention for preservation – which will in the end give way in any case – nor does it wish to turn it into the wild falls of laissez-faire. Here, too, a third method will be adopted: the flow will be channeled, whilst its course will be shortened as much as possible.

The neoliberal economist outlines a new international order, which in reality is very similar to the classical one, based on free trade and gold money, in which nations, including European ones, become open and communicating spaces once again. The novelty is that Röpke, precisely in order to save the market, considers it necessary, among other things, to protect competition and adapt to the ever-changing market balances. The reference model was Switzerland, which would later be defined as "a Europe in miniature", with a federalism, the Swiss one, aimed at ensuring maximum autonomy to states that are like cantons and that must be able to carry out interventions in accordance with the market.

At the heart of Mises's analysis is the distinction between comparative advantages and absolute advantages. In Ricardo's nineteenth-century economy, in which only or mainly goods circulated, a division of labour based on the principle of comparative advantages was possible, and only one freedom, that of trade, was sufficient to ensure the harmony of national interests. In the economy that emerged during the *belle époque*, in which people and capital also began to circulate intensively, the Ricardian hypothesis was dropped, the principle of absolute advantages reappeared, and the factors of production moved to where conditions were better. In order to ensure the harmony of national interests, one single freedom, that of trade, is no longer sufficient; the free movement of inputs must also be recognised. In the world, and therefore also in Europe, there are only over- and under-populated areas. The interest of every nation is to have the optimum population by ensuring the free movement of goods, people and capital. Any attempt to increase national prosperity by restricting the movement of the population results in an escalation that leads to higher production costs, consequent protectionism, the formation of cartels, and finally and violently the search for a living space. The only alternative to war is integral liberalism. Mises (1940 [1949]: 161) writes:

> Now, in a world in which there is free mobility not only for products, but no less for capital goods and for labor, a country so little suited for production would cease to be used as the seat of any human industry. If people fare better without exploiting the – comparatively unsatisfactory – physical conditions of production offered by this country, they will not settle here and will leave it as uninhabited as the polar regions, the tundras and the deserts. But Ricardo deals with a world whose conditions are determined by settlement in earlier days, a world in which capital goods and labor are bound to the soil by definite institutions. In such a milieu free trade, i.e., the free mobility of commodities only, cannot bring about a state of affairs in which capital and labor are distributed on the surface of the earth according to the better or poorer physical opportunities afforded to the productivity of labor. Here the law of comparative cost comes into operation. Each country turns toward those branches of production for which its conditions offer comparatively, although not absolutely, the most favorable opportunities.

Mises, like Röpke, sees at the origin of the international and European disorder the rising tide of a non-conformable interventionism, even if he does not like and does not use the expression coined by Röpke, maintaining a basic skepticism both towards antitrust legislation and towards interventions to adapt to the new equilibriums. For Mises, the problem is the "hampered market", a market hampered by the many limitations to the free movement of inputs and outputs introduced by governments in a vain attempt to defend a misunderstood national interest at the time of the emerging global economy. The problem is most acute in Eastern Europe where, due to the scattered presence of linguistic minorities, the principle of nationality cannot be applied and original solutions must therefore be sought.

In his writings of the 1940s, Mises updated and completed the history of Europe already outlined in his 1919 book and other writings of the 1920s, showing the incidence of the great economic ideas in the political events of the time.

For ages, Europe had been the ground of absolute monarchies where despots, more or less enlightened, ruled in the name of God over territories they considered their own property. When a king conquered a new land, he certainly did not ask permission of its inhabitants, who passively submitted to their new master. The idea that the borders of nations and states could coincide was simply unthinkable:

> As long as nations were ruled by monarchical despots, the idea of adjusting the boundaries of the state to coincide with the boundaries between nationalities could not find acceptance. If a potentate desired to incorporate a province into his realm, he cared little whether the inhabitants – the subjects – agreed to a change of rulers or not.
>
> *Mises 1927: 118*

The French Revolution destroyed the *ancien régime*, proclaiming human rights, among them the right of self-determination, that is, the right of people to freely choose their political destiny. The principles of the French Revolution spread all over Europe, from West to East, conquering Central Europe too: "From Western Europe new ideas began to penetrate into Germany. The people, accustomed to obey blindly the God-given authority of the princes, heard for the first time the words liberty, self-determination, rights of man, parliament, constitution" (Mises 1944: 19). Thanks to Smith and Ricardo, Classical Liberalism won the battle of ideas against Mercantilism and inspired a new economic culture and policy across Europe. In a few years, the long-lasting Mercantilist System was destroyed and economic freedom triumphed in internal relationships as well as in external ones. Liberalism beat Mercantilism but encountered an unforeseen obstacle that divided Europe. In Western Europe, in particular in Britain and France, where people spoke the same language and shared common values and culture, the principle of self-determination could easily be applied and it was possible to consolidate genuine nation-states developing, according to Mises (1919: 25), a "Liberal or Pacifistic Nationalism". In East-Central Europe, on the other hand, due to the phenomenon of "mixed populations" of diverse linguistic, religious and ethnic backgrounds, it was impossible to draw the boundaries of homogeneous nation-states, and so a "Militant or Imperialistic Nationalism" spread all over the region (Mises, 1919: 32). Strong minorities of Germans, Polish, Hungarians and Czechs were disseminated everywhere in East-Central Europe. How to apply the self-determination principle? How to allow people belonging to the same nation to live together? A twofold trial was conducted to solve the "national question". In Germany, under the leadership of Bismarck's Prussia, a *National* Empire was established, the so-called Lesser Germany, which hosted the majority of Germans but not the Austrian ones. In Austria-Hungary, under the leadership of Franz Joseph's House of Habsburg, a *Multinational* Empire was consolidated, where lived people belonging to eleven nationalities. Both regimes adopted an interventionist policy. The Habsburg Monarchy approved discriminatory laws against linguistic, ethnic or religious groups. The German Empire ran a social policy (*Sozialpolitik*) that triggered a vicious cycle leading to the Great War.

In particular, according to Mises (1919: 46–70), Bismarck made a dramatic mistake. During the seventies, at the beginning of the First Globalisation, when workers and capitals began to move, he tried to defend the national interest of Germany – an over-populated country – instead of enforcing the three freedoms, running a *Sozialpolitik* in favour of the working classes with the support of the trade unions. He should have raised the standard of living of people and allowed the emigration of unnecessary workers. Instead, he tried to achieve the same goal by promoting an increase in nominal wages above the average labour productivity. The final result was, according to Mises, a catastrophe. The social policy increased the costs of production, forcing the country to abandon the free trade policy and to embrace a protectionist strategy. Germany was the first European country to approve a restrictive law in 1879. It was not only a measure to defend the "infant industries", as suggested by List some decades earlier, but a universal protectionism with tariffs on industry and agriculture (on "iron and rye"). Protectionism, in turn, further increasing the costs of production, threatened to squeeze exports, slowing down the growth of the country. Bismarck's response was to promote a cartel policy aimed at differentiating domestic and external prices. Germany's big companies were able to impose higher prices on domestic householders in order to make sufficient profits to lower prices for foreign consumers and conquer new market shares. According to Mises, it was only a temporary solution. The final solution was to build a self-sufficient Great Empire. Starting in the nineties, after Bismarck's resignation, Germany undertook a "living space" policy (inspired by Historicists) that led to the war.

In a global economy, where everything can circulate, the only alternative to freedom is war. After World War I, the Paris Peace Conference tried to establish a New International (and European) Order based on the principle of self-determination. The European map was redesigned to give each nation a State. In Wilson's view, the spread of democracy would cut the roots of war, and the League of Nations would be a watchdog of peace. In particular, the Treaties provided a twofold system to solve the problem of linguistic minorities building homogeneous nation-states: protection by international law and territorial exchange. Mises argued that both methods were ineffective, the first because governments could discriminate against linguistic minorities through specific economic policy measures without violating international law. Mises (1941: 12–13) wrote:

> A law cannot protect anybody against measures dictated purely by considerations of economic expediency. If a law in one of these countries discriminated against the members of the minority group – for instance, by refusing them educational opportunities – the international tribunal could interfere. But, if the government injures a minority, by economic measures that make no specific mention of minority distinctions but whose effect is virtually discriminatory, the international provisions are in vain. If, for instance, members of the minority are alone engaged in a specific branch of business, the government can ruin them by means of customs provisions. In other words, they can raise

the price of essential raw materials and machinery. In these countries, every measure of government interference – taxes, tariffs, freight rates, labor policy, monopoly and price control, foreign exchange regulations – was used against the minorities.

The second method – exchange of minorities – could only work in a world without significant geographical disparities:

> This method would be excellent in a world where all regions offer the same opportunities for production. In our actual world, it is absolutely inadequate. It can only aggravate and stabilize the inequalities already existing, those very inequalities that are the economic causes of war.
>
> *Mises, 1941: 13*

In Mises's view, the only way to prevent war and foster peace was to enforce the three freedoms abolishing any attempt to interfere in the market via politics. In a global economy, the national interest is to achieve the optimum level of population that considers self-determination a right of individuals and local communities rather than the right of an entire nation to erect its own state.

Mises proposed to establish a large Eastern European Union comprising approximately 150 million people and without Germany and Russia. It was to be a Liberal Union, not a Federation, which could only function if there was a culturally homogeneous population and which, in the case of Eastern Europe, would lead to new discriminatory actions by member states against linguistic minorities:

> A federation of the Eastern European nations could neither solve the minority problem nor the boundaries problem. All the factors which make these nations fight one another would remain and would shatter the union. The only possible constitution for such an Eastern Union would be a strictly centralized organization. But this, too, presupposes the absence of all kinds of economic intervention. If the government is limited to the preservation of security, it could avoid measures that some linguistic groups consider prejudicial.
>
> *Mises 1941: 17*[6]

Röpke and Mises see the cause of European and international disorder in an interventionism that does not conform, in the broadest sense, to the market. For both, the solution lies in a Europe of nations that recognises the three basic economic freedoms. The difference is that Röpke fights for the new liberalism of conformist interventions and looks to the Swiss model, and therefore to a "light" federation that respects the autonomy of the canton states, while Mises, who only justifies actions to preserve an unhampered market, prefigures a liberal Union (not a federation) of Eastern Europe which recognises the individual (not national) right to self-determination. In both cases, we are dealing with a vision of Europe (and of the world) that is different, at least in part, from that of the "pure" federalists: the nature and aims of the institutions proposed to re-establish a supranational order differ.

If federalism and internationalism had a history prior to the war years, in 1943 David Mitrany, the Romanian-born economist (but naturalised British scholar at the London School of Economics), published *A Working Peace System*, thus "inventing" a new (and decisive) approach to European unity: functionalism.

Mitrany (1943, 1975) discards as an effective solution the failed model of the Union or Confederation of States already attempted with the League of Nations. There are only two possible solutions: a world federation or a set of functional supranational institutions. However, the federation only works where there is a strong cultural unity. For this reason, only national federations are successful. It is much more difficult to set up internationals, as the experience of the British Empire shows:

> Federations have still been national federations; the jump from national states to international organization is infinitely more hazardous than was the jump from provincial units to national federations. None of the elements of neighborhood, of kinship, of history are there to serve as steps. The British Empire is bound closely by old ties of kinship and history, but no one would suggest that there is among its parts much will for federation.
>
> *Mitrany 1943: 6*

It is therefore illusory to imagine setting up a world federation. Theoretically, continental (geographical) or ideological (among democratic countries) federations could be set up. However, according to Mitrany, both would be doomed to failure: the former because of their intrinsic tendency to be closed and therefore conflictual towards the outside world, while the latter would be exposed to the precariousness of a flimsy ideological glue. There is also a common and radical objection. If wars arise from the division of the world into political units, there is little point in moving the borders:

> If the evil of conflict and war springs from the division of the world into detached and competing political units, will it be exorcised simply by changing or reducing the lines of division? Any political reorganization into separate units must sooner or later produce the same effects; any international system that is to usher in a new world must produce the opposite effect of subduing political division.
>
> *Mitrany 1943: 6*

Functionalism is the only effective alternative to federalism. It would be a matter of rendering national political borders harmless, almost invisible, by setting up supranational technical (functional) institutions that, without requiring any changes to the borders or legal systems of the various countries, could satisfy common interests. The decisive example, for Mitrany, is the Tennessee Valley Authority (TVA), established by Roosevelt in 1933 to deal with the widespread economic depression that had hit the American states. A special institution was set up, of a technical or functional nature, to meet a need common to different states, without changing the constitutional structure of the country. According to Mitrany, the same model should be adopted in post-war Europe to manage the various common interests, starting with the network of railway communications that crosses national borders. Functionalism does not require the establishment of a higher political authority. However, by reducing territorial disparities and demonstrating the effectiveness of common institutions, it creates the basis for a solid federation:

> There is nothing incompatible between the two conceptions [federalism and functionalism]: the functional arrangements might indeed be regarded as organic elements of a federalism by instalments. But such a federalism if it came would be the solid growth of a natural selection and evolution, tested and accepted by experience, and not a green-table creation, blown about and battered by all the winds of political life.
>
> *Mitrany 1943: 43*

Interestingly, in Mitrany's original vision, there is only an implicit reference to the priority to be given to economic integration (common interests are predominantly economic) and to the progressive extension of integration itself. It will be the neofunctionalists who will explicitly refer to the spillover effect and economic integration as a way of achieving an accomplished political union on a federal basis.

Thus, in the immediate post-war period, Eastern Europe is caught between an ideal popular democracy and a real Soviet socialism, while Western Europe is uncertain about the first step on the road to unification. This uncertainty vanished when, in the spring of 1947, the Americans proposed an economic aid package known as the Marshall Plan.

The Marshall Plan and the Separated Unification of Europe

On 5 June 1947, the US Secretary of State, George Marshall, announced in a speech at Harvard University the decision by the US government to launch an extraordinary economic aid plan for the reconstruction of Europe, a plan that was to be called the European Recovery Program (ERP). The Americans made it clear that the funds would be given to and managed by a group of European countries rather than individual national governments. On 16 April 1948, sixteen European countries (including Turkey) signed the Convention in Paris establishing the Organisation Européenne de Coopération Economique (OECE), the body responsible for managing the ERP funds. It was a decisive act, one that activated the process of "separate unification" of the two Europes. The Eastern European countries decided, under Soviet pressure, not to join either the Marshall Plan or the GATT–Bretton Woods system. In other words, they decided to remain outside the international (western) community and to build their own (socialist) supra-national community. Western European countries, on the other hand, joined both the Marshall Plan and the GATT–Bretton Woods system (Hogan 1987).

The twenty-five years of history between 1948 and 1973 can be read as an attempt to build two parallel single markets: that of the Western European countries and that of the Eastern European countries. This attempt underwent a turning point with the end of the Bretton Woods monetary agreements in 1971, the transition to a flexible exchange rate regime in 1973, and the simultaneous oil shock that threw the economies of the two Europes into crisis.

The aim of Yalta, as we have seen, was to transform Eastern Europe into a group of genuine democratic countries friendly to Russia. It soon became clear, however, that this was not possible. One could not be both democratic and a friend of Russia: sovereign and subordinate. A choice had to be made. And the choice was made by Russia. In February 1948, the communists in Czechoslovakia carried out a coup d'état that put an end to the Third Republic by forcing the democratic ministers to resign. In June of that year came the excommunication of Tito's Yugoslavia to mark the end of the experiments. There was only one established model, the Soviet model, which provided for the nationalisation of enterprises, the planning of industry, and the collectivisation of agriculture.

Russia feared European unification under the auspices of America and preferred to build another, its own, Europe. Fejtö (1955: 242, my translation from Italian) writes:

> The USSR certainly feared that if it took part in an economic cooperation tending to unify Europe under the auspices of the United States, the countries of the East would escape it without compensation; moreover, Molotov [the Foreign Minister] reproached his colleagues for wanting to separate their countries and all those who would follow them from the other European states, "which will result in the division of Europe into two groups of states". But what Molotov did not say was that Soviet policy preferred the division of Europe into two blocs, one dominated by the United States, the other by the Soviet Union, rather than a united Europe which, according to the Kremlin leadership, would have neither the strength nor the will to break away from American domination.

The Soviet response to the Marshall Plan was the establishment in 1949 of Comecon, the Council for Mutual Economic Assistance between the major countries of the Soviet bloc. Eastern Europe was divided into two complementary areas: an industrial north and an agricultural south, with Hungary in the middle. In June 1962, at the third Comecon Conference, a document on the "Fundamental Principles of the International Socialist Division of Labour" was approved. Each country was called upon to participate in the construction of a common socialist economy. However, impatience with compressed economic freedom smouldered under the ashes. Romania, for example, did not want to become the breadbasket of

Eastern Europe and, more generally, suffered from Soviet intrusiveness in its internal affairs (Bottoni 2011: 205).

In 1968, the Prague Spring broke out, showing the world how impatient the various peoples of Europe had become with ongoing violations of their fundamental civil and political freedoms. Russia responded first with tanks that invaded Prague (20 August), then with a speech by Leonid Brezhnev in November 1968, to the Fifth Congress of the Polish United Workers Party, justifying the use of force: "When internal and external forces that are hostile to Socialism try to turn the development of some socialist country towards the restoration of a capitalist regime", said Brezhnev,

> when socialism in that country and the socialist community as a whole is threatened, it becomes not only a problem of the people of the country concerned, but a common problem and concern of all Socialist countries. Naturally an action such as military assistance to a fraternal country designed to avert the threat to the social system is an extraordinary step, dictated by necessity.
>
> *quoted by Cain and Harrison 2001, vol. 2: 104*

The socialist division of labour created inequalities and inefficiencies and showed the world the difficulty – Mises would say the impossibility – of planning an economy. Some Eastern European countries, in particular Hungary, Poland and Romania, tried to reactivate trade relations with the West in hopes of attracting the capital needed to finance their growing external debt. "It was hoped", Fejtö (1998: 89, my translation from Italian) argues, "that they would be able to pay off that debt with profits made from exports, once they had restructured their industrial equipment and reached maximum production capacity". But the 1973 crisis abruptly halted the attempt to open up and again forced the Eastern countries to adopt restrictive measures. Paradoxically, the oil shock did not even benefit Russia, an oil-producing country, which was forced by superior socialist reason to offer its allies reduced prices (Bottoni 2011: 231).

Between 1948 and 1973, therefore, a major effort was made to build a single socialist market in Eastern Europe.

During these same years, a similar attempt was made in Western Europe. After joining the Marshall Plan and the bodies of the reconstituted international community, federalist discussions on the division of economic tasks between the member states and the federal government in the area of the free movement of goods, persons, and capital or of money and taxation were put aside or postponed. All attention was focused on the stages of the economic integration process that should gradually lead to the desired political union. The functionalist approach, conceived by Mitrany, is reworked and adopted by the men most directly involved in European integration: Jean Monnet, Robert Schuman, and Walter Hallstein. The basic idea was that progressive economic integration would require parallel political unification. The strategy is clearly expressed in Robert Schuman's declaration of 9 May 1950: "Europe will not be made all at once, or according to a single plan. It will be built through concrete achievements which first create a *de facto* solidarity".

Meanwhile, the debate among economists takes place within the shared IS-LM model, and the focus shifts from the particular and extreme case of a major crisis to the general or normal case of an economic system that, with an appropriate policy mix, can reach the equilibrium of full employment of available resources.

If the establishment of the ECE in Paris in April 1948 can be considered the start of the European unification process, other steps were taken in 1950 with the establishment of the European Payments Union and in 1951 with the creation of the European Coal and Steel Community. There was also the misstep of the European Defence Community, a military cooperation agreement, promoted by France and Italy, but then withdrawn due to a change of heart by France.

The first decisive step, however, was taken in Rome on 25 March 1957 when six countries (Italy, France, the Federal Republic of Germany, Belgium, the Netherlands and Luxembourg) signed the Treaty establishing the European Economic Community. There they took the crucial decision to start a process that would lead to the formation of a single European market as a way of achieving a wider integration.[7]

The main objective of the Treaty of Rome was to establish the single market. In reality, it prefigured an "imperfect economic union". The Treaty provided for the establishment of a customs union, a partial movement of production factors, and an initial common policy (the Common Agricultural Policy and antitrust rules). Monetary union, on the other hand, was not a problem because in 1957 the Bretton Woods agreements were in full force and a fixed exchange rate regime was still a form of monetary union (there was an exchange rate parity between currencies). The aim of the Treaty was clearly expressed in the opening words and in Article 2: the common market (later called the single or internal market) and the gradual coordination of economic policies were to promote the harmonious development of the Community of European peoples. For the founding fathers who signed the Treaty of Rome, Europe was a Community of peoples.[8]

The essential instrument with which the objective of the harmonious development of the Community was to be pursued was the formation, over time, of an economic union based on the pillars of a common market, regulated by antitrust rules, and a common policy, ensuring monetary stability.[9] The competition regime was governed by Articles 85 and 86. The former only prohibited agreements between undertakings that resulted in consumer harm. The second article, likewise, prohibited only the abuse of a dominant position (and not the dominant position itself), which always resulted in consumer harm.[10] The coordination of economic policies was regulated in Articles 104 and 105. It is noteworthy that in Article 104, the priority objective of economic policy remains balance of payments equilibrium and thus the exchange rate stability required by the Bretton Woods agreements. At the same time, however, a high level of employment and domestic price stability appear as desirable secondary or joint objectives. In other words, monetary stability is understood simultaneously and compatibly as exchange rate stability and domestic price stability.[11]

The German ordoliberals played a decisive role in drafting Articles 85 and 86, which foresee a discretionary intervention of the antitrust authorities in determining whether and when agreements between companies or market dominance should be prohibited. Gerber (1994: 73) writes:

> The Rome Treaty reflects this influence. It contains two main competition law provisions: a prohibition of cartels (article 85) and of abuse of a market-dominating position (article 86). This structure closely tracked ordoliberal thought and the patterns established in the GWB, and bore little resemblance to anything found in other European competition laws at the time. Moreover, while the prohibition of cartel agreements had analogues in US antitrust law, the concept of prohibiting abuse of a market-dominating position was an important new development closely associated with ordoliberal and German competition law thought, and very different from U.S. concepts.

On 1 January 1958, the Treaties of Rome came into force. On 7 January, Walter Hallstein was appointed the first President of the European Commission. The same year, Ernst B. Haas (1958 [2004]) published *The Uniting of Europe*, the cornerstone of neofunctionalism, which was adopted as the "official doctrine" of Brussels. The distinguishing feature of neofunctionalism is spillover, the idea that integration in one sector triggers a process that necessitates further integration in the sector itself and extension to close sectors, until a complete form of economic and political unification is achieved. It was, therefore, a way of deepening and widening the process of European integration. Ben Rosamond (2000: 60) summarises Haas's seminal thinking as follows:

> In Haas's original formulation ... spillover referred to the way in which the creation and deepening of integration in one economic sector would create pressures for further economic integration within and beyond that sector, and greater authoritative capacity in the European level.
>
> *see also Lindberg 1963*

The architects of European integration themselves contributed to the elaboration, and practical implementation, of neofunctionalism. Hallstein (1961: 12), for instance, saw economic integration (from the single market to the monetary union) as already a form of political unification and not merely a way of achieving it in the future:

> It is not only a step on the way to political integration, it is already part and parcel of it. For it is not the "economy" which is being integrated, it is not production, trade or consumption, nor is it the action of employers, workers,

merchants, or consumers. What is being integrated is the part played by the states in creating the conditions in which economic activity takes place.[12]

After 1958, criticism of the neofunctionalist approach and another idea of Europe also emerged. Particularly significant are those of the economist Röpke and the politician Erhard, who came from the same influential circles of German ordoliberalism as Hallstein. The other idea of Europe is a community of nations that are culturally united but open and integrated into the wider international community. In order to achieve this ambitious goal, according to these two authoritative Germans, it was sufficient to apply the rules of the GATT–Bretton Woods system, if anything drawing inspiration, as Röpke hoped, from the model of Switzerland's "unity in diversity", the "*Europe en miniature*". The European Economic Community, on the other hand, is said to have committed "two capital errors": it pursued maximum economic integration and subordinated it to achieving a form of political union. But there is a substantial difference between the national single market and the international single market: the former follows and does not precede political union, while the latter is only achieved if it remains open and integrated. Instead, the European Community has forced member countries to adopt a common policy in order to achieve sufficient internal convergence, acting as a closed block or tending to be closed to the outside world, generating the negative effects of trade "creation" and "diversion" highlighted by Jacon Viner:

> In other words, the more the member governments must subordinate themselves to a common economic policy, the more the bloc must be confined to those countries which are already so close to each other as to make such maximum integration not altogether unrealistic.
>
> *Röpke 1964: 242*

The ordoliberals Erhard and Röpke outline an idea of Europe that comes close to De Gaulle's Europe of the homelands and moves away from that pursued and implemented by the European Commission under the leadership of the ordoliberal Hallstein, while economists debate whether and under what conditions it is possible to achieve a single market in the absence of a strong European economic government. The debate focused on the issue of convergence needed for a well-functioning single market. In Italy, Marco Fanno, one of the most authoritative economists, argued that a single market could only function among economies that were in substantial internal and external equilibrium, while Walter Hallstein, in a lecture given in 1962 and published as *The Economics of European Integration*, quoted James Meade, who in 1953 had argued that three conditions were necessary:

> First, the individual member-states must not be too out of line with each other in their domestic policies concerning the distribution of income and property. Second, the individual member-states must not be too out of line with each other in their choice among direct controls, fiscal policy, and

monetary policy for the stabilization of their domestic economies. Third, the individual member-states must not be too out of line with each other in those social and economic policies which determine their domestic demographic trends.[13]

The years after 1958 were a transitional period for the application of the rules laid down in the Treaties. In 1973, for the first time, the Community enlarged to include three new countries: Denmark, Ireland, and the United Kingdom. But 1973 was a watershed year for Western Europe, and not just because of the oil shock. On 15 August 1971, US President Nixon announced to the world that he was suspending the gold convertibility of the dollar, and in 1973, there was a shift to a flexible exchange rate regime. The Bretton Woods order came to an end: it came to an end as a result of a growing divergence in the conduct of monetary policy between the United States and the Federal Republic of Germany, the leading country in Western Europe, that is, as a result of a lack of cooperation or, if you like, as a result of the prevalence of nationalistic impulses. For Western Europe, the unprecedented prospect of a single market without a monetary union was opening up.

In Short

Immediately after World War II, Europe was divided into two blocs by what Churchill called an "iron curtain". In the East, Marxism–Leninism dominated; in the West, a multifaceted interventionism that, from time to time, was coloured by the Keynesianism of the neoclassical synthesis and the controversy between federalism and functionalism that animated the debate on European unification. Eastern Europe oscillated between an ideal popular democracy and a real Soviet socialism, while Western Europe remained undecided about the path to unification. The Marshall Plan dissolved all uncertainty by activating a process of "separate unification" of Europe, which took the form of the (imperfect or incomplete) construction of two parallel single markets.

What is the influence of the great economic ideas on the process of the "separate unification" of Europe that took place between 1944 and 1973? In the East, the prevailing idea, derived from the prevailing Marxism–Leninism, was that the Eastern European countries should participate in the "socialist division of labour" in order to contribute to the construction of world socialism; in the West, the functionalist idea prevailed, according to which, in order to achieve a complete political union, it was first necessary to build an economic union. The 1973 crisis marked a turning point for the two Europes: in the East, perhaps for the first time, the fallacy of a socialism that trampled on fundamental human rights and also generated widespread poverty became evident; in the West, not for the first time, the limits of nationalism emerged, undermining the foundations of international cooperation and depriving the single market being created of the necessary monetary union.

The founding values of Europe find their first "constitutional" recognition in the Treaties of Rome, where the Community explicitly undertakes to promote, through the market and common economic policies, the harmonious development of the peoples of Europe. Implicit in that intention is the commitment to respect the values of freedom (positive and negative), work and intermediate communities, avoiding any process of unjustified concentration of power.

The lesson of this story is that Europe is united by economic and cultural ties that are stronger than any artificial political division. François Fejtö (1955: 596, my translation from Italian) concluded his classic *History of the People's Democracies* quoting Montesquieu as follows:

«In Europe things are so arranged that all states depend on each other», Montesquieu wrote. – «France needs the opulence of Poland and Muscovy, just as Guienne needs Brittany and Brittany needs Anjou. Europe is a state composed of several provinces». The history of the last thirty years has tragically confirmed these words.

Notes

1 On the history of Europe in the World War II aftermath, see Swann (1989), Cesarano (2006), Eichengreen (2007), Judt (2007), Gilbert (2020). On the history of economic thought during the same period, see Rodano (1997), Coats (2000), Screpanti and Zamagni (2005, Part II), Romani (2009), Jones (2012), Steil (2013), Carabelli and Cedrini (2014).
2 See Hall (1989), Romani (2009), Mirowski and Plehwe (2015).
3 On Eastern Europe in the communist era, see, among others, Rupnik (1989).
4 On the complex idea of social order held by Robbins, see Masini (2018).
5 On the debate in Italy, see Magliulo (1993) and Gioli (1997).
6 Mises (1944: 275) writes:

The EDU would have to include all the territories between the eastern borders of Germany, Switzerland, and Italy and the western borders of Russia, including all Balkan countries. It would have to take in the area which in 1933 formed the sovereign states of Albania, Austria, Bulgaria, Czechoslovakia, Danzig, Estonia, Greece, Hungary, Latvia, Lithuania, Poland, Rumania, and Yugoslavia. It would have to include the territory that in 1913 comprised the Prussian provinces of East Prussia, West Prussia, Posen, and Silesia … Italy must cede to the EDD all the European countries which it has occupied since 1913, including the Dodecanese Islands, and furthermore the eastern part of the province of Venice, Friuli, a district inhabited by people speaking a Rhaeto-Romanic idiom. Thus the EDD will include about 700,000 square miles with some 120,000,000 people using 17 different languages.

See also Bibó (1946 [2015])

7 It may be useful to recall the elementary vocabulary of economic integration theory. It is like a Matryoshka doll in which the larger doll contains the smaller ones. The first level of economic integration is the "free trade area", which eliminates internal customs barriers

and leaves individual countries free to set their own external tariffs; the second level is the "customs union", which adds a common external tariff to the free trade area; the third level is the "common market", which adds the free movement of productive factors (labour and capital) to the customs union; the fourth and final level is the "economic and monetary union", which adds the coordination of national economic policies to the common market.

8 The Treaty's incipit states: The representatives of the six countries, "Determined to lay the foundations of an ever-closer union among the peoples of Europe ...". Article 2 continues:

> The Community shall have as its task, by establishing a common market and progressively approximating the economic policies of Member States, to promote throughout the Community a harmonious development of economic activities, a continuous and balanced expansion, an increase in stability, an accelerated raising of the standard of living and closer relations between the States belonging to it.

9 Article 3 states: "For the purposes set out in Article 2, the activities of the Community shall include, as provided in this Treaty and in accordance with the timetable set out therein": the elimination of internal tariffs; the establishment of a common external customs tariff; the abolition of obstacles to the free movement of persons, services and capital; a competition regime in the internal market; a common agricultural policy and the coordination of economic policies to reduce balance of payments imbalances; the creation of the European Social Fund and the European Investment Bank; and the association of overseas countries and territories.

10 Article 85 states:

> 1. The following shall be prohibited as incompatible with the common market: all agreements between undertakings, decisions by associations of undertakings and concerted practices which may affect trade between Member States and which have as their object or effect the prevention, restriction or distortion of competition within the common market, and in particular those which: (a) directly or indirectly fix purchase or selling prices or any other trading conditions; (b) limit or control production, markets, technical development, or investment; (c) share markets or sources of supply ... 2. Any agreements or decisions prohibited pursuant to this Article shall be automatically void. 3. The provisions of paragraph 1 may, however, be declared inapplicable in the case of: any agreement or category of agreements between undertakings; any decision or category of decisions by associations of undertakings; any concerted practice or category of concerted practices; which contributes to improving the production or distribution of goods or to promoting technical or economic progress, while allowing consumers a fair share of the resulting benefit.

Article 86 continues:

> Any abuse by one or more undertakings of a dominant position within the common market or in a substantial part of it shall be prohibited as incompatible with the common market in so far as it may affect trade between Member States. Such abuse may, in particular, consist in: (a) directly or indirectly imposing unfair purchase or selling prices or other unfair trading conditions; (b) limiting production, markets or technical development to the prejudice of consumers.

11 Article 104 states:

> Each Member State shall pursue the economic policy needed to ensure the equilibrium of its overall balance of payments and to maintain confidence in its currency, while taking care to ensure a high level of employment and a stable level of prices.

Article 105 continues: "In order to facilitate attainment of the objectives set out in Article 104, Member States shall co-ordinate their economic policies".

12 On Hallstein's work, see Loth, Wallace and Wessels (1998), Malandrino (2006). On neofunctionalism, see Navari (1996) and Rosamond (2000).

13 On Fanno, see Magliulo (1993); the Meade quotation is in Hallstein (1962: 45).

7

DECLINE OF ETATISM, REBIRTH OF NEOLIBERALISM AND UNITED EUROPE (1974–2007)

Introduction

On 11 December 1974, in Stockholm, Friedrich August von Hayek, the prophet of the ineluctable end of communism, Keynes's losing rival, was unexpectedly awarded the Nobel Prize for Economics for his contributions to the advancement of business cycle theory in the tumultuous 1930s.

On 9 November 1989, the Berlin Wall fell, communism imploded, and Hayek's prophecy came true.

Within a few years, Eastern Europe joined Western Europe and together they continued along the functionalist path that the founding fathers had intended would lead to political unity.

In this chapter, we attempt to understand the role of economic ideas in the epochal transition from the two separately united Europes to a single Europe on its way to a federal union.

The debate among economists and the major political choices that marked the start of the second globalisation, with the associated processes of privatisation and liberalisation of the economy, will only be evoked, while we will pause to examine the construction phase of the Economic and Monetary Union (EMU).[1]

We shall examine, first, the crisis of Keynesianism and the collapse of Marxism; second, the rebirth of Neoliberalism; and third, the enlargement of the EEC and the establishment of the EU and EMU.

The Crisis of Keynesianism and the Collapse of Marxism

Thus it was that in 1974 Hayek received the Nobel Prize for Economics. In 1976, the prize was awarded to Milton Friedman, also a founding member of the Mont Pèlerin Society and the acknowledged father of modern monetarism, who

DOI: 10.4324/9781003188889-7

explained that the inverse relationship between the rate of inflation and the rate of unemployment – known as the Phillips curve – was only valid in the short run, while in the long run all relationships ceased and the curve became a vertical line indicating that the causes of unemployment were independent and real.

From the 1970s onwards, alongside the IS-LM model, which remains central to neo-Keynesian macroeconomics, a complementary and increasingly popular AS-AD model was developed, where AS stands for aggregate supply and AD for aggregate demand. AS indicates a direct relationship between the general price level (P) and the general level of output (Y): it is assumed that an increase in output (Y) requires an increase in employment (i.e. a reduction in unemployment), an increase in wages and a consequent increase in prices (P) in accordance with the Phillips curve. The correlation between P and Y ends (and the AS becomes vertical) when the relationship between inflation and unemployment ceases, that is, when the Phillips curve also becomes vertical. The vertical AS represents "potential GDP", that is, the maximum level of production that can be stably achieved in an economic system by making the best use of existing resources and thus without generating inflation. The AD, on the other hand, indicates an inverse relationship between P and Y: it is assumed that a reduction in the general price level increases the real money supply and, by reducing the interest rate, stimulates investment and aggregate demand, as predicted by the underlying IS-LM model.

In 1973, the world economy, including the European economy, entered an unprecedented "stagflation". Contrary to what the Phillips curve had predicted and Keynesian economists had theorised, both unemployment (due to a stagnating economy) and inflation increased. The historical–political reason for this is the quadrupling of the price of oil from $3 to $12 a barrel in a short period of time. In terms of the AS-AD model, this is a negative shock to the AS which, moving left and upwards along an immobile AD, determines a new macroeconomic equilibrium characterised by a higher general price level (P) and a lower level of output (Y) and therefore by higher unemployment. The new equilibrium, characterised by higher unemployment and higher inflation, is called stagflation.

On 28 September 1976, Labour Prime Minister James Callaghan, in a famous speech to the annual conference of the British Labour Party, certified the failure and the end of Keynesianism in government with these words:

> We used to think that you could spend your way out of a recession, and increase employment by cutting taxes and boosting Government spending. I tell you in all candour that that option no longer exists, and that in so far as it ever did exist, it only worked on each occasion since the war by injecting a bigger dose of inflation into the economy, followed by a higher level of unemployment as the next step. Higher inflation followed by higher unemployment. We have just escaped from the highest rate of inflation this country has known; we have not yet escaped from the consequences: high unemployment.[2]

The 1973 crisis, followed by a second major oil shock in 1979, also brought the increasingly indebted Eastern European economy to its knees. But it is the development of the entire socialist economy, based on the dogmatic doctrine of Marxism–Leninism, that is increasingly unsustainable. This is demonstrated by just one fact: "In the countries of 'real socialism'", writes Fejtö (1998: 96, my translation from Italian), "nine out of ten people were paid by the state".

The Rebirth of Neoliberalism

The crisis of etatism favours (and is at the same time favoured by) the resurgence of neoliberalism. While the new Keynesian liberalism, which aspired to govern and direct the market economy, declined, Hayek's Austrian neoliberalism, Friedman's monetarist neoliberalism, and Röpke's ordoliberalism ascended.

Historians of economic thought try to identify affinities and divergences among the three approaches within modern neoliberalism, which had a major impact on the start of the second globalisation of the economy. The Washington Consensus doctrine inspired the choices of international institutions, Margaret Thatcher and Ronald Reagan explicitly referred to Hayek and Friedman, and the social market economy of the ordoliberals became the reference model for the new Europe on its way to unity.[3]

The epochal shift from Keynesian neoliberalism to monetarist neoliberalism is symbolised by Reagan's famous statement in his White House inauguration speech on 20 January 1981: "In this present crisis, government is not the solution to our problem; government is the problem".[4]

In the 1970s, neoliberal economic thought became highly relevant to the political history of Europe. Hayek, for example, after receiving the Nobel Prize for Economics, returned to be a protagonist of the economic debate and seemed to come closer to the positions advocated by Röpke in the 1930s by recognising that, in a great crisis like that of 1929, one can, and indeed must, use Keynesian manoeuvres of an expansive type, not only for political considerations but also for purely economic ones (see Magliulo 2016).

This is a highly relevant issue that cannot be examined here. We limit ourselves to a single observation. If Keynes's neoliberalism is characterised by the attempt to entrust the government with the decision-making power to direct the economy, the other souls of neoliberalism seem to be united, albeit with different nuances, by the attempt to return decision-making power to the market or to re-establish the primacy of the economy over politics. Centeno and Cohen (2012: 317) write:

> For more than three decades, neoliberalism reshaped the global political economy. Broadly, neoliberalism stresses the necessity and desirability of transferring economic power and control from governments to private markets. Beginning in the 1970s, this perspective dominated policy making in the West, and it spread globally after the Cold War.

The Enlargement of the EEC and the Establishment of the EU and EMU

The end of the Bretton Woods agreements, announced in 1971, and the move to a flexible exchange rate regime in 1973 led to a contraction in intra-EU trade. A trade guerrilla war broke out between European countries: some of them undertook competitive devaluations to the detriment of their partners, who reacted by imposing duties and quotas. The end result is a reduced European division of labour and thus a destruction of common wealth.

The upswing began with a monetary agreement known as the Monetary Snake, but the turning point, a positive one, came in 1979 with the first direct election of the European Parliament and the entry into force of the European Monetary System (EMS), which established a quasi-fixed exchange rate regime allowing national currencies to fluctuate within margins no greater than 2.25%. The new monetary system, which favoured the recovery of intra-European trade, was inspired by a logic of cooperation, providing for multilateral management of realignments and agreed management of national monetary policies.

In the early 1980s, the European Community expanded from nine to twelve members with the accession of Greece (1981), Portugal and Spain (1986).

In 1984, an unexpected cry for help and hope came from the writer Milan Kundera who, in a famous article, spoke of "the tragedy of Central Europe" as a "kidnapped" West in the indifference of the West itself. Central Europe, including Poland, Czechoslovakia and Hungary is, according to Kundera, an area of small vulnerable states between Germany and Russia. An area that has no political borders does not form a state, because it is first and foremost a "culture or a fate". The free West did not realise that a part of it had been seized by Eastern communism because it had lost its cultural identity. Kundera (1984: 34) explains:

> Boxed in by the Germans on one side and the Russians on the other, the nations of Central Europe have used up their strength in the struggle to survive and to preserve their languages. Since they have never been entirely integrated into the consciousness of Europe, they have remained the least known and the most fragile part of the West — hidden, even further, by the curtain of their strange and scarcely accessible languages. The Austrian empire had a great opportunity to create a strong state in central Europe. But the Austrians, alas, were divided between an arrogant Pan-German nationalism and their own Central European mission. They did not succeed in building a federation of equal nations, and their failure has been the misfortune of the whole of Europe. Dissatisfied, the other nations of Central European blew apart their empire in 1918, without realizing that, in spite of its inadequacies, it was irreplaceable. After the First World War, Central Europe was therefore transformed into a region of small, weak states, whose vulnerability ensured first Hitler's conquest and ultimately Stalin's triumph.

In 1985, the Intergovernmental Conference, convened by the European Council, decided that by 1 January 1993 the European single market should be completed by removing the remaining obstacles to the free movement of goods, services, persons and capital: the four freedoms enshrined in the Single European Act of 1986. The liberalisation of capital movements was then brought forward to 1990.

In 1989, the Berlin Wall fell and, with the Iron Curtain lifted, diversity reappeared. Fejtö (1998: 428, my translation) writes:

> Once the unifying pillory of Soviet hegemony was lifted, the historic separation between Central Europe and Balkan Europe reappeared, the former dominated and westernised for centuries by the Habsburg Empire and Prussia, the latter, of Byzantine tradition, subjugated and delayed in its development by the Turkish Empire.

In 1991, the Visegrad group was founded, uniting the countries of Central Europe (Czechoslovakia, Poland and Hungary), and later attempts to reach an understanding between the countries of Balkan Europe began.[5]

At the beginning of the 1990s, the first major step on the European path can be considered substantially completed: the construction (albeit incomplete) of a single market to ensure the free movement of goods, services, people and capital. And here is the first obstacle, foreseeable in neofunctionalist logic: the single market does not work without a monetary union.

The reason is explained by the theory of the "inconsistent quartet" formulated, perhaps for the first time explicitly, by the Italian economist Tommaso Padoa-Schioppa (1992), one of the architects of the construction of the Euro.

There are four objectives, all desirable in themselves:

a. The free movement of goods and services, which makes it possible to achieve the territorial division of labour that the classical economists had already noted as the fundamental condition for increasing the productivity of human labour and thus the wealth of nations.

b. The free movement of capital, which enables countries rich in savings to finance the most profitable investments and countries poor in savings to attract the capital needed to finance their development.

c. A system of fixed or stable exchange rates, which, by instilling certainty in operators, favours the territorial division of labour.

d. Autonomy in the conduct of monetary policy, which represents a significant part of the economic sovereignty of nations.

Although desirable in themselves, these objectives are incompatible with each other. Something must be given up. In particular, and taking the free movement of goods as a given, if national monetary policies are too divergent, it becomes necessary to place limits on the free movement of capital in order to maintain exchange rate stability. That is, it is not possible to have, at the same time, stable exchange rates, capital mobility, and autonomy in the management of monetary policy. In this sense, the "inconsistent quartet" becomes an "economic trilemma".

European countries, in order to enjoy free trade and exchange rate stability, give up monetary sovereignty.

In retrospect, 1988 was a crucial year. The European Monetary System had been in place for almost ten years, but in June of 1988, the European Council mandated a committee chaired by Jacques Delors to study the feasibility of an EMU. Until then, and in particular in the Werner Report of 1970, monetary union had been understood as a regime that fulfils three conditions: convertible currencies, capital mobility and fixed exchange rates. In practice, a regime of fixed or stable exchange rates was considered a substitute for the single currency.

In April 1989, the European Commission approved the Delors Report. The Report envisages a strong EMU with a single currency and a common monetary policy geared to the objective of price stability. The fundamental reason for moving from the "weak" monetary union of a fixed exchange rate regime to the "strong" monetary union of the single currency is economic and psychological and aims to make the process of European economic integration irreversible:

> The adoption of *a single currency*, while not strictly necessary for the creation of a monetary union, might be seen for economic as well as psychological and political reasons as a natural and desirable further development of the monetary union. A single currency would clearly demonstrate the irreversibility of the move to monetary union, considerably facilitate the monetary management of the Community and avoid the transaction costs of converting currencies.
>
> *Delors Report 1989: 15, original italics*

The essential condition for implementing a common monetary policy geared towards price stability, and thus for achieving an EMU, is attaining a sufficient degree of convergence of the economies of the participating countries and compliance with binding fiscal rules. Indeed, it is considered that, once the exchange rate compensation valve is closed and in the absence of a large Community budget, national fiscal policies will have to fulfil the task of mitigating economic cycles caused also by asymmetric shocks:

> an economic and monetary union could only operate on the basis of mutually consistent and sound behaviour by governments and other economic agents in all member countries. In particular, uncoordinated and divergent national budgetary policies would undermine monetary stability and generate imbalances in the real and financial sectors of the Community. Moreover, the fact that the centrally managed Community budget is likely to remain a very small part of total public sector spending and that much of this budget will not be available for cyclical adjustments will mean that the task of setting a

> Community-wide fiscal policy stance will have to be performed through the
> coordination of national budgetary policies.
>
> *Delors Report 1989: 19*

The ultimate goal is to define an appropriate policy mix to manage the completed single European market:

> Without such coordination it would be impossible for the Community as a whole to establish a fiscal/monetary policy mix appropriate for the preservation of internal balance, or for the Community to play its part in the international adjustment process. Monetary policy alone cannot be expected to perform these functions.
>
> *Delors Report 1989: 20*

At the crucial moment when Europe was busy defining the next step towards the completion of the single market, the Berlin Wall fell and the reunification of Germany became possible. Padoa-Schioppa (2004a: 27, my translation from Italian) writes:

> Both the hope of closing the wounds of the Second World War and fears of a revival of German hegemony regained strength. This situation gave decisive impetus to the implementation of the single currency. By supporting its adoption, the German government sent a clear signal that German reunification and further European integration were inseparable aspects of a single policy.

The Maastricht Treaty, negotiated in 1991 on the basis of the Delors Report, was signed on 7 February 1992 by the twelve member countries of the European Community. With the exception of the United Kingdom and Denmark, which were granted an "opting out" clause, the signatories undertook to adopt a single currency by 1 January 1999.

In the summer of that year, the European Monetary System went into crisis. The EMS crisis confirms the validity of the "economic trilemma" theory. The German central bank, the Bundesbank, raised interest rates on its own to counter the feared rise in inflation (and also to attract the foreign capital needed to finance the country's reunification). In order to stem the flight of capital and prevent the devaluation of their currencies, Italy and Great Britain were forced to follow Germany in raising interest rates. The restrictive manoeuvre exacerbated an economic crisis that was already under way and, in September 1992, forced the two countries to devalue their currencies and leave the EMS. The German mark quickly appreciated by more than 50% against the Italian lira.

The EMS went into crisis and was formally rescued in August 1993 with the decision to widen the margins of exchange rate fluctuation from 2.25% to 15%. In fact, we can no longer speak of a quasi-fixed exchange rate regime. The EMS crisis, like the previous Bretton Woods crisis, shows that in a fixed exchange rate regime, with perfect capital mobility, no autonomous management of monetary policy is possible. The single market only works with a solid monetary union. And in Maastricht it was decided to establish the most solid form of monetary union: a single currency managed by a single European Central Bank.

The Maastricht Treaty was signed on 7 February 1992 and came into force on 1 November 1993. The second major stage in the process of European unification began. In Maastricht, the European Union was born, built on three "pillars": The European Community (the single market), the Common Foreign and Security Policy (CFSP) and cooperation in Justice and Home Affairs (JHA).

In 1997, the Treaty of Amsterdam was approved, which, by transposing the Stability and Growth Pact signed in 1996, regulates the fiscal policy of the EMU member states. In particular, they undertake to achieve a structural deficit (the public deficit corresponding to potential GDP) of zero, so as to be able, during recessionary phases, to implement expansive counter-cyclical manoeuvres by financing public spending plans, up to a ratio between deficit and GDP not exceeding 3%.

Some scholars argue that, since Maastricht, Europe has been a fragile "market without state" and an undemocratic "Union without Constitution". These considerations can be shared, although it should be noted that, with the approval of the Maastricht and Amsterdam treaties, a "material constitution" was consolidated in Europe, that is, a body of rules that determines the aims and instruments of European economic governance.

The main aim is to extend and reconcile economic freedoms and social rights or, in the words of Article 2 of the Amsterdam Treaty, "to promote economic and social progress and a high level of employment and to achieve balanced and sustainable development". The instruments provide for an active economic policy in accordance with three principles. The first is the principle of "an open market economy with free competition", which prevents the political authorities from adopting duties, premiums or other instruments that distort competition. The second is the principle of "stable prices, sound public finances and monetary conditions and a sustainable balance of payments": this requires that European monetary policy be oriented towards the objective of domestic price stability, understood as an inflation rate below but close to 2%, and that member states' fiscal policy be oriented towards the objective of financial stability, understood as keeping public deficits and debts within certain sustainability parameters. The last one is the subsidiarity principle, and it implies the renunciation of any prospect or strategy of centralising power.

These seem to be typical principles of liberal constitutions, which entrust the invisible hand of the market with the mission of reconciling economic freedoms and social rights. In reality, the two treaties, in order to achieve their aim, set out in Article 2, assign to the national and Community political authorities a series of "common actions" that are unusual for a classic liberal constitution and closer to modern social constitutions.

By signing the Maastricht Treaty, the twelve countries undertook to pursue an "ever closer union", starting with the construction of an EMU that includes a single currency, a European central bank and a common monetary policy. It was established that the EMU would be formally established at the end of a process comprising three consecutive stages: (a) the completion of the European single market by 1993; (b) the creation of a European Monetary Institute and the renunciation by member states of the financing of public debt in the period 1994–1996; and (c) the admission of candidate countries to the EMU by 1997 or 1999 at the latest, as decided by the European Council on the basis of a series of convergence criteria or parameters.

Five convergence parameters measure the health of national economies:

1. the inflation rate, which may not be more than 1.5 percentage points above the average of the three most virtuous countries;
2. the long-term interest rate, which may not exceed 2 percentage points above the average of the three most virtuous countries;
3. the percentage ratio of public deficit to GDP, which cannot exceed 3%;
4. the percentage ratio of public debt to GDP, which cannot exceed 60%;
5. the exchange rate requires "the observance of the normal fluctuation margins provided for by the exchange-rate mechanism of the European Monetary System, for at least two years, without devaluing against the currency of any other Member State" (Maastricht Treaty, Article 109j).

The basic idea is that only countries with converging economies can participate in the EMU: convergence measured by a set of quantitative indicators. The basic reason, which emerges in the debate within the Union, is that the presence of divergent economies, for example with excessive public deficits, would make the implementation of a common monetary policy problematic. Financially weaker countries might demand an expansionary policy while financially stronger countries might want a restrictive one. Moreover, distributional conflicts could arise with creditor countries, which would be urged or forced to bail out debtor countries. For this twofold reason, it was basically decided to admit only those countries that had met the convergence criteria.

There has been much debate, indeed there is ongoing debate, over the scientific validity of the numbers used to measure the sustainability of the deficit (3%) and debt (60%) in relation to GDP. The choice, as regards the debt, fell, once again, on an average value: 60% was, more or less, the average of the public debts of the Community countries, while 3% was the public deficit rate that, in relation to the GDP growth forecasts of the member countries, would have made it possible to keep the debt/GDP ratio substantially unchanged (Padoa Schioppa 2004b: 290–292).

It is interesting to note that two Italian economists, Paolo Savona and Carlo Viviani, in a small book published in 1996, *L'Europa dai piedi d'argilla* (*Europe of the Clay Feet*), argued that the Maastricht Treaty required countries such as Italy – which had a trade surplus and thus, according to the national income equation, an excess of savings over investment – to reduce their excessive public debt, while it allowed countries such as Germany, that had a trade deficit (and thus a shortage of savings over investment), to increase their public debt under the Maastricht parameters. The Maastricht negotiators, according to the two Italian economists, forgot that there may be unused ("aborted") savings, which the public authorities have a duty to return into circulation with expansionary manoeuvres. Europe was in danger of repeating the mistake it made after World War I when, by forcing the Weimar Republic to implement a deflationary policy, it favoured Hitler's rise.

The reference to the case of "abortive savings" is interesting but, as we have seen, it is a special case that only rarely takes the malignant form of the great deflation that favoured Hitler's rise or prolonged the Great Depression. Moreover, a distinction must be made between flow and stock magnitudes. Italy, a candidate for the EMU, had a (temporary) trade surplus but a (consolidated) public debt, which posed and still poses a serious problem of sustainability.

The economic philosophy of the Maastricht and Amsterdam treaties is simple. During expansionary phases, when the private economy does not require public support, governments should aim at restoring a substantial balance in the public budget, while during recession or stagnation phases, when the private economy requires public support, governments can increase public deficit spending up to a maximum of 3% in relation to the GDP and, in the case of severe recessions, go even further, like a kind of public accordion that widens and narrows to compensate for the inverse and parallel movements of the private sector.

The drafters of the treaties probably underestimated the difficulties that national governments would face in implementing fiscal consolidation policies in expansionary phases for fear of interrupting or slowing down growth, or overestimated their ability to incur the risk of unpopularity in the name of higher general interest. In any case, that was the economic philosophy of the planned EMU.

On 1 January 1999, the euro was born. For three years, the new currency was only used for electronic payments, and on 1 January 2002, banknotes and coins came into circulation. At present, the euro is the currency of nineteen countries comprising the Eurozone.

The Maastricht Treaty inaugurated the erosion of national economic sovereignty. In particular, the governments of the member states lost the availability of the traditional instruments of economic policy: currency, exchange rates, duties, public deficits and State aid.

At the beginning of the new millennium, Europe tried to give itself a formal constitution. After a special meeting of the European Council in Lisbon in March 2000 to launch a new strategy for growth and social cohesion (the so-called Lisbon Strategy), the Council met again in Laeken in December 2001 to convene a "Convention on the Future of Europe" to write a constitution. The inaugural session took place on 28 February 2002, and during the debate, two members of the Convention, Joschka Fischer and Dominique de Villepin, proposed a joint motion in which explicit reference was made to a model of a social market economy (see Joerges 2011: 9).

On 29 October 2004, the "Treaty establishing a Constitution for Europe" (TEC) was signed. Article I-3 states:

> The Union shall work for the sustainable development of Europe based on balanced economic growth and price stability, a highly competitive social market economy, aiming at full employment and social progress, and a high level of protection and improvement of the quality of the environment. It shall promote scientific and technological advance.

For the first time, the (ordoliberal) term social market economy appears in a European treaty. But the process of ratifying the treaty was interrupted after a vote against it in two referendums held in France and the Netherlands in 2005.

In the meantime, Europe, without a constitution, expanded eastwards, welcoming some countries of the former Soviet bloc. In 2004, Poland, the Czech Republic, Slovakia, Hungary, Estonia, Latvia, Lithuania, Slovenia, Cyprus and Malta joined, and in 2007 Bulgaria and Romania, bringing the total number of EU members to 27 (the 28th being Croatia, which joined in 2013).

A significant part of the contents of the rejected Constitutional Treaty is transposed in the Lisbon Treaty, which was approved on 13 December 2007 and which entered into force on 1 December 2009. Article 2.3 states:

> The Union shall establish an internal market. It shall work for the sustainable development of Europe based on balanced economic growth and price stability, a highly competitive social market economy, aiming at full employment and social progress, and a high level of protection and improvement of the quality of the environment. It shall promote scientific and technological advance.

In Short

In 1974, Hayek received the Nobel Prize for Economics and in 1989 the Berlin Wall fell: neoliberalism was reborn from the ashes of communism. The process of European unification proceeded along the functionalist path of progressive economic integration. After the end of Bretton Woods, it was decided first to create a European Monetary System (1979) and then (in 1986) to complete the construction of the Single Market by removing the remaining obstacles to the free movement of goods, services, people and capital. But the Single Market only works with a Monetary Union. This led to the approval of the Maastricht Treaty, which prefigured an Economic and Monetary Union. The European Union was born, incorporating a (ordoliberal) model of a social market economy, a model included in the Constitution rejected in 2005 and taken up in the Lisbon Treaty of 2007, which came into force in 2009.

What was the influence of the great economic ideas in the epochal transition from the two separate Europes to the reunified Europe on its way to federal union?

The decline of Keynesian interventionism and the rise of German ordoliberalism favoured the formation of a Europe that adopted, at least programmatically, a model of social market economy that saw monetary and financial stability as an indispensable condition for pursuing the social goal of full or maximum employment.

Europe's founding values are further recognised in the treaties of Maastricht, Amsterdam, and Lisbon where, as we have seen, explicit reference is made to the principle of subsidiarity and the objectives of maximum employment and balanced and sustainable development. The Maastricht Treaty includes, among the aims of the Union, that of preserving and developing the *acquis communautaire*, that is, Europe's identity heritage, while the Lisbon Treaty, in Article 2, summarises the constitutive European values as follows:

> The Union is founded on the values of respect for human dignity, freedom, democracy, equality, the rule of law and respect for human rights, including the rights of persons belonging to minorities. These values are common to the Member States in a society in which pluralism, non-discrimination, tolerance, justice, solidarity and equality between women and men prevail.

The history of recent years teaches us that Europe is one in its diversity, but it can only live or survive as a community of nations if it adopts and respects a set of common rules, designed and used for the common good of people and peoples.

Notes

1 On the history of Europe of the period, see Dayson and Featherstone (1999), Majone (2009), James (2012), Dyson and Maes (2016), Brunnermeier, James and Landau (2016), De Grauwe (2018). On the history of economic thought, see Yergin and Stanislaw (2002), Screpanti and Zamagni (2005, ch. 9), Overtveldt (2007), Jones (2012), Mirowski and Plehwe (2015). On the history of macroeconomics, see Nerozzi and Ricchiuti (2020).
2 www.britishpoliticalspeech.org/speech-archive.htm?speech=174.
3 On M. Friedman (1912–2006), see Ebenstein (2007). For a comparison between the Austrian School and the Chicago School, see Skousen (2005). On ordoliberalism, see Nicholls (1994) and Bonefeld (2017). For a comparison between the Austrian School and ordoliberalism, see Kolev (2015).
4 https://avalon.law.yale.edu/20th_century/reagan1.asp.
5 On Southern European capitalism, see Rangone and Solari (2012).

8

CRISIS OF NEOLIBERALISM, THE GREATEST RECESSION AND UNFINISHED EUROPE (2008–)

Introduction

In 2018, British historian Adam Tooze published a volume entitled *The Crash. How a Decade of Financial Crisis Changed the World*. Tooze's volume added to, and almost summarised, the many previous works in which economists and historians had tried to explain the Great Recession of 2008 by comparing it with the Great Depression of 1929. Many believed that the decade of crisis was over and that the world would experience a new era of prosperity. Instead, just around the corner, the black swan of Coronavirus disease 2019 (COVID-19) was preparing to enter the scene, prolonging the crisis and turning the Great Recession of 2008 into the greatest recession in modern capitalism.

The Great Recession reignited the old dispute between Hayek and Keynes. The main explanations for the crisis that had hit the world economy, and the consequent remedies proposed, were based on alternative explanations for the macroeconomic imbalances that exploded in 2008, attributable either to overinvestment theories or, conversely, to an excess of savings over investments (saving glut explanations). The economists who ascribed the crisis to the sin of greed suggested, as a remedy, a policy of "expansive austerity", which envisaged a reduction in (unproductive) public spending, a parallel lowering of taxation, and a consequent increase in (productive) investment. On the other hand, the advocates of the sin of greed believed that, in order to escape the deep throes of a Keynesian crisis that paralysed both private consumption and investment, the intervention of a public entity was needed to bolster the private economy with public investment and/or consumption.

During the Great Recession, the third and final obstacle separating Europe from the goal of federal political union was raised. Until the crisis, the single market and the euro had been sufficient to dispense the benefits of European integration to all member countries. Experience and economic theory had shown that a single

DOI: 10.4324/9781003188889-8

market requires a solid monetary union. But the crisis revealed another truth: the Economic and Monetary Union (the euro and the European Central Bank), in the presence of asymmetric shocks, requires the support of a fiscal union, that is, a larger EU budget. The issue was no longer only economic but also involved the upper echelons of politics, since the transfer of greater financial resources from the national states to the community bodies also implied a strengthening of Europe's model of democracy. The economic trilemma became a political trilemma. What was at stake was no longer merely the compatibility of economic goals, all desirable in themselves, but also the reconciliation of democracy and the market: the two pillars of European and Western civilisation.

The pandemic shock brought about a dramatic acceleration in the process of European integration, forcing the EU authorities to launch the historic Recovery Plan that marks the beginning of a common fiscal policy.

In this chapter, we will try to understand how great economic ideas have guided European choices in the years of modern capitalism's greatest recession.[1]

The reasons for the crisis and the debate among economists will remain in the background and will only be evoked, while centre stage will be occupied by those events that have most marked European history.

We shall examine, first, the Great Recession of 2008 and the last obstacle to European unity; second, how the economic trilemma becomes a political trilemma; and third, the crisis of neoliberalism, the pandemic shock and the Recovery Plan.

The Great Recession of 2008 and the Last Obstacle to European Unity

The 2008 crisis, like the previous great crisis of 1929, remains shrouded in a fog of mystery that economic historians are still trying to dispel. To be at least partly understood, the crisis must be contextualised within the economic cycle of the 2000s.

The cycle began with the dramatic attack on New York's Twin Towers on 11 September 2001, which paralysed the US economy and dealt a severe blow to the entire world economy. In the United States, the crisis had in fact already begun in March 2001. Moreover, it was an expected crisis, after a long period of economic expansion. The concern was, if anything, to ensure that the American economy had a soft landing (the recurrent expression in the media) while waiting for a new take-off.

The attack on the Twin Towers – the lexical combination sounds dramatic today – plunged the economy into a state of total uncertainty and fear that pushed all private operators to postpone any significant consumption and investment decision. The economy risked being dragged down by the fall in domestic demand, with the impossibility of stimulating foreign demand in any way.

In this dramatic situation, the American authorities decided to resort to shock therapy, obviously not only for economic reasons, and to a strong mix of expansive fiscal and monetary policies. The federal government reduced taxes on households and businesses and increased public spending, in particular spending to finance the so-called war on terror. The federal budget, which had closed with a large surplus over GDP in 2000, closed with a large deficit in 2003. At the same time, the Federal Reserve drastically lowered interest rates in an effort to stimulate consumption and investment.

The combination of an expansive fiscal policy and an expansive monetary policy was like a whip to a tired horse. The horse, against all odds, began to run again. Despite the terrorist attack, which exacerbated a crisis already under way, the American economy began to grow again at an average annual rate of more than 3%: the increase in consumption, investment and public spending, that is, domestic demand, was such that it drove up GDP and employment, but also led to general indebtedness. Households, businesses and the government went into debt. America appeared to be a country that demanded more than it produced, invested more than it saved, and imported more than it exported.

The American administration, partly in order to strengthen a patriotic feeling of belonging to the nation, relaunched the American Dream of an Ownership Society: if there were more homeowners, it was thought, the feeling of belonging to the nation would be strengthened. And so it was that, as part of the deregulation of the financial markets that began in 1999 with the abolition of the Glass-Steagall Act, subprime mortgages were also granted to those unable to offer adequate financial security. It was thought that "the price of houses never goes down" and that those who could not pay the mortgage could repay the loan by selling the house, at worst at its initial purchase value.

The bottom line, from a macroeconomic perspective, is that Americans were buying houses; that is, they were demanding more than they were producing, using the savings of the Chinese. In other words, there was a global imbalance whereby the trade deficit of America (and more generally of the West) corresponded to the trade surplus of China (and more generally of the East). In 2007, that is, on the eve of the crisis, the American trade deficit was around 6% of the GDP while China's trade surplus was around 10% of its GDP. The Chinese were saving about 30% of their national income, which the Chinese authorities also used to buy US government debt securities to finance the US trade deficit.

After an unheeded warning in the summer of 2007, the crisis exploded in the summer of 2008 with the indelible image of traders leaving the headquarters of the failed Lehman Brothers carrying the boxes containing their personal belongings. Starting in 2005, the Federal Reserve began a policy of gradually raising interest rates in an attempt to counteract the expected inflation resulting from the excessive amount of money in circulation. The parallel increase in (variable) mortgage rates put less affluent borrowers at risk. Fears spread that many people might default, and house sales began to increase steeply, leading to an unexpected fall in prices. The Fed first stabilised and then reduced the key interest rate – but it was too late. Panic spread throughout the economic system among savers and mutual distrust among banks stuffed with bad bonds. With the failure of Lehman Brothers, a catastrophic domino effect began.

The immediate cause of the crisis was the excessive provision of subprime mortgages, granted to subjects highly exposed to the risk of insolvency, but the remote and structural cause was the global imbalance between America and China, between West and East. More precisely, the cause was not the global imbalance per se, because the fact that a large country like China, which had too much savings compared to opportunities for domestic investment, transferred part of its savings to a country like America, which had a shortage of savings, was in itself a positive fact for both countries. Moreover, the imbalance is normally reduced or absorbed by a change in the relationship between the currencies involved, with an appreciation in the currency of the surplus country and a depreciation in that of the deficit country. The global imbalance became the remote cause of the crisis both because the US debt was excessive and not sustainable over time and because China obstructed the adjustment process by refusing to revalue or appreciate the yuan.

America, after the Lehman Brothers bankruptcy, changed its strategy by launching a series of measures aimed at bailing out troubled banks and supporting domestic demand (stimulus package).

In 2010, Europe adopted a ten-year strategy known as "Europe 2020", and in 2012 approved the fiscal compact, a treaty that tightened fiscal policy by requiring signatory countries to return to a debt-to-GDP ratio of no more than 60% within 20 years. But above all, Europe discovered the existence of a second major obstacle to the achievement of political union: monetary union (the euro), under the given conditions, could only work well if there was also a form of fiscal union. Robert Mundell, winner of the Nobel Prize for Economics in 1999 and a theorist of optimal currency areas, explained the fundamental reason for this *ante litteram*. A monetary union can only function well without fiscal union if there are no (unrealistic) asymmetric shocks, that is, if all areas of the union are in the same phase of the economic cycle. If, on the other hand, as can happen and as usually happens, one area (e.g., Germany) is in an expansionary phase and another area (e.g., Greece) sinks into a recession, then a problem of rebalancing between the two areas arises. There are three alternative adjustment mechanisms. First, the area in crisis devalues its currency and regains some international competitiveness. Second, the unemployed in the crisis area move to the expansion area. Third, a central authority finances the recovery and revival of the depressed area. In the United States, for example, when Louisiana is in crisis, the federal government provides substantial funding for the recovery and revitalisation of the local economy and a proportion of the unemployed move to more prosperous regions of the country. In Europe, the three mechanisms were essentially blocked. Greece could not devalue the drachma simply because it no longer existed. Unemployed Greeks did not go to Germany or other expanding countries because there is little labour mobility in Europe. The last solution remained: a fiscal union that could conduct a fiscal policy to stabilise and grow the EU economy. But how could Europe, if it wanted to, implement a common fiscal policy if its budget amounted to 1% of Europe's GDP? This is the problem with fiscal union: in the face of asymmetric shocks, that is, in the face of reality, the common monetary policy is no longer sufficient and, alongside the pillar of monetary union, the pillar of fiscal union must be built. If the crisis then degenerates into a great depression, like those of 1929 and 2008, then those extraordinary expansionary deficit spending policies proposed by Keynes in the 1930s and accepted, albeit as rare exceptions, first by Röpke and then also by Hayek, might be necessary.

In fact, however, there is an alternative. Some scholars believe that a monetary union could be sufficient and self-consistent, provided that the European Central Bank has no obligation to intervene to support countries in crisis. Padoa-Schioppa (2004b: 191, my translation from Italian), for example, writes: "In this way, financial markets would be certain that neither the central bank nor any other EU institution would – even implicitly – stand in support of the financial commitments of national governments". Thus, monetary union could function on its own, without fiscal union, only on condition that national governments, in exchange for fiscal sovereignty, accept the risk of default. In other words, solidarity between the peoples of Europe would be renounced, so that if an area goes into crisis it must fend for itself.

Europe needs to complete the path of economic integration it embarked on after World War II by adopting a fiscal union, but in order to create one, to share, at least in part, public debts and credits, tax revenues, and expenditures, it is necessary to know what form the political union will take and which Europe is hiding behind the hedge: the democratic Europe of the people or the technocratic Europe of the elites. The economic question is becoming political and brings into play the controversial relationship between democracy and the market.

The Economic Trilemma Becomes a Political Trilemma

The American economist Dani Rodrik (2011) has argued that the world is now faced with a fundamental political trilemma: it is no longer possible to have democracy, national sovereignty, and globalisation simultaneously. In fact, to develop globalisation or deeper economic integration, whether at the European or global level, that is, to guarantee the four basic economic freedoms, it would be necessary for individual countries to accept, and respect, a set of common rules dictated by neoclassical orthodoxy: monetary stability, fiscal discipline, privatisation, liberalisation and minimum government. Without these rules, it would be difficult to transform the many local and national economies into a single, large, integrated European or world market.

The common rules can be imposed either by international authorities – for example by the so-called troika comprising representatives of the European Commission, the European Central Bank, and the International Monetary Fund – or by national governments willing to conform their economic sovereignty to the directives of supranational bodies (e.g., Latin American governments in the 1990s, in order to obtain loans from the IMF, had to accept the rules of the Washington Consensus by adopting the policies of privatisation and liberalisation of the economy required by the IMF itself). In both cases, a political trilemma arises in the sense that it is not possible to have, at the same time, national sovereignty, democracy (i.e., decisions that stem from the will of the people) and greater economic globalisation.

There are three hypothetical ways out of the political trilemma. The first is to defend national democracy and contain economic globalisation (more democracy and less market); the second is to develop economic globalisation and restrict the space of national democracy (more market and less democracy); and the third is to build a transnational democracy to govern globalisation (more democracy and more market).

The first is historically the Keynesian path that led to the Bretton Woods order when, in a framework of international cooperation, national governments had sufficient economic sovereignty to implement the aggregate demand management policies needed to achieve full employment equilibrium. The cost of that model was a limited or imperfect mobility of the factors of production, that is, the chosen combination was more (national) democracy and less (global) market.

The second is historically the Austrian way, which considers only a liberal democracy that limits itself to protecting the fundamental civil and political rights of the individual to be compatible with a free and large market. Any promise of social justice in this world, that is, full employment and distributive equity, implies a policy of market interference and control that ends up destroying or compressing the fundamental rights of the individual and disregarding the very promise of economic welfare and social justice. The chosen combination, in this case, is less (national) democracy, with all the associated risks, and more (global) market, with all the associated benefits.

The third is historically the way of those who, starting with the English School of International Relations, believe that it is possible to build a transnational democracy that can also govern a transnational economy.

Today, many scholars, starting with Rodrik, consider the prospect of building a cosmopolitan democracy a chimera. Thus, at a global level, the trilemma reduces to a dilemma. The trivium is reduced to a fork in the road. It is a question of choosing between the first and second way. Either the Keynesian way, which takes us back to the Bretton Woods world and restores some of the lost economic sovereignty to the nation-states, albeit within a framework of international cooperation, or the Austrian way, which leads to a new and somewhat disturbing world where democracy renounces the protection of certain fundamental social rights and entrusts the market with the task of determining the personal and territorial distribution of resources.

Rodrik's (2011: XIX, original italics) preference is for the first route: "*Democracies have the right to protect their social arrangements, and when this right clashes with the requirements of the global economy, it is the latter that should give way*".

The Crisis of Neoliberalism, the Pandemic Shock and the Recovery Plan

In Europe, the three ways out of the political trilemma all remain open and it is a matter of choosing the best one. Rodrik himself, in the *Preface* to the new Italian edition of his book written in 2014, observes:

When I wrote the book, I could not imagine that the eurozone would provide us with such a perfect illustration of the ongoing trilemma. Europe's economic and political difficulties are rooted in the fact that monetary and financial integration has gone further than its political and institutional foundations. Democracy and economic performance are both victims of this imbalance. Saving democracy requires either more political integration or less economic integration. Because Europe's leaders refuse to make a choice, the crisis continues to drag on.

my translation from Italian

So let us see where the three ways out lead. The first way, the Keynesian way, which calls for more national democracy and less economic globalisation, can lead either to a new Bretton Woods or to a confederal Europe. For example, the German sociologist Streeck (2013: 213, my translation from Italian) writes:

The European Monetary Union was a political mistake because it abolished devaluation despite the enormous heterogeneity of the eurozone countries, without at the same time abolishing nation-states and democracy at the national level. Instead of compounding the mistake through a flight forward and completing monetary union through "political union", which would be nothing more than the final crowning of the consolidated state, one can try, as long as the crisis keeps the door open, to remedy that mistake by returning Europe to an orderly system of flexible exchange rates.

In an interview with the Italian newspaper *La Repubblica* on 9 October 2016, Polish nationalist leader J. Kaczynski expressed instead a preference for a confederation of nation-states: "All of us in Europe must return to the concept of the nation-state, the only institution capable of guaranteeing democracy and freedom" (my translation from Italian). This is also the perspective of Brexit. In the referendum of 23 June 2016, the British people rejected the prospect of an "ever closer union" with other European States, confirming their long-standing aspiration for national self-government. The British authorities initially thought and hoped that they could leave the European Union by remaining in the single market without respecting one of the four fundamental freedoms, the one that ensures the free movement of people. However, faced with the clear position expressed by the European authorities, they then had to take note that the four freedoms are indivisible and they formed an agreement with the European Union. In a speech in Florence on 22 September 2017, the then PM Theresa May admitted, "The United Kingdom is leaving the European Union. We will no longer be members of its single market or its customs union. For we understand that the single market's four freedoms are indivisible for our European friends".[2]

The second way, the Austrian way, which envisages less national democracy and more of a global market, in Europe takes the form of a federation that imposes on the member states strict compliance with the rules and principles necessary for a well-functioning community economy, starting with respect for the "austere" principles of monetary and financial stability enshrined in the founding treaties of the Union.

The third way, that of the English School of International Relations of Wight and Bull, which envisages the construction of a transnational democracy, takes the form in Europe of a federal political union between a restricted group of countries that share differentiated models of cooperation with other European countries. It is the image of a small circle of countries, which complete the process of economic integration to form a political union, around which a series of concentric circles are formed that contemplate different modes of economic and political cooperation. One author who has thoroughly explored this theme is the Italian political scientist Sergio Fabbrini, who speaks of a "Federal Union in a differentiated Europe".

For Fabbrini (2015, 2019), Europe should complete the unification process that began in the post-war period with the approval of a constitution that formalises and legitimises the differentiation that has already taken place between a group of countries that want to reach the goal of political union and other countries that only wish to access differentiated levels of economic integration. To complete the unification process, it is not necessary to assume, as the German Constitutional Court does, the existence of a European *demos*. All one needs is a constitution that enshrines the separation, the differentiation, between political and economic Europe. The political union should be inspired by the American model of compound democracy, that is, a union of states and citizens which, unlike the traditional federal states created by splitting up pre-existing centralised states, provides for both vertical (between the centre and the periphery) and horizontal (at the centre) separation of power, typical of those federal unions, such as the United States, which were created by the aggregation (not the sundering) of pre-existing sovereign states. Economic union, on the other hand, according to Fabbrini, requires lighter forms of political union.[3] The European Union is the answer to the need to ensure peaceful coexistence among peoples with different identities. It is sufficient to recognise an additional cultural identity without denying pre-existing ones:

> Europe has many *demoi* that cannot and must not be streamed into a single *demos* … A union of states must maintain the pluralism of national identities and the languages and cultural traditions of its citizens, even if it must encourage reciprocal knowledge, a condition necessary for mutual respect and tolerance. The point is that democratic unions of states cannot be based on a common cultural identity. They add a new (political) identity to the existing (national) identities … Federal unions should acknowledge national diversity among their member states, in addition to their similarities. Such diversity must be compounded, as already encapsulated in the motto of the EU (*in varietate concordia*). If a state or a people cannot hold a federal union together, where does the glue for such a union reside? The comparative analysis of federal unions (of the United States and Switzerland) has led us to a single response: That glue resides in the

constitution. A federal union of asymmetrical and differentiated states requires a founding pact between its members to establish the purely political reasons of the aggregation project.

Fabbrini 2019: 127–128

In the early 2020s, as Europe was looking for a way out of the Rodrik trilemma, the dark menace of COVID-19 appeared. From a macroeconomic point of view, the pandemic was a devastating, twofold adverse shock. First, on the aggregate supply side, with a temporary suspension of production of many consumer goods during the lockdown months and a subsequent contraction of production capacity with a reduction in available seats in airplanes, trains, buses, theatres, cinemas and restaurants. No bombs fell, as in war, destroying production capacity, but in fact it was as if they had fallen, as the actual and potential supply of goods and services contracted. The shock quickly spread to the aggregate demand side, with a fall in incomes, consumption, investments and exports. The contraction in demand was accentuated by growing uncertainty, which led to an increase in the average propensity to save: even households that had not suffered a reduction in income or businesses that had planned new investments preferred to postpone spending decisions by depositing those sums of money in current accounts. In other words, the typically Keynesian phenomenon occurred whereby, in times of great uncertainty, the preference for liquidity grows and the savings deposited in banks are not used to finance investments but remain at a standstill, creating a vacuum in the spending circuit. The primary, devastating, economic consequences of COVID-19 have been a falling GDP, rising unemployment and poverty, rising deficits and public debt, and a sharp rise in the deficit-to-GDP and debt-to-GDP ratios.

The European Union has shown that it has learned the lesson of 2008: that it is not possible, and indeed wrong, to demand austerity during a severe recession. This time it intervened promptly with a series of expansionary measures. It immediately suspended the Stability and Growth Pact, allowing individual countries to borrow to the extent necessary to support their economies. It suspended State aid rules, allowing individual governments to directly help companies in difficulty. Lastly, it launched a major Recovery Plan for Europe called the Next Generation EU, allocating 750 billion euros for loans and grants, financed, in part, by the issuance of common European debt securities. The ECB also intensified its expansionary monetary policy by continuing to buy sovereign debt securities to enable European countries to finance an increasing share of public spending.

The European Union's interventions made it possible to contain the fall in aggregate demand and thus in incomes and employment in the countries most affected by the pandemic. The Next Generation EU, in particular, linked to the new European strategy, the Green Deal, marked the beginning of a common fiscal policy and the strengthening of that *de facto* solidarity that Schuman had indicated as being essential to European construction.

However, Rodrik's trilemma is not solved and the three hypothetical ways out remain open. Let us try to make a comparative assessment of those three paths, because Europe cannot remain for too long in the middle of the road.

The first way out, the Keynesian way out, takes us back to a Europe of sovereign nation-states that accept a system of common rules on the Bretton Woods model. The advantage is to save a tried and tested form of democracy, the national one. The disadvantage is to deprive oneself of some of the benefits – and not only economic ones – deriving from greater economic integration and to give up the prospect (the challenge) of building a supranational democracy for an economy and a society that will be increasingly supranational. The risk, which Keynes himself wanted to avoid, is to fall back into the trap of opposing nationalisms that end up destroying both democracy and the market.

The second way, the Austrian way, leads us into the unknown land of a Europe that increasingly renounces the protection of social rights in order to defend economic freedoms. This is a Europe in which sovereignty belongs fundamentally to the market, that is, to the consumers who, with their preferences – some of them free, some manipulated by companies – direct production, employment, and the distribution of wealth. The advantage is to enjoy the full benefits of globalisation and fundamental economic freedoms. The disadvantage is to give up a democracy, understood as a representative government of the citizens, which pursues an ideal of common good and social justice by entrusting an impersonal mechanism, the market, with the power to direct the lives of millions of people. Perhaps the crisis of neoliberalism, even before the accusations of having fostered, with the deregulation of the financial markets, the Great Recession, stems from the prefigured prospect of a society regulated by the market and of a democracy that renounces the protection of social rights.

The third way, that of supranational democracy, takes us to the partly unknown land of a federal and differentiated Europe. The great advantage is that we can enjoy the benefits of both the market (and thus economic freedom) and democracy (and thus political freedom). The great disadvantage is that the last obstacle is the highest. It is not easy to build a federal and differentiated Europe. Fabbrini argues that a constitution is enough and recognises that there is a common European identity in addition to the national identity. The problem is how can a community, the European community, enter into a constitutional pact that makes the union between certain peoples even closer if it does not recognise the existence and value of a common European identity. Beyond any technical solution, the rich countries of Europe will only be willing to help countries or areas in difficulty if they feel part of the same community, albeit a supranational one, which does not preclude but rather makes it possible for different peoples to live together. Fabbrini argues that some states can limit themselves to participating in the single market. The problem is, as historical experience and economic theory show, that the single market requires the acceptance of the four economic freedoms and a more or less solid form of monetary union. In other words, it always presupposes the existence and recognition of a common identity or a feeling of belonging to the same community. In short, if nationalist tendencies prevail, participation in the single market or monetary union alone becomes difficult, if not impossible.

However, the best way forward seems to be the third: a federal and differentiated Europe. A multi-speed Europe, as it has been called, with a group of countries – for example, the nineteen countries of the Eurozone – that could accelerate the pace towards a federal union by establishing differentiated forms of cooperation with other countries wishing to remain in the single market or in the monetary union itself, and always leaving the door open to those who want to join the political union. A Europe united around the three founding values – *libertas, opus, communitas* – which underpin and shape the "European economic and social model" recognised and often appreciated throughout the world: a model that translates the idea of freedom into the *de facto* recognition of fundamental civil, political, economic and social rights, the idea of industriousness into a constant commitment to promoting inclusive growth, that is, growth that generates the highest sustainable level of employment and community by regulating vertical relations between institutions and horizontal relations between civil and political society on the basis of the principles of subsidiarity and solidarity.[4]

The economics has run out of steam: the functionalist race is over. In order to complete the process of economic integration, a fiscal union must be established, and in order to establish a fiscal union, that is, to share the "wealth of nations", it is necessary to know which accomplished model of democracy Europe intends to adopt. In other words, a form of political union must be chosen.

In Short

During the Great Recession, the last obstacle to European political union was raised: it was realised that, in the face of asymmetric shocks, monetary union could only work with a joint fiscal union. But it was also realised that, in order to establish a fiscal union, a model of political union must be chosen. The question turns from economics to politics, and Europe, like the rest of the world, falls into a political trilemma that highlights the incompatibility among national sovereignty, democracy and economic globalisation. Around the world, the trilemma boils down to a dilemma between a return to national democracy and the development of the global market. In Europe, however, the third way remains open, the possibility of building a supranational democracy to govern a community economy. This is a path that the pandemic shock has dramatically made more viable.

So which economic ideas guided European choices during the years of modern capitalism's greatest recession? The Great Recession illustrated the limits of the functionalism and neoliberalism that have accompanied the process of European unification in recent years. Functionalism has served its purpose: the initial promise was that, at the end of a prolonged and progressive process of economic integration, the need would arise to establish a full political union. The promise has been fulfilled, and it is now a question of choosing a model of that political union. Neoliberalism, which won the battle of ideas against etatism, showed its limits when it upheld and practised the principle of the primacy of economics over politics, and thus of the market over democracy.

The lesson of history is that, in Europe, sovereignty cannot belong either to the market or to an elite of technocrats lacking the full democratic legitimacy that only comes from popular participation in collective deliberations and from a use of power for the common good of the peoples. Neither economic freedom alone (the market) nor political freedom alone (formal democracy) is sufficient, because Europe was born and lives to pursue an ideal of full and equal freedom, economic and political, negative and positive – in other words, to guarantee a common good for individuals and peoples.

Notes

1 On the recent history of Europe, see Majone (2014), Amato and Galli della Loggia (2014), Fabbrini (2015, 2019), Tooze (2018), Gilbert (2020). On the history of economic ideas, see Skidelsky (2009), Woods (2009), Rodrik (2011).
2 On the issue of Brexit, see Fabbrini (2021).
3

> An economic community requires competition policy but does not require the adoption of a common foreign or security policy, nor does it require a common policy for home affairs or immigration. It does not even require a single currency, once balanced exchange rates between the different currency regimes are established. For the federal union, instead, the challenge will be more complex. Here it is a question of creating a constitutionally anti-centralizing system, and yet capable of making legitimate and effective decisions, if organized according to the model of multiple separation of powers. A federal union does not imply the transfer of sovereignty from member states to the center. Rather, it is based on a division of sovereignty, distinguishing between the policies and resources that must remain national and the policies and resources that are shared at the supranational level.

Fabbrini 2019: 148

4 On the European economic and social model, see Sapir (2006), Gill and Raiser (2012).

CONCLUSION

The European story is only one face of a much larger prism: in only a few decades, we have abruptly moved from a world of independent nations to a world of interdependent transnational communities, populated by people with multiple identities. The rise of the melting-pot society has led to a rediscovery of the comparative method in the social sciences and also in historiography, where World History studies transnational and intercultural interaction phenomena occurring on a planetary scale, sometimes resorting to comparison to identify similarities and differences among human groups destined to live together.

This research was born with the aim, and in an attempt, to extend the three-dimensional approach of the history of economic thought (theories–cultures–policies), fruitfully experimented in national contexts, to a supranational dimension such as the European one, thus linking the history of economic thought to World History. We asked ourselves how the history of economic thought can contribute to our knowledge and understanding of history and thus of European identity, illustrating the role of economic culture in the development of Europe, from its origins to the present day.

We have chosen a "realistic" approach to history, avoiding falling into either idealistic determinism, according to which "ideas shape the course of history" (Keynes), or materialistic determinism, according to which history is class struggle (Marx). Man learns from experience, which reason judges. Human reason, including economic reason, by judging a social order, orients the actions of men, which change history.

We have reconstructed the secular European journey through eight major stages. It is now time to briefly recall the path we have travelled and to answer, at least partially, the question that prompted our research.

In Chapter 1, we saw how Europe, after a long conception that began with Greco-Roman civilisation and continued with the "Germanic-Byzantine" empire,

DOI: 10.4324/9781003188889-9

was born, just as Bloch had surmised, when the Roman Empire died. Not the Western Roman Empire, as someone may perhaps imagine, but the Eastern Roman Empire, which collapsed in 1453. At that time, there was no longer a strong universalist power but already fully formed nations; however, none of them aspired to play a hegemonic role. Europe was born as a "community of Christian nations", united and diverse. Centuries later it would be called "unity in diversity". Unity was not ensured by the power of a great empire, which no longer existed, or by the strength of one or a few large nation-states, which did not yet exist. Europe was born as a "stateless society". Its unity was based on Christianity which, having healed the wounds of the two schisms in the West and the East, inspires and spreads shared values of freedom, hard work, and community, from which common institutions also spring: a market economy and a municipal democracy. Europe was Christianity: Europeans were Christians and Christians were only in Europe. Outside, there was Eastern despotism. The Christian nations were united but diverse, with cohesive nation-states in the West, a surviving multinational empire (the Habsburg empire) at the centre, and former Byzantine territories populated by linguistic minorities of the Orthodox faith in the East: a triplet birth. Medieval economic thought (Scholastic and Byzantine) contributed to the birth of Europe by elaborating and disseminating its constitutive values (*libertas*, *opus* and *communitas*) and by orienting the economic ethics of commercial capitalism and the political ethics of municipal democracy towards an idea of common good: the idea that one's own good is always in relation to that of others, is a common good, which individuals and social groups must directly and responsibly care for. The European identity, which is strengthened in the confrontation with external despotism, is marked by the unceasing search for an ever more extensive and at the same time just freedom.

In Chapter 2, we examined the epochal transition – which occurred (symbolically) between 1517, the year of the beginning of the Protestant Reformation, and 1776, the year of the last attempt to save the *ancien régime* – from a Europe as a "society without a State" to a Europe as a "society of absolute States". Christian Europe dissolved when religion, from a unifying factor, became the cause of devastating wars while the absolute state emerged to ensure peace. With the Protestant Reformation and the subsequent Catholic Counter-Reformation, another identity corridor was added to the East–West axis, crossing Europe along the North–South axis and inspiring two distinct models of capitalism: northern and southern. Between the mid-sixteenth and mid-eighteenth centuries, mercantilism contributed to the formation of a Europe of despotic monarchies by elaborating and spreading the doctrine that entrusted the sovereign, and his stewards, with the task of directing the economy to achieve the commercial surplus needed to accumulate the gold and silver with which to buy the goods needed to ensure the material well-being and military supremacy of the kingdom in an international competition between opposing and irreconcilable national interests. This was a zero-sum game where the gain of one corresponds to the loss of others. In the second half of the eighteenth century, Physiocracy, which supplanted Mercantilism, contributed to the formation of a Europe of enlightened absolute monarchies with the doctrine of natural order that entrusted the sovereign with the task of re-establishing the primacy and centrality of agriculture over trade and manufacturing in accordance with natural economic laws. The spread of absolutism strengthened unity in the diversity of the Three Europes, with Western Europe consolidating national states experiencing an agricultural and industrial revolution that loosened the old feudal shackles, Eastern Europe experiencing new forms of serfdom, and an enigmatic Central Europe, subject to Habsburg rule, still predominantly agricultural. Unity is represented by a king, despotic or enlightened, creator of the law or its first servant, who becomes the sole interpreter and guarantor of the common good of national and multinational monarchies. The lesson of history for Europe is that fundamental personal freedoms, such as religious freedom, cannot be suppressed without triggering a process of dissolution of the established order.

In Chapter 3, we saw the passage – which took place between 1776, the year of the American Revolution, which was the prelude to the French Revolution, but also the year Smith's *Wealth of Nations* appeared, to 1870, when the process of national unification of Germany and Italy ended – from a Europe of a "society of absolute monarchies" to a Europe of a "concert of liberal nation-states" of which Tsarist Russia was a fully-fledged member. Absolutism, despotic and enlightened, failed because of a double crisis of effectiveness (the elite lived in luxury and the people in poverty) and of legitimacy (people rebelled against a power exercised in the name of God and without the people). Classical economists contribute to the formation of a Europe of liberal nation-states by explaining, with economic reason, the failure of mercantilist and enlightened nationalism and by pointing out the social institutions that make cooperation between nation-states (and hence the harmony of national interests) possible and mutually beneficial. In a world where there is limited mobility of capital and people, two major social institutions are sufficient: a gold-based monetary system and a free trade regime. In other words, only one economic freedom is needed: the freedom to exchange goods and services. The spread of liberalism accentuates the distinctive features of the Three Europes. In Western Europe (particularly in England and France), homogeneous national states were consolidated that overthrew the mercantilist system and developed a policy of liberalisation and deregulation of the economy, both in internal and external relations: a form of "liberal nationalism" as defined by Mises or, if you like, "national liberalism". In Central and Eastern Europe, on the other hand, the widespread presence of strong linguistic minorities prevented the formation of cohesive nation-states and, after a brief period of classical liberalism, the roots of a nationalism that Mises described as "aggressive" emerged. The market becomes the supreme and impersonal guarantor of the common good of a society comprising only individuals whose only responsibility towards the community is to pursue their own interests, trusting in the thaumaturgical capacity of the invisible hand of the market to transform private selfishness into national wealth. The lesson of history for Europe is that, under certain conditions, cooperation between nation-states is possible and mutually beneficial.

In Chapter 4, we examined the epochal transition – which took place between 1871, the year in which the Second German Reich was founded, and 1918, the last year of the Great War – from a Europe of a "concert of liberal nation-states" to a Europe of "empires at war". Liberal Europe dissolved in the face of a twofold major crisis: political and economic. The political crisis was triggered by Bismarck, who deluded himself into believing that he could maintain the European order solely on the balance of power by renouncing the principle of royal legitimacy restored at the Congress of Vienna. When Bismarck left the scene in 1890, the balance broke down and the great powers, no longer united by a Holy Alliance, prepared for war. The economic crisis was triggered in 1873 by the First Globalisation, which, by moving not only goods but also people and capital, broke the assumption on which the Ricardian theory of free trade was based and reopened the question of the possible and mutually beneficial harmony of national interests. In these years, between 1871 and 1918, a fierce battle of ideas was fought between the new neoclassical orthodoxy and the new etatist heresy. The neoclassics conquered economic science but not civil and political society where etatist ideas prevailed, in the double version of Marxist socialism, which conquered tsarist Russia, and historicist interventionism, which spread to the German Second Reich. The empire became the horizon, the vital space, necessary to ensure the interest of the nation and Europe was transformed into the land of warring empires: British, Austro-Hungarian, German and Russian. The lesson of history is that, at the time of the First Globalisation, the common good of Europe, a "community of nations", is assured neither by traditional free trade, which everyone abandons, nor by an imperialist etatism that leads to World War I. One might even add neither by the economic power of the market, nor by the political power of the state. Power is not enough; we also need legitimacy.

In Chapter 5, we saw the epochal transition – which took place between 1919, the year of the Paris Peace Conference outlining a new European order, and 1943, when the fate of the war was already sealed – from a Europe of sovereign nations to a Europe once again at war. In Paris, a Europe of sovereign nations was designed within the framework of a reconstituted international economic community based on free trade and the gold standard – a Europe from which Soviet Russia would withdraw. American President Woodrow Wilson, unlike Bismarck, renounced the balance of power and staked everything on the legitimate principle of the self-determination of peoples. The Europe of Paris collapsed in the face of a new, twofold major crisis: political and economic. The economic crisis was triggered by repeated violations of the rules of the gold standard monetary system, which were perceived as golden cages preventing national governments from implementing the economic policies necessary to ensure national prosperity. The political crisis was triggered by Hitler, who used the principle of self-determination of peoples to invade – in the name of the unity of the German people – Austria, Czechoslovakia and Poland, leading to the devastation of World War II. In the inter-war years, the years of "high theory", the challenge was between a multifaceted neoliberalism, which included rivals such as Hayek and Keynes, and an enigmatic and magmatic corporatism. Until the crisis, faith in the classical liberal order had dominated. Since the crisis, currents of economic thought have prevailed, justifying the abandonment of the classical order and the recovery of full national economic sovereignty. Prior to the crisis, the great guardian of Europe's common good had been gold, an impersonal mechanism that makes nation-states independent of each other and all of them dependent on a common set of rules that, in this sense, allows nations to repeat the Westphalian *"superiorem non recognoscens"*. Following the crisis, the common good of Europe was entrusted to individual national governments, who pursued only national interests – thus preparing for a catastrophic war. The lesson of this story, for Europe, is that nations exist and refuse to be subjected to any automatic mechanism that could coerce their sovereignty. Rules are not enough. But neither is popular legitimacy. We also need a balance of power and therefore a system of shared rules geared to the common good of individuals and national communities.

In Chapter 6, we examined the transition – between 1944, the year of the Bretton Woods Conference, and 1973, the year of the definitive end of those monetary agreements and the concomitant oil shock – from a Europe initiating a political process of "separate unification" to a Europe entering a crisis, both in the East and in the West. After World War II, in some respects, the debate that followed World War I was repeated. At first, there seemed to be an emerging tendency to reconstitute a Europe of sovereign nations within the framework of an international community still founded on the traditional pillars of free trade and the gold currency. The Americans, with the Marshall Plan, then offered the opportunity to build the third pillar of a united or at least integrated Europe. And it is here that the process of "separate unification" began. Western Europe accepted the Plan, while Eastern Europe, under Soviet pressure, rejected it. Europe was now divided in half by an ideological iron curtain that erased Central Europe. There was a return to the balance of power and thus to a limitation of national sovereignty. Soviet Russia returned to Europe, albeit via intervening governments. In the East, a socialist order was established based on the territorial division of labour and a popular democracy that made national sovereignty conditional on participation in the construction of Soviet socialism. In the West, a liberal order was re-established, based on the participation of nation-states in new international institutions (GATT and Bretton Woods), while adherence to the Marshall Plan triggered a process of unification along the functionalist path of economic integration that preceded and prepared for political union. The thirty glorious years (*les trente glorieuses*) were dominated, in the East, by the obligatory acceptance of Marxism–Leninism and, in the West, by the spread of a Keynesianism mitigated by the neoclassical synthesis, but still interventionist. In the West, liberal democracy and the market economy, within the international framework of Bretton Woods, jointly played the role of guarantors of the common good, while in the East that role was played, under the supervision of the Soviet Union, by popular democracy and the planned economy. The 1973 crisis revealed to Europeans and to the world at large the limits of a socialism without a human face and of a resurgent nationalism which, by irreparably violating the Bretton Woods monetary agreements, deprived the nascent European single market of the necessary monetary union. The lesson of history for Europe is that centuries-old cultural unity is stronger than any temporary and artificial political separation.

In Chapter 7, we examined the transition from a Europe still divided by the Iron Curtain to a Europe once again united after the collapse of the Berlin Wall, between 1974, the year in which Hayek's Nobel Prize for Economics marked the beginning of the liberal revolution in the West, and 2007, the year that heralded the Great Recession. During these years, Europe continued along the functionalist path, completing the Single Market, which recognised the "four freedoms" (free movement of goods, services, people and capital), and building the Economic and Monetary Union, which ensured price stability. These years were marked by the decline of Keynesian interventionism, the rebirth of Austrian neoliberalism and monetarism, and the rise of German ordoliberalism, which inspired the adoption by the European Union, born with the 1992 Maastricht Treaty, of a model of social market economy that considers monetary and financial stability an indispensable condition for pursuing the social goal of maximum and stable employment. It is precisely the ordoliberal model of the social market economy, regulated by a special anti-trust authority, that represents the mechanism through which the common good is sought in a Europe that, after the fall of the Wall, is once again divided into three distinct areas: western, central and eastern. The lesson of history is that Europe is united in its diversity and can only develop if it is able to direct the market towards desired social goals.

Lastly, in Chapter 8, we saw Europe in the stormy open sea of the greatest crisis of modern capitalism, with Brexit and the revolt of the nationalists. The crisis has shown the limits of both functionalism and neoliberalism. The former has run out of steam by holding out the promise that economic integration would necessitate a more accomplished form of political unification. The latter, which won the battle of ideas against etatism, raised the legitimate issue that the government of a complex society cannot be entrusted to the market, even if it is well regulated and protected. Europe has fallen into a political trilemma and must decide whether to turn back towards a new Bretton Woods that restores sovereignty to national governments, to fall back on a model that still limits national sovereignty to the benefit of an increasingly global market, or to move forward to the constitution of a federal union that can and does govern the European market. In the Europe grappling with this political trilemma, hit by the pandemic shock, unity is renewed thanks to the historic Recovery Plan, and so is diversity, with three increasingly compact areas: that of the western founders (France, Germany and Italy), the Visegrad group, and the Balkan region, with the singular appearance of a "Hanseatic neo-league" that recalls the existence of an identity axis between a northern and southern capitalism. The final lesson is that sovereignty in Europe cannot belong either to the market, that is, to a population of consumers often influenced by businesses, or to a power legitimised only by procedural rules. Europe was born for something more.

In conclusion, what role has economic culture, resulting from the systematic reflection of economists, played in the formation of Europe? Economic culture has helped to steer Europe's course, from its birth to the present day, towards a certain idea of the common good, blaming, correcting or corroborating current political experiences. Economic culture, the expression of economic knowledge, is a manifestation of human reasoning which, by judging reality, contributes to changing it for the better or for the worse. The idea of the common good that takes root in Europe is the awareness that the good of each person and nation is realised together with that of others and depends largely on the possibility, offered to the greatest number of people, of being free, of being able to work, and of being able to participate in the life of the community. Freedom is understood as the possibility to act and to want, as negative and positive freedom, as complete freedom. Work is understood no longer as punishment and suffering or as expiation of an ancestral guilt, but as participation in human (and, for those who believe, divine) creative work. Communities are understood as areas in which the human personality is fully expressed. These are the three values that underpin the "European economic and social model".

It is a unity in diversity. The constitutive values that unite Europe have in fact declined in different ways in the three Europes. In Western Europe, the idea of freedom as individual independence prevails, industriousness as creative entrepreneurship, community as subsidiary autonomy of intermediate bodies, while in Central and Eastern Europe the idea of freedom as voluntary acceptance of authority, industriousness as dependent participation in the work of the enterprise and community as trust in state institutions prevails even more. A unity in diversity that is at the origin of a variety of capitalisms that unites and distinguishes Europe internally, along the dual East–West and North–South axes, and that differentiates it from other economic models: American, Asian and Islamic.

Europe was born as a "community of nations", united by Christianity, when its three constitutive values blossomed. Before that there was the freedom of the ancients, the Greeks and Romans, which recognised the (positive) freedom of some to take part in collective deliberations, but denied the (negative) freedom of many to act protected from the abuse of political authority, work was a punishment reserved for slaves and the community was restricted to the *polis* or *civitas*, that is, the legal community of citizens. Medieval economic thought contributed to the birth of Europe by clarifying, harmonising and spreading those three constituent values as a single ideal of common good immortalised in Ambrogio Lorenzetti's frescoes of Good Government (or Common Good) in Siena.

After its birth, Europe zigzagged in search of the best form of government to ensure the common good. Hence, from time to time, the sceptre of power passes from the hands of despotic and enlightened kings to the invisible hand of the market, to more or less sacred emperors, to delegates of the people. Europe falls in wars and always rises again in search of the ideal of a common good that distinguishes it from other peoples and nations.

Today, Europe is grappling with a fundamental political trilemma: it is no longer possible to have national sovereignty, democracy, and economic globalisation all at once. A choice must be made by giving something up. Globalisation, that is, the gradual but rapid unfolding of the four economic freedoms, is turning Europe into a single country. In a particular country, it would be inconceivable to raise a customs barrier between one region and another, or to prohibit a citizen from transferring his savings from one city to another, or to prevent an unemployed person from changing his residence. The same is happening in Europe. Here the trilemma arises, as does the urgency of making a choice. In the vision of Mises and Hayek, the European government should behave like a national government: limit itself to ensuring the four economic freedoms. Any attempt to defend the national interest by adopting restrictive measures would end up harming the national community itself. Each country, like each region, should only accommodate the number of people for whom the highest possible standard of living can be ensured using existing resources. Politics cannot increase the wealth of nations, and the optimum population can only be determined by the market. In the Keynesian view, on the other hand, the European government should limit the four freedoms, in particular the free movement of production factors, in order to protect national sovereignty and democracy.

Europe has so far chosen a third way. By building a single market, it has fully recognised the four freedoms, effectively renouncing to follow the Keynesian path. It must now choose a model of supranational democracy capable of governing the single market. From the perspective of Austrian neoliberalism, this should be a minimal government, one that only protects fundamental civil and political rights and one that could not and should not do anything about the depopulation or impoverishment of a country by letting the free market operate. From an ordoliberal perspective, on the other hand, the government should intervene to protect and modify certain structural data of the market, which would however maintain its role as the supreme mechanism for allocating productive resources. The three constitutive values remain central to European history and identity. Europe remains a community of nations in search of the common good. There can be no European common good, and therefore no united Europe, without freedom, industriousness and community. A Europe that could not guarantee complete freedom, starting with economic freedom, or that did not fight unemployment, or that accepted the depopulation or impoverishment of nations, would no longer be Europe. The point is that the market alone cannot ensure the common good of peoples and nations. What is needed is democratic governance and therefore an innovative model of supranational democracy capable not only of protecting but also of orienting the market.

Europe was born as a community of nations striving for a common good. If she loses her soul, she loses herself.

BIBLIOGRAPHY

Acton, J.E. (1907). *History of Freedom and Other Essays,* London: Macmillan.

Agnelli, A. (1971 [2005]). *La genesi dell'idea di Mitteleuropa,* Trieste: MGS Press.

Amato, G. and Galli della Loggia, E. (2014). *Europa perduta?,* Bologna: Il Mulino.

Anderson, P. (1979). *Lineages of Absolutist State,* London and New York: Verso.

Aquinas, S.T. (1270 [1947]). *Summa Theologiae,* New York: Benziger Bros.

Aquinas, S.T. (1267ca [1949]). *De regimine principum ad regem Cypri,* Toronto: The Pontifical Institute of Mediaeval Studies.

Arnason, J.P. and Doyle, N.J. (eds.) (2010). *Domains and Divisions of European History,* Liverpool: Liverpool University Press.

Ashley, P. (1920 [1970]). *Modern Tariff History. Germany – United States – France,* New York: Howard Fertig.

Asso, P.F. (ed.) (2001). *From Economists to Economists. The International Spread of Italian Economic Thought, 1750–1950,* Firenze: Edizioni Polistampa.

Augello, M.M. and Guidi, M.E.L. (eds.) (2001). *The Spread of Political Economy and the Professionalisation of Economists,* London and New York: Routledge.

Avtonomov, V. (2019). Russian and European Economic Thought: Several Stories of Interconnection. *History of Economic Thought and Policy,* 1: 93–107.

Backhouse, R.E. (1985). *A History of Modern Economic Analysis,* Oxford: Basil Blackwell.

Backhouse, R.E. (1994). Why and How Should We Study the History of Economic Thought? *History of Economic Ideas,* 2: 115–123.

Backhouse, R.E. (2001). How and Why Should We Write the History of Twentieth-Century Economics. *Journal of the History of Economic Thought,* 2: 243–251.

Backhouse, R.E. (2002). *The Penguin History of Economics,* London: Penguin Books.

Baeck, L. (1994). *The Mediterranean Tradition in Economic Thought,* London and New York: Routledge.

Baldi, B. (2003). Enea Silvio Piccolomini e il "De Europa": umanesimo, religione e politica. *Archivio Storico Italiano,* 4: 619–683.

Balot, R.K. (ed.) (2009). *Greek and Roman Political Thought,* Chichester: Blackwell Publishing.

Barnett, V. (ed.) (2014). *Routledge Handbook of the History of Global Economic Thought,* London and New York: Routledge.

Barucci, P. (2005). On the Circular Process of Evolution of Economic Theory. *Storia del pensiero economico*, 2: 81–96.

Bergamini, O. (2003). *Storia degli Stati Uniti*, Roma-Bari: Laterza.

Berggren, H. and Trägårdh, L. (2011). Social Trust and Radical Individualism. In World Economic Forum, *Shared Norms for the New Reality*, Davos: 13–27.

Berlin, I. (1958 [1969]). Two Concepts of Liberty. In *Four Essays On Liberty*, Oxford: Oxford University Press, pp. 118–172.

Bibó, I. (1946 [2015]). The Miseries of East European Small States. In *The Art of Peacemaking*, New Haven and London: Yale University Press.

Black, A. (2003). *Guild & State. European Political Thought from the Twelfth Century to the Present*, New Brunswick and London: Transaction Publishers (fourth printing 2009).

Black, A. (2008). *The West and Islam. Religion and Political Thought in World History*, Oxford: Oxford University Press.

Black, A. (2009a). *A World History of Ancient Political Thought*, Oxford: Oxford University Press.

Black, A. (2009b). Toward a Global History of Political Thought. In T. Shogimen and C.J. Nederman (eds.), *Western Political Thought in Dialogue With Asia*, Lanham: Rowman & Littlefield Publishers, pp. 25–42.

Black, A. (2011a). *The History of Islamic Political Thought. From the Prophet to the Present*, Edinburgh: Edinburgh University Press, second edition (first published 2001 and reprinted 2012).

Black, A. (2011b). Islamic and Western Political Thought: Does History Have Any Lessons? *Khazar Journal of Humanities and Social Sciences*, 3: 5–12.

Blanning, T. (2007). *The Pursuit of Glory. Europe 1648–1815*, London: Penguin Books.

Blaug, M. (2001), No History of Ideas, Please, We're Economists. *Journal of Economic Perspectives*, 1: 145–164.

Bobbio, N. (1978 [2009]). *Eguaglianza e libertà*, Torino: Einaudi.

Böhm-Bawerk, E., Hilferding, R. and Bortkiewicz, L. (1971). *Economia Borghese ed economia marxista*, Firenze: La Nuova Italia.

Bonefeld, W. (2017). *The Strong State and the Free Economy*, Lanham: Rowman & Littlefield.

Bottoni, S. (2011). *Un altro novecento. L'Europa orientale dal 1919 a oggi*, Roma: Carocci editore.

Bresciani Turroni, C. (1958). *Corso di economia politica*, Milano: Giuffrè.

Bresciani-Turroni, C. (1918). *Mitteleuropa. L'impero economico dell'Europa centrale*, Roma: L'Universelle Imprimerie Polyglotte.

Bruni, L. (2018). *La pubblica felicità. Economia civile e political economy a confronto*, Milano: Vita e pensiero.

Bruni, L. and Milbank, J. (2019). Martin Luther and the Different Spirits of Capitalism in Europe. *International Review of Economics*, 66: 221–231.

Bruni, L. and Zamagni, S. (2004). *Economia civile. Efficienza, equità, felicità pubblica*, Bologna: Il Mulino.

Bruni, L. and Zamagni, S. (2016). *Civil Economy. Another Idea of the Market*, Newcastle upon Tyne: Agenda Publishing.

Brunnermeier, M.K., James, H. and Landau, J.-P. (2016). *The Euro and the Battle of Ideas*, Princeton and Oxford: Princeton University Press.

Bull, H. (1977). *The Anarchical Society*, London: Red Globe Press.

Cain, P.J. and Harrison, M. (eds.) (2001). *Imperialism: Critical Concepts in Historical Studies*, London and New York: Routledge.

Cain, P.J. and Hopkins, A.G. (2002). *British Imperialism 1688–2000*, London: Pearson Education.

Campagnolo, G. (2019). Some Reflections on China and Europe. *History of Economic Thought and Policy*, 1: 109–138.

Canning, J. (2003). *A History of Medieval Political Thought, 300–1450*, London and New York: Routledge.

Canning, J. (2011). *Ideas of Power in the Late Middle Ages, 1296–1417*, Cambridge: Cambridge University Press.

Capaldi, N. (2009). *John Stuart Mill. A Biography*, Cambridge: Cambridge University Press.

Carabelli, A. and Cedrini, M. (2014). *Secondo Keynes. Il disordine del neoliberalismo e le speranze di una nuova Bretton Woods*, Roma: Castelvecchi.

Cardini, F. and Montesano, M. (2006). *Storia medievale*, Firenze: Le Monnier.

Cardoso, J.L. and Psalidopoulos, M. (eds.) (2016). *The German Historical School and European Economic Thought*, London and New York: Routledge.

Centeno, M.A. and Cohen, J.N. (2012). The Arc of Neoliberalism. *Annual Review of Sociology*, August: 317–340.

Cesarano, F. (2006). *Monetary Theory and Bretton Woods. The Construction of an International Monetary Order*, Cambridge: Cambridge University Press.

Chabod, F. (1964). *Storia dell'idea d'Europa*, Bari: Laterza.

Chaplygina, I. and A. Lapidus (2016). Economic Thought in Scholasticism. In Gilbert Faccarello and Heinz D. Kurz (eds.), *Handbook of the History of Economic Analysis*, Vol. 2, *Schools of Thought in Economics*, Cheltenham: Edward-Elgar, pp. 20–42.

Cipolla, C.M. (1974). *Storia Economica Dell'europa Pre-industriale*, Bologna: Il Mulino.

Coats, A.W. (1968). Political Economy and the Tariff Reform Campaign of 1903, *Journal of Law and Economics*, 1: 181–229.

Coats, A.W. (2014). *The Historiography of Economics*, compiled and edited by R.E. Backhouse and B. Caldwell, London and New York: Routledge.

Coats, A.W. Bob (ed.) (2000). *The Development of Economics in Western Europe Since 1945*, London and New York: Routledge.

Colletti, L. and Napoleoni, C. (1970). *Il futuro del capitalismo. Crollo o sviluppo?*, Bari: Laterza.

Conrad, S. (2016). *What Is Global History?*, Princeton: Princeton University Press.

Constant, B. (1819 [2011]). *The Liberty of Ancients Compared With That of Moderns*, Indianapolis: Liberty Fund.

Crotty, J. (2019). *Keynes Against Capitalism. His Economic Case for Liberal Socialism*, London and New York: Routledge.

Curcio, C. (1978). *Europa. Storia di un'idea*, Roma: ERI.

Davies, N. (1996). *Europe. A History*, Oxford: Oxford University Press.

Dawson, Ch. (1950). Preface. In O. Halecki (ed). *The Limits and Divisions of European History*, London: Sheed & Ward, pp. vii–xi.

Dawson, Ch. (1956). *The Making of Europe*, New York: Meridian Books.

De Grauwe, P. (2018). *Economics of Monetary Union*, Oxford: Oxford University Press.

De Roover, R. 1955. Scholastic Economics: Survival and Lasting Influence From the Sixteenth Century to Adam Smith. *The Quarterly Journal of Economics*, 69 (2): 161–190.

De Roover, R. 1958. The Concept of the Just Price: Theory and Economic Policy. *The Journal of Economic History*, 18 (4): 418–434.

Delors Report (1989), *Committee for the Study of Economic and Monetary Union*, Presented April 17, 1989.

Demetracopoulos, J.A. (2012). Thomas Aquinas' Impact on Late Byzantine Theology and Philosophy: The Issues of Method or 'Modus Sciendi' and 'Dignitas Hominis'. In A. Speer and Ph. Steinkrüger (eds.), *Knotenpunkt Byzanz. Wissensformen und kulturelle Wechselbeziehungen*, Berlin: De Gruyter, pp. 333–410.

Di Bello, A. (2009). Ordine e Unità nel Medioevo: La rappresentanza del *Corpus Mysticum* all'*Universitas*, *Esercizi filosofici*, 4: 1–37.

Di Fiore, L. and Meriggi, M. (2011). *World History. Le nuove rotte della storia*, Roma-Bari: Edizioni Laterza.

Droz, J. (1960). *L'Europe centrale. Évolution historique de l'idée de «Mitteleuropa»*, Paris: Payot.
Duroselle, J.-B. (1964). *L'idea d'Europa nella storia*, Milano: Edizioni Milano Nuova.
Duroselle, J.-B. (1990). *Europe. A History of its Peoples*, London: Viking.
Dyson, K. and Featherstone, K. (1999). *The Road to Maastricht. Negotiating Economic and Monetary Union*, Oxford: Oxford University Press.
Dyson, K. and Maes, I. (eds.) (2016). *Architects of the Euro. Intellectuals in the Making of European Monetary Union*, Oxford: Oxford University Press.
Ebenstein, A. (2001). *Friedrich von Hayek. A Biography*, New York: St. Martin's Press.
Ebenstein, L. (2007). *Milton Friedman. A Biography*, New York: Palgrave Macmillan.
Eichengreen, B. (1992). *Golden Fetters*. New York-Oxford: Oxford University Press.
Eichengreen, B. (2007). *The European Economy Since 1945: Coordinated Capitalism and Beyond*, Princeton and Oxford: Princeton University Press.
Einaudi, L. (1949 [1975]). *Lezioni di politica sociale*, Torino: Einaudi Editore.
Ermiş, F. (2013). *A History of Ottoman Economic Thought*, London and New York: Routledge.
Evans, R. J. (2017). *The Pursuit of Power. Europe 1815–1914*, London: Penguin Books.
Fabbrini, F. (2021). *Brexit and the Future of the European Union*, Oxford: Oxford University Press.
Fabbrini, S. (2015). *Which European Union? Europe After the Euro Crisis*, Cambridge: Cambridge University Press.
Fabbrini, S. (2019). *Europe's Future. Decoupling and Reforming*, Cambridge: Cambridge University Press.
Fanfani, A. (1935). *Catholicism, Protestantism and Capitalism*, London: Sheed & Ward.
Febvre, L. (1944–45 [1999]). *L'Europa. Storia di una civiltà*, Roma: Donzelli Editore.
Fejtö, F. (1955). *Storia delle democrazie popolari*, Firenze: Vallecchi Editore.
Fejtö, F. (1998). *La fine delle democrazie popolari. L'Europa orientale dopo la rivoluzione del 1989*, Milano: Mondadori.
Feuchtwanger, E. J. (1985). *Democracy and Empire: Britain 1865–1914*, London: Arnold.
Fieldhouse, D.K. (1980). *Politica ed economia del colonialismo 1870–1945*, Roma-Bari: Laterza.
Fonzi, P. (2015). Il Nuovo Ordine Europeo nazionalsocialista: storia e storiografia. In *1943: strategie militari, collaborazionismi, resistenze*, Roma: Viella, pp. 101–119.
Foreman-Peck, J. (1999). *Storia dell'economia internazionale dal 1850 a oggi*, Bologna: Il Mulino.
Gerber, D.J. (1994). Constitutionalizing the Economy: German Neoliberalism, Competition Law and the "New" Europe, *American Journal of Comparative Law*, 1: 25–84.
Gerber, D.J. (1998). *Law and Competition in Twentieth Century Europe: Protecting Prometheus*, Oxford: Clarendon Press.
Geremek, B. (1996). *The Common Roots of Europe*, Oxford: Polity Press.
Gilbert, M. (2020). *European Integration. A Political History*, Lanham: Rowman & Littlefield.
Gill, I.S. and Raises, M. (eds.) (2012). *Golden Growth. Restoring the lustre of the European economic model*, Washington: International Bank for Reconstruction and Development.
Gioli, G. (ed.) (1997). *L'Europa e gli economisti italiani nel Novecento*, Milano: Franco Angeli.
Greengrass, M. (2015). *Christendom Destroyed. Europe 1517–1648*, London: Penguin Books.
Gregg, S. (2010). *Wilhelm Röpke's Political Economy*, Cheltenham and Northampton: Edward Elgar.
Gregg, S. (2013). *Becoming Europe. Economic Decline, Culture, and How America Can Avoid a European Future*, New York and London: Encounter Books.
Groenewegen, P.D. (1995). *A Soaring Eagle: Alfred Marshall 1842–1924*, Cheltenham: Edward Elgar.
Haas, E.B. (1958 [2004]). *The Uniting of Europe. Political, Social, and Economic Forces 1950–1957*, Notre Dame: University of Notre Dame Press.

Haberler, G. (1963). *Prosperity and Depression*, New York: Atheneum.

Hagemann, H. (ed.) (2002). *Business Cycle Theory: Selected Texts, 1860–1939*, London: Pickering and Chatto.

Halecki, O. (1950). *The Limits and Divisions of European History*, London and New York: Sheed & Ward.

Halecki, O. (1963). *The Millennium of Europe*, Notre Dame: University of Notre Dame Press.

Hall, P.A. (ed.) (1989). *The Political Power of Economic Ideas: Keynesianism across Nations*, Princeton: Princeton University Press.

Hall, P.A. and Soskice, D. (eds.) (2001). *The Varieties of Capitalism. The Institutional Foundations of Comparative Advantage*, Oxford: Oxford University Press.

Hallstein, W. (1961). Economic Integration as a Factor of Political Unification. Available at: aei.pitt.edu/14775/

Hallstein, W. (1962). The Economics of European Integration. In *United Europe. Challenge and Opportunity*, Cambridge: Harvard University Press, pp. 30–57.

Harrison, L.E. and Huntington, S. (eds.) (2000), *Culture Matters. How Values Shape Human Progress*, Library of Congress Cataloging-in-Publication Data.

Harrod R. (1951 [1963]). *The Life of John Maynard Keynes*, London: Macmillan.

Hartwich, O.M. (2009). *Neoliberalism: The Genesis of a Political Swearword*, Sidney: The Centre for Independent Studies Limited.

Hay, D. (1968). *Europe. The Emergence of an Idea*, Edinburgh: Edinburgh University Press.

Hayek, F.A. (1932). Das Schicksal der Goldwährung. *Deutsche Volkswirt*, February, reprinted under the title The Fate of the Gold Standard. In McCloughry, R. (ed). *Money, Capital and Fluctuations. Early Essays*. London: Routledge & Kegan, pp. 118–135.

Hayek, F.A. (1933). *Monetary Theory and the Trade Cycle*. London and Toronto: Jonathan Cape (German edition, Vienna 1929).

Hayek, F.A. (1935). *Prices and Production* (2nd edn), London: Routledge and Kegan.

Hayek, F.A. (1939 [1948]). The Economic Conditions of Interstate Federalism. In *Individualism and Economic Order*, Chicago: The University of Chicago Press.

Hayek, F.A. (1943 [1999]). A Commodity Reserve Currency. In *Good Money*, Part II. The Standard, edited by S. Kresge, Indianapolis: Liberty Fund, pp. 106–114.

Hayek, F.A. (1944 [2006]). *The Road to Serfdom*, London and New York: Routledge.

Hayek, F.A. (1982). *Law, Legislation and Liberty*, London: Routledge.

Hayes, B.B. (1994). *Bismarck and Mitteleuropa*, London and Toronto: Associated University Press.

Heckscher, E. (1935 [1994]). *Mercantilism*, London and New York: Routledge, 2 vols.

Hermet, G. (1997). *Nazioni e nazionalismi in Europa*, Bologna: Il Mulino.

Hobsbawm, E.J. (1996). *L'età degli imperi 1875–1914*, Milano: Mondadori.

Hobsbawm, E.J. (1999). *L'età della rivoluzione 1789–1848*, Milano: Rizzoli.

Hofstede, G., Hofstede, G.J. and Minkov, M. (2010). *Cultures and Organizations. Software of the Mind*, New York: McGraw Hill.

Hogan, M.J. (1987). *The Marshall Plan. America, Britain, and the Reconstruction of Western Europe, 1947–1952*, Cambridge: Cambridge University Press.

Horvath, J. (2019). The Evolution of Central European Economic Thought. *History of Economic Thought and Policy*, 1: 15–28.

Horvath, J. (2020). *An Introduction to the History of Economic Thought in Central Europe*, Basingstoke: Springer Nature.

Islahi, A.A. (2014). *History of Islamic Economic Thought*, Cheltenham: Edward Elgar.

James, H. (2012). *Making the European Monetary Union*, Cambridge: Harvard University Press.

Joerges Ch. (2011). *Unity in Diversity as Europe's Vocation and Conflicts Law as Europe's Constitutional Form*, Bremen, TranState Working Papers, No. 148.

Johnson, L.R. (1996). *Central Europe. Enemies, Neighbours, Friends*, New York – Oxford: Oxford University Press.

Jones, D.S. (2012). *Masters of the Universe. Hayek, Friedman, and the Birth of Neoliberal Politics*, Princeton and Oxford: Princeton University Press.

Jordan, W. (2002). *Europe in the High Middle Ages*, London: Penguin Books.

Judt, T. (2007). *Postwar. A History of Europe Since 1945*, London: The Penguin Press.

Kemp, T. (1969). *Teorie dell'imperialismo. Da Marx a oggi*, Torino: Einaudi Editore.

Kennedy, P.M. (1980). *The Rise of the Anglo-German Antagonism 1860–1914*, London: The Ashfield Press.

Kershaw, I. (2016). *To Hell and Back. Europe 1914–1949*, London: Penguin Books.

Keynes, J.M. (1923). *A Tract on Monetary Reform*, London: Macmillan.

Keynes, J.M. (1930 [1971]). *A Treatise on Money*. In *The Collected Writings of J.M. Keynes*. Vols. V and VI. London: Macmillan.

Keynes, J.M. (1931 [1973]). An Economic Analysis of Unemployment. In *The Collected Writings of J.M. Keynes*. Vol. XIII. London: Macmillan, pp. 343–367.

Keynes, J.M. (1933). *Essays in Biography*, New York: The Norton Library.

Keynes, J.M. (1934). Poverty in Plenty: Is the Economic System Self-Adjusting?, *The Listener*, November.

Keynes, J.M. (1936). *The General Theory of Employment, Interest and Money*, London: Macmillan.

Kindleberger, C.P. (1986). *The World in Depression 1929–1939*. Berkeley: University of California Press. Revised and Enlarged Edition.

Kissinger, H. (1995). *Diplomacy*, New York: Simon & Schuster.

Kissinger, H. (2014). *World Order*, New York: The Penguin Press.

Klein, D. (2010). Convictions Opposed to Certain Popular Opinions: The 1903 Anti-Protectionism Letter Supported by 16 British Economists, *Economic Journal Watch*, 2: 157–161.

Kolev, S. (2015). Ordoliberalism and the Austrian School. In C.J. Coyne and P.J. Boettke (eds). *The Oxford Handbook of Austrian Economics*, Oxford – New York: Oxford University Press, pp. 419–444.

Kundera, M. (1984). The Tragedy of Central Europe. *The New York Review of Books*, April: 33–38.

Kurz, H.D. (2006). Whither the History of Economic Thought? Going Nowhere Rather Slowly? *European Journal of the History of Economic Thought*, 4: 463–488.

Kurz, H.D. (2016). *Economic Thought. A Brief History*, New York: Columbia University Press.

Lai, C.-C. (ed.) (2000), *Adam Smith Across Nations. Translations and Receptions of* the Wealth of Nations, Oxford: Oxford University Press.

Laiou, A.E. (ed.) (2002). *The Economic History of Byzantium*, 3 vols., Washington: Dumbarton Oaks.

Laiou, A.E. and Morrison, C. (2007). *The Byzantine Economy*, Cambridge: Cambridge University Press.

Landreth, H. and Colander, D.C. (1994). *History of Economic Thought*, Boston: Houghton Mifflin Company.

Langholm, O. (1998). *The Legacy of Scholasticism in Economic Thought*, Cambridge: Cambridge University Press.

Le Goff, J. (1990). *Your Money or Your Life. Economy and Religion in the Middle Ages*, New York: Zone Books.

Le Goff, J. (2007). *The Birth of Europe 400–1500*, Oxford: Blackwell Publishing.

Le Goff, J. (2011). *La città medievale*, Firenze: Giunti.

Le Goff, J. (2012). *Money and the Middle Ages*, Cambridge: Polity.

Lindberg, L.N. (1963). *The Political Dynamics of European Economic Integration*, Stanford: Stanford University Press.

Livezeanu, I. and Klimó, Á. von (ed.) (2017). *The Routledge History of East Central Europe Since 1700*, London and New York: Routledge.

Lopez, R.S. (1962 [2004]). *Nascita dell'Europa. Storia dell'età medievale*, Milano: Il Saggiatore.

Loth, W., Wallace, W. and Wessels, W. (1998). *Walter Hallstein. The Forgotten European?*, New York: Macmillan.

Luzzatto, G. (1934). *Storia economica. L'età moderna*, Padova: Cedam.

Luzzatto, G. (1960). *Storia economica. L'età contemporanea*, Padova: Cedam.

Macmillan, M. (2003). *Paris 1919. Six months that changed the world*, New York: Random House.

Magliulo, A. (1993). Economia e politica dell'integrazione europea in Italia (1941–1958). *Rassegna Economica*, 4: 783–819.

Magliulo, A. (2007). La politica economica di Ezio Vanoni negli anni del centrismo, *Studi e Note di Economia*, 1: 77–114.

Magliulo, A. (2012). The Great Depression of 1929 in Italy: Economists' Views and Government Policy. In M. Psalidopoulos (ed), *The Great Depression in Europe: Economic Thought and Policy in a National Context*, Athens: Alpha Bank, Historical Archives, pp. 153–185.

Magliulo, A. (2016). Hayek and the Great Depression of 1929. Did He Really Change His Mind? *European Journal of the History of Economic Thought*, 1: 31–58.

Magliulo, A. (2018). Before Hitler: The Expansionary Program of the Brauns Commission. In R. Leeson (ed.), *Hayek: A Collaborative Biography*, New York: Palgrave Macmillan, pp. 129–159.

Magliulo, A. (2019). Towards a History of European Economic Thought: An Introductory Note. *History of Economic Thought and Policy*, 1: 5–13.

Maiolo, F. (2007). *Medieval Sovereignty. Marsilius of Padua and Bartolus of Saxoferrato*, Delf: Erubon Academic Publishers.

Majone, G. (2009). *Europe as the Would-be World Power. The EU at Fifty*, Cambridge: Cambridge University Press.

Majone, G. (2014). *Rethinking the Union of Europe Post-Crisis. Has Integration Gone Too Far?*, Cambridge: Cambridge University Press.

Makrides, V. (2019). Orthodox Christianity and Economic Development: A Critical Overview, *Archives des sciences sociales des religions*, 185: 23–43.

Malandrino, C. (2006). *«Tut etwas Tapferes»: compi un atto di coraggio. L'Europa federale di Walter Hallstein (1948–1982)*, Bologna: Il Mulino.

Mancini, O., Perillo, F. and Zagari, E. (1982). *La teoria economica del corporativismo*, Napoli: ESI.

Maniatis, G.C. (2001). The Domain of Private Guilds in the Byzantine Economy, Tenth to Fifteenth Centuries, *Dumbarton Oaks Papers*, vol. 55: 339–369.

Maranesi, P. (2015). *Labor sapientiae melior est corporeo labore*. La visione di Bonaventura del lavoro manuale. In P. Maranesi and M. Melone (eds.), *"La grazia di lavorare". Lavoro, vita consacrata, francescanesimo*, Bologna: EDB, pp. 455–500.

Marcuzzo, M.C. and Rosselli, A. (1990). *Ricardo and the Gold Standard. The Foundations of the International Monetary Order*, London: Palgrave Macmillan.

Marinova, T. and Nenovsky, N. (2019). Towards Understanding Balkan Economic Thought: Preliminary Reflections. *History of Economic Thought and Policy*, 1: 29–50.

Marshall, A. (1890 [1930]). *Principles of Economics*, London: Macmillan (Eighth edition).

Masala, A. (2017). *Stato, società e libertà. Dal liberalismo al neoliberalismo*, Soveria Mannelli: Rubbettino.

Masini, F. (2018). Decision-Making Processes and Multilayered Institutional Order: Lionel Robbins's Legacy. *Cambridge Journal of Economics*, 5: 1459–1471.

Massie, R.K. (2007). *Dreadnought. Britain, Germany and the Coming of the Great War*, London: Vintage.

McCloskey, D.N. (2010). *Bourgeois Dignity. Why Economics Can't Explain the Modern World*, Chicago: The University of Chicago Press.

McCloskey, D.N. (2016). *Bourgeois Equality. How Ideas, Not Capital or Institutions, Enriched the World*, Chicago: The University of Chicago Press.

McNeill, W. (1963). *The Rise of the West*, Chicago: The University of Chicago Press.

Menger, C. (1871 [2007]). *Principles of Economics*, Auburn: Ludwig von Mises Institute.

Meyer, H.C. (1955). *Mitteleuropa in German Thought and Action 1815–1945*, The Hague: Martinus Nijhoff.

Mikkeli, H. (1998). *Europe as an Idea and an Identity*, Basingstoke: Palgrave Publishers.

Mill, J.S. (1848 [2009]). *Principles of Political Economy*, Gutenberg EBook.

Mirowski, P. and Plehwe, D. (2015). *The Road from Mont Pèlerin. The Making of the Neoliberal Thought Collective*, Harvard: Harvard University Press.

Mises, L. von (1919 [2006]). *Nation, State, and Economy*. Indianapolis: Liberty Fund.

Mises, L. von (1922 [1951]). *Socialism. An Economic and Sociological Analysis*, New Haven: Yale University Press.

Mises, L. von (1927 [1985]). *Liberalism in the Classical Tradition*, San Francisco: Cobden Press.

Mises, L. von (1929 [2011]). *A Critique of Interventionism*, Alabama: Ludwig von Mises Institute.

Mises, L. von (1938 [2018]). Speech. In Reinhoudt, J. and Audier, S. (2018), pp. 124–125.

Mises, L. von (1940 [1949]). *Human Action: A Treatise on Economics*, La Vergne: Lightning Source (reprint).

Mises, L. von (1941 [2000]). Postwar Reconstruction. In Richard M. Ebeling (ed), *Selected Writings of Ludwig von Mises*, vol. 3, Indianapolis: Liberty Fund, pp. 1–19.

Mises, L. von (1944). *Omnipotent Government. The Rise of the Total State and Total War*, New Haven: Yale University Press.

Mitrany, D. (1943). *A Working Peace System*, London: The Royal Institute of International Affairs.

Mitrany, D. (1975). *The Functional Theory of Politics*, London: Martin Robertson.

Mizuta, H. and Sugiyama, C. (eds.) (1993). *Adam Smith. International Perspectives*, New York: St. Martin's Press.

Mokyr, J. (2016). *A Culture of Growth. The Origins of the Modern Economy*, Princeton and Oxford: Princeton University Press.

Monsalve, F. (2014). Scholastic Just Price Versus Current Market Price: Is It Merely a Matter of Labelling?, *The European Journal of the History of Economic Thought*, 1: 4–20.

Montaigne, M. (1580 [1910]), *Essays of Montaigne*, New York: Edwin C. Hill.

Montani, G. (1996). *L'economia politica e il mercato mondiale*, Roma-Bari: Laterza.

Montecinos, V. and Markoff, J. (eds.) (2009). *Economists in the Americas*, Cheltenham: Edward Elgar.

Naumann, F. (1918–1919). *Mitteleuropa*, 2 vols., Bari: Laterza.

Navari, C. (1996). Functionalism Versus Federalism: Alternative Visions of European Unity. In P. Murray and P. Rich (eds.). *Visions of European Unity*, edited by Boulder: Westview Press, pp. 63–91.

Nerozzi, S. and Ricchiuti, G. (2020). *Pensare la macroeconomia. Storia, dibattiti, prospettive*, Milano, Pearson.

Neumann, F. (1942). *Behemoth. The Structure and Practice of National Socialism*, Toronto: Oxford University Press.

Neumann, K. (2017). Inter-war Germany and the Corporatist Wave, 1918–39. In Pinto (2017), Ch. 6.

Nicholls, A.J. (1994). *Freedom with Responsibility. The Social Market Economy in Germany, 1918–1963*, Oxford: Clarendon Press.

North, D.C. (1990). *Institutions, Institutional Change and Economic Performance*, Cambridge: Cambridge University Press.

O'Brien, D.P. (1984). *Gli economisti classici*, Bologna: Il Mulino.

O'Rourke, K.H. and Williamson, J.G. (2005). *Globalizzazione e storia. L'evoluzione dell'economia atlantica nell'Ottocento*, Bologna: Il Mulino.

Ostrogorsky, G. (1968). *History of the Byzantine State*, Oxford: Basil Blackwell.

Overtveldt, J.V. (2007). *The Chicago School. How the University of Chicago Assembled the Thinkers Who Revolutionized Economics and Business*, Chicago: Agate.

Overy, R.J. (1996). *The Nazi Economic Recovery 1932–1938* (2nd ed). Cambridge: Press Syndicate of the University of Cambridge.

Padoa-Schioppa, T. (1992). L'Unione monetaria europea e l'Italia. *Bollettino Economico della Banca d'Italia*, 18: 61–68.

Padoa-Schioppa, T. (2004a). *L'euro e la sua banca centrale. L'unione dopo l'Unione*, Bologna: Il Mulino.

Padoa-Schioppa, T. (2004b). *La lunga via per l'euro*, Bologna: Il Mulino.

Pagden, A. (ed.) (2002). *The Idea of Europe. From Antiquity to the European Union*, Cambridge: Cambridge University Press.

Palma, N.P.G. (2008). History of Economics or a Selected History of Economics. *Journal of the History of Economic Thought*, 1: 93–104.

Pantaleoni, M. (1889 [1931]). *Principii di economia pura*, Milano: Treves.

Pasetti, M. (2017). The Fascist Labour Charter and its transnational spread. In Pinto (2017), Ch. 3.

Pasinetti, L.P. and Schefold, B. (eds.) (1999). *The Impact of Keynes on Economics in the 20th Century*, Cheltenham: Edward Elgar.

Penchev, P. and Özgur, M.E. (2019). The Role of the State in the Economic Policy and Thought of Bulgaria and Turkey During the Interwar Period. *History of Economic Thought and Policy*, 1: 51–66.

Phelps, E.S. (2006). *Economic Culture and Economic Performance: What Light Is Shed on the Continent's Problem?* Conference of CESifo and Center on Capitalism and Society, Venice, July 21–22, 2006, www.columbia.edu/~esp2/Center3rdAnnualConf2006Sept27.pdf

Phillipson, N. (2010). *Adam Smith. An Enlightened Life*, London: Penguin Books.

Piccolomini, A.S. (1458 [2013]). *Europe.* Translated by R. Brown. Introduced and Annotated by N. Bisaha, Washington: The Catholic University of America Press.

Pinto, A.C. (ed.) (2017). *Corporatism and Fascism. The Corporatist Wave in Europe*, London and New York: Routledge.

Pirenne, H. (1937). *Economic and Social History of Medieval Europe*, New York: Harvest Books.

Plested, M. (2012). *Orthodox Readings of Aquinas*, Oxford: Oxford University Press.

Popescu, O. (1997). *Studies in the History of Latin American Economic Thought*, London and New York: Routledge.

Price, S. and Thonemann, P. (2010). *The Birth of Classical Europe: A History from Troy to Augustine*, London: Penguin Books.

Prodi, P. (2009). *Settimo non rubare. Furto e mercato nella storia dell'Occidente*, Bologna: Il Mulino.

Rangone, M. and Solari, S. (2012). Southern European Capitalism and the Social Costs of Business Enterprise. *Studi e Note di Economia,* 1: 3–28.

Reinhoudt, J. and Audier, S. (2018). *The Walter Lippmann Colloquium. The Birth of Neo-Liberalism*, London: Palgrave Macmillan.

Ricardo, D. (1821 [2001]). *On the Principles of Political Economy and Taxation*, Kitchener: Batoche Books.

Robbins, L. (1937). *Economic Planning and International Order*, London: Macmillan.

Rodano, G. (1997). La scuola neoclassica nella macroeconomia contemporanea. *Rivista italiana degli economisti*, 3: 383–424.

Rodrik, D. (2011). *The Globalization Paradox*, New York and London: W.W. Norton.

Roggi, P. (1978). *L'economia politica classica 1776–1848*, Firenze: Le Monnier.

Roggi, P. (ed.) (1994). *Quale mercato per quale Europa. Nazione, mercato e grande Europa nel pensiero degli economisti dal XVIII sec. ad oggi*, Milano: Franco Angeli.

Romani, R. (2009). *L'economia politica dopo Keynes. Un profilo storico*, Roma: Carocci editore.

Roncaglia, A. (2005). *The Wealth of Ideas. A History of Economic Thought*, Cambridge: Cambridge University Press.

Röpke, W. (1936). *Crises and Cycles*. London: William Hodge (originally published in German in 1932).

Röpke, W. (1942 [1950]). *The Social Crisis of Our Time*, Chicago: The University of Chicago Press.

Röpke, W. (1944). *Civitas Humana. A Humane Order of Society*, London: William Hodge.

Röpke, W. (1945 [1946]). *L'ordine internazionale*, Milano: Rizzoli.

Röpke, W. (1964). European Economic Integration and Its Problems. *Modern Age. A Quarterly Review*, summer: 231–244.

Rosamond, B. (2000). *Theories of European Integration*, New York: St. Martin's Press.

Rosser, G. (2015). *The Art of Solidarity in the Middle Ages. Guilds in England 1250–1550*, Oxford: Oxford University Press.

Rossi, P. (2007). *L'identità dell'Europa*, Bologna: Il Mulino.

Rousseau, J.-J. (1761 [1993]). Estratto dal progetto di pace perpetua dell'Abbé de Saint-Pierre. In a cura di P. Rossi (ed), *Opere*, Milano: Sansoni Editore, pp. 139–154.

Roversi, A. (1984). *Il magistero della scienza. Storia del Verein für Sozialpolitik dal 1872 al 1888*, Milano: Franco Angeli.

Rupnik, J. (1989). *The Other Europe. The Rise and Fall of Communism in East-Central Europe*, New York: Pantheon Books.

Rüstow, A. (1938 [2018]). Speech. In Reinhoudt, J. and Audier, S. (2018), p. 124.

Santori, P. (2020). *Donum*, Exchange and Common Good in Aquinas: The Dawn of Civil Economy, *The European Journal of the History of Economic Thought*, 1: 276–297.

Santori, P. (2021). *Thomas Aquinas and the Civil Economy Tradition: The Mediterranean Spirit of Capitalism*, London: Routledge.

Sapir, A. (2006). Globalization and the Reform of European Social Models. *Journal of Common Market Studies*, 2: 369–390.

Savona, P. and Viviani, C. (1996). *L'Europa dai piedi d'argilla. Basi empiriche, fondamenti logici e conseguenze economiche dei parametri di Maastricht*, Milano: Libri Scheiwiller.

Schoorl, E. (2013). *Jean-Baptiste Say: Revolutionary, Entrepreneur, Economist*. London: Routledge.

Schulze, H. (1996). *States, Nations and Nationalism*, Hoboken: Wiley.

Screpanti, E. and Zamagni, S. (2005). *An Outline of the History of Economic Thought*, Oxford: Oxford University Press.

Sen, A. (2004). How Does Culture Matters? In V. Rao and M. Walton (eds.), *Culture and Public Action*, Stanford: Stanford University Press, pp. 37–58.

Seton-Watson, H. (1967). *Eastern Europe Between the Wars 1918–1941*, New York: Harper & Row.

Skidelsky, R. (1998). *Keynes*, Bologna: Il Mulino.

Skidelsky, R. (2009). *Keynes. The Return of the Master*, New York: Public Affairs.

Skousen, M. (2005). *Vienna and Chicago. Friends or Foes? The Tale of Two Schools of Free-Market Economics*, Washington: Regnery Publishing.

Smith, A. (1776 [2005]). *An Inquiry Into the Nature and Causes of the Wealth of Nations*, The Pennsylvania State University. www.academia.edu/38658864/AN_INQUIRY_INTO_THE_NATURE_AND_CAUSES_OF_THE_WEALTH_OF_NATIONS_A_PENN_STATE_ELECTRONIC_CLASSICS_SERIES_PUBLICATION

Slobodian, Q. (2018). *Globalists. The End of the Empire and the Birth of Neoliberalism*, Harvard: Harvard University Press.

Spinelli, A. and Rossi, E. (1941 [2011]). Towards a Free and United Europe. A Draft Manifesto, *Eurostudium*, luglio-settembre.

Stanziani, A. (2018). *Eurocentrism and the Politics of Global History*, London: Palgrave Macmillan.

Stassinopoulos, Y. (2019). Mare Nostrum, Œconomica Nostrum: Mediterranean Economic Thought, From the Early Nineteenth Century to the Interwar Period. *History of Economic Thought and Policy*, 1: 67–91.

Steil, B. (2013). *The Battle of Bretton Woods. John Maynard Keynes, Harry Dexter White, and the Making of a New World Order*, Princeton and Oxford: Princeton University Press.

Streeck, W. (2013). *Tempo guadagnato. La crisi rinviata del capitalismo democratico*, Milano: Feltrinelli.

Stürmer, M. (1986). *L'impero inquieto. La Germania dal 1866 al 1918*. Bologna: Il Mulino.

Subrahmanyam, S. (2014). *Aux origines de l'histoire globale*, Collège de France / Fayard.

Swann, D. (1989). *L'economia del Mercato comune europeo*, Bologna, Il Mulino.

Szűcs, J. (1996). *Disegno delle tre regioni storiche d'Europa*, Soveria Mannelli: Rubbettino.

Todeschini, G. (2004). *Ricchezza francescana. Dalla povertà volontaria alla società di mercato*, Bologna: Il Mulino.

Tooze, A. (2007). *The Wages of Destruction. The Making and Breaking of the Nazi Economy*, London: Penguin Books.

Tooze, A. (2018). *The Crash. How a Decade of Financial Crisis Changed the World*, London: Penguin Books.

Treadgold, W. (1997). *A History of the Byzantine State and Society*, Stanford: Stanford University Press.

Vito, F. (1949). La comunità economica internazionale. In Atti della XXII Settimana Sociale dei Cattolici Italiani, *La comunità internazionale*, Roma: Icas, pp. 166–190.

Voltaire (1764 [1900]). *The Philosophical Dictionary*, New York: Carlton House.

Wapshott, N. (2012). *Keynes Hayek. The Clash That Defined Modern Economics*, New York: W.W. Norton & Co.

Wasserman, J. (2019). *The Marginal Revolutionaries. How Austrian Economists Fought the War of Ideas*, New Haven: Yale University Press.

Weatherall, D. (2011). *David Ricardo: A Biography*, New York: Springer.

Weber, M. (1915 [1946]). The Social Psychology of the World Religions. In H. Gerth and C.W. Mills (eds.), *From Max Weber: Essays in Sociology*, New York: Oxford University Press, pp. 267–301.

Wickham, C. (2010). *The Inheritance of Rome. A History of Europe from 400 to 1000*, London: Penguin Books.

Wood, D. (2012). *Medieval Economic Thought*, Cambridge: Cambridge University Press.

Wood, J.C. (1983). *British Economists and the Empire*, London and New York: St. Martin's Press.

Woods, T.E. (2009). *Meltdown. A Free-Market Look at Why the Stock Market Collapsed, the Economy Tanked, and Government Bailouts Will Make Things Worse*, Washington: Regnery Publishing.

Yergin, D. and Stanislaw, J. (2002). *The Commanding Heights. The Battle for the World Economy*, New York: Touchstone.

Zagari, E. (2000). *L'economia politica dal mercantilismo ai giorni nostri*, Torino: Giappichelli.

Zamagni, V. (2017). *An Economic History of Europe Since 1700*, Newcastle upon Tyne: Agenda Publishing.

Zanardo, A. (1972). Il marxismo. In C.M. Cipolla *et al.*, *Storia delle idee politiche, economiche e sociali*, Vol. V, Torino: UTET, pp. 411–550.

INDEX

1848, revolutions of 36, 39, 71
1929 crisis: British reflationary response 93; classical liberalism discredited by 95; fixed exchange rates vs. devaluation 94; German austerity response 90; Italian neoclassical response 93; US reflationary response 90; weak recovery 94

abortive savings 145
Acton, John Dalberg xv, 4
Alexander the Great 3, 4
America, discovery of 20
antitrust action 74, 98–99, 119, 121, 129, 130
Aquinas 9–10, 12, 13, 14, 23
Aristotle 12
AS-AD model 137
Austrian School 65, 67, 69
Austro-Hungarian Empire 59; discrimination against ethnic and linguistic minorities 75, 122; failure to create federation of equal nations 139; League of the Three Emperors 64; as multinational empire 59, 122; Triple Alliance 64

Bagehot rule 84, 89
Balfour, Arthur 74
Barnett, Vincent xii
Basil of Caesarea 13
Berdjaev, Nikolai 17
Berlin, Congress of 63
Berlin, Isaiah 3

Berman, Harold J. 7
Bernadine of Siena 11
Beveridge, William 95
Bismarck, Otto von 35n4, 56, 62, 63, 64, 73, 74, 75, 122, 163
Blaug, Mark xii
Bloch, Marc xiii, 1, 6, 17, 161
Bodin, Jean 35n5
Böhm-Bawerk, Eugen von 65, 69, 86
Bonaventure 11–12
Bretton Woods 107–110; demise of 127, 132, 139; European Community underpinned by 129, 131, 157; prefigured by Keynes 98, 153; as substantial return to gold 105
Brexit 154, 165
Brezhnev, Leonid 128
Briand, Aristide 103n8
Britain: 1929 crisis, restrictive policy response 92; absolutism, decline of 29; Bank Charter Act 58, 59, 103n2; Bank of England 59; Corn Laws xi, 39, 51, 56, 57, 58, 72; Eden, Treaty of 57, 58; East India Company 28; Entente Cordiale 74; general strike (1926) 83; gold standard 38, 58, 92; imperial protectionism 74, 75, 94; mercantilist trading regime 26, 27; Navigation Acts 28, 45, 57, 58; neo-mercantilist nationalism 39; new cities, rise of 29; Poor Laws 28, 45, 52, 56; Statute of Apprentices 29, 34; Statute of Artificers 27, 45, 56; Trade Union Act 64
Brüning, Heinrich 90, 92, 93, 94–95

bubonic plague 12, 14, 19
Bull, Hedley 16, 115, 155
Burke, Edmund 33
Byzantine Empire: economic thought 9, 12–14; fall of Constantinople 16, 20, 161; mixed economy 8; state's retreat from economy 15; as unified political and ecclesiastical entity 6

Caesaropapism 6, 17, 21, 28
Callaghan, James 137
Calvin, Jean 21
Cambridge School 65, 68, 69
Cantillon, Richard 29
Cardoso, José Luis xiii
Caritas/charity 9, 10, 20, 46
Carolingian period 1, 2
Catherine II 32
Chabod, Federico 3
Chamberlain, Joseph 74
charity *see Caritas*
Charlemagne 1, 2, 6–7
Charles V 22
Chevalier, Michel 56
Churchill, Winston 105, 132
classical political economy: absentee liberalism 118, 119; absolute and relative gains, failure to distinguish between 55; economic globalisation, failure to foresee 55; economic nationalism, condemnation of 55; free trade 55, 60, 74, 162; gold standard 55, 60, 74, 162; imperfect mobility of labour and capital 55, 60, 74, 162; labour theory of value as limitation of 55; long-term national development, focus on 66; nationalism, coeval with 37; orthodox and heterodox versions of 40; political influence of 56, 60; self-interest as key to common good 60–61, 100, 162; spontaneous division of labour and capital 55, 60; *see also* Malthus, Thomas; Mill, John Stuart; Ricardo, David; Say, Jean-Baptiste; Smith, Adam
Cobden, Richard xi, 56, 58
Colbert, Jean-Baptiste 27, 29, 31, 34
Comecon 127–128
commercial revolution (medieval Europe) 14
common good, idea of 19–20, 34, 60–61, 100, 162, 166, 167
comparative method in the social sciences x
Constant, Benjamin 3, 4
corporatism: command economy 101, 102; individual identification with the state 100–101; Fascist version 88, 100–101;

Nazi version 101; neoclassical frame of reference 101–102; post-WWII survival of 106
Counter-Reformation 22, 161
COVID-19 pandemic 148, 149, 156, 158, 165
Crimean War 55
Czechoslovakia 113, 127

Dawson, Christopher xi, xiii, 1
de Gaulle, Charles 131
Delors, Jacques 141
de Nemours, Dupont 30, 32
disintegration of Christian Europe: absolute monarchy, rise of 23–24, 34, 161; Atlantic trade, rise of 20; humanist challenge to *fides et ratio* 20; ideal of common good, economic and political strains on 19–20, 34; long-distance trade 20, 25; Nordic vs. Meridian models of capitalism 22, 161, 165; Protestant challenge to *fides et ratio* 20; Protestant individualism, economicism and nationalism 21–22, 24–25; wars of religion 22–23, 34, 161; *see also* mercantilism
Disraeli, Benjamin 62, 64
Dominican scholasticism 10, 11
Duroselle, Jean-Baptiste xiii

Eastern Europe after WWII: Bretton Woods system, rejection of 126; Comecon regime 127–128, ethnic and linguistic minorities, problem of 121, 123–124; European Union, expansion into 146; GATT, rejection of 126; initial precarious democracy 113–114; iron curtain 105, 132, 140, 164; Marshall Plan, rejection of 127, 164; Mises' proposal for Eastern European Union 124; oil shock crises of 1970s 138; socialist division of labour 127–128, 132, 164; structural imbalance between agriculture and industry 113; "tragedy" of (Kundera) 139; Visegrad group 140, 165
Eastern schism of Christianity 16
economic culture: difficulty of determining influence of 17; economists as producers of xi, xii, 65, 68; European xiv, 9, 37, 68, 160, 165–166; Keynes, revolutionised by 95; national histories of xii; Smith, revolutionised by 37, 122
Eichengreen, Barry 92
Einaudi, Luigi 27, 29, 56, 57, 89, 115
emphyteusis contract 15

Engels, Friedrich 64
England *see* Britain
English School of international relations theory 153, 155
enlightened absolutism 32, 36, 56, 161–162
Erasmus 21
Erhard, Ludwig 131
etatism *see* interventionist etatism; socialism
European Coal and Steel Community 129
European Community/European Union: *acquis communautaire* 147; Amsterdam Treaty 143, 145, 147; antitrust rules 129, 130; Bretton Woods demise, challenge of 132; Common Agricultural Policy 129; constitution, attempt to adopt 145–146; constitutive values 147; convergence 144; *demos* vs. *demoi* 155, 157–158; eastward expansion in 2000s 146; Economic and Monetary Union (EMU) 141–145, 154, 165; economic trilemma 141, 142; European Monetary System 139, 141, 142–143; Eurozone 145; exchange rate stability and domestic price stability as joint aims 129–130; expansion in 1980s 139; four freedoms 140, 154, 157, 165, 166–167; freedom, work and community as values 133, 158, 166; Great Recession, lack of fiscal union exposed by 158; Green Deal 156; Lisbon Treaty 146, 147; Maastricht Treaty 142–145, 147, 165; Monetary Snake 139; national economic sovereignty, erosion of 145; nationalism as disruptive force 132, 157–158, 164, 165; Next Generation EU 156; ordoliberal criticism of 131–132; ordoliberal influence on 130, 146, 165; political trilemma 149, 152–158, 165; Rome, Treaties of 106, 129, 130, 133, 134–135nn8–11; Single European Act (1986) 140; single market as core aim of 129, 140, 165; spillover doctrine 130; Stability and Growth Pact 143, 156; subsidiarity principle 143, 147, 158; supranational democracy, search for 157, 158, 167; "troika" 152; unity in diversity 147, 155, 165, 166; *see also* Great Recession
European Defence Community 129
European Payments Union 129

Fabbrini, Sergio 155, 157, 159n3
famine (1315) 19
Fanno, Marco 131
Febvre, Lucien xiii, 1, 2, 4, 33, 36, 60

federalism: common goal of 114; Christian 117–118; international impracticability of 125; liberal 115–117; socialist 114–115
Fejtö, François 106, 113, 127, 128, 133, 138, 140
First Globalisation 74, 76, 123, 163
Fisher, Irving 26
Florence, Republic of 15
France: absolutism, decline of 29; agriculture damaged by Colbert's policies 29, 34; Chapelier law 38, 56, 57; Eden, Treaty of 57, 58; eighteenth-century quest to contain 33; Entente Cordiale 74; French Revolution 36, 37–38, 60, 122, 162; mercantilist trading regime 26–27; Paris Commune 64; protectionism (1892) 74; *see also* physiocracy
Francis I 32
Francis II 38
Franciscan scholasticism 11–12
Franco-Prussian War 56, 62
Frederick II 7, 14, 15
Frederick III 15
Frederick Barbarossa 7, 8
Frederick the Great 32, 33
freedom: absolutist states, effects of 34, 121–122, 161; early Christian conception of 4–5; economic freedom, early medieval battle for 7–8; European freedom vs. Asiatic despotism 3, 33; fundamental freedoms, revolt as inevitable consequence of constraining 34; Greek conception of 3–4, 166; individualistic turn in century of revolutions 60; *libertas ecclesiae* 7, 9; negative vs. positive 3–4, 76, 166; Roman *libertas* 4, 166
Friedman, Milton 112, 136–137, 138
functionalism 125–126, 128, 132, 136, 158, 164, 165; *see also* European Community

Gasperi, Alcide de 117
General Agreement on Tariffs and Trade (GATT) 105, 106, 110–111, 131, 164
Gerber, David J. 130
German Confederation 39, 56, 73
German Historical School xiii, 73
Germany: 1929 crisis, deflationary response to 90–92, 94–95, 145; Berlin Wall, fall of 136, 140, 146; Bismarckian protectionism 64, 74, 75, 123, 142; Bismarckian social policy 63, 64, 75, 122–123; Brauns Kommission 90–91, 94; cartels 74, 75, 123; command economy established

by Hitler 94; Dawes Plan 83; economic imperialism 64; gold standard 83, 92; Lautenbach Plan 91, 93; League of the Three Emperors 64; *Lebensraum* 73, 75, 77n7, 101, 123; Müller government, collapse of 90; Nazis, rise of 90, 91, 94, 95, 145; Reassurance Treaty with Russia 64, 74; Triple Alliance 64; unification of 59, 62, 63, 75, 162, 163; *see also* Holy Roman Empire; Prussia

gold standard: abandoned in US (1973) 132; Banking School vs. Currency School 58–59; Bretton Woods compromise 109; demise in 1929 crisis 92, 93, 94, 102, 103, 164; domestic price flexibility 81; fixed exchange rates 80, 81, 103n3, 107; gold bloc 93, 94, 102; gold exchange standard 82–83, 119; Mill on 55; money supply adjustment in proportion to gold reserves 81, 103n2; reintroduction in 1920s 79, 80; restored in Britain (1821) 58; Ricardo on 51; suspended in Britain (1797) 38; suspended in Britain (1931) 92

Gonella, Guido 117

Gournay, Vincent de 32

Great Depression (1873) 63, 75–76

Great Depression (1929) 84, 94, 148

Great Recession (2008): COVID-19, compounding effect of 148, 149, 156; "expansive austerity" 148; fiscal compact (EU) 151; Hayek–Keynes debate reignited 148; lack of EU fiscal union exposed by 148–149, 151–152, 158; neoliberalism's limitations exposed by 158–159, 165; subprime mortgages 150; US expansionary policy after 9/11 149–150; West–East trade imbalance 150, 151; yuan, lack of revaluation 151

Gregory VII 7

guilds: Byzantine 8, 14, 21; decline under absolute monarchies 34; early lack of autonomy 9; Fascist 100; French 27, 32, 38, 56; Italian 15; just price, control of 10; medieval centrality of 12, 14, 15, 17; physiocracy and 32

Haas, Ernst B. 130

Habsburg Empire 15, 16, 22, 23, 28, 32, 39, 161, 162

Halecki, Oscar x–xi, xiii, 1–2, 17

Hallstein, Walter 128, 130, 131

Hanseatic League 14

Harmenopoulos, Constantine 13

Harrod, Roy 108–109

Hayek, Friedrich von xv, 65; Brauns Kommission, criticism of 91; central banks, blames for 1929 crisis 87; communism, opposition to 136; domestic price flexibility as goal 87, 89; gold standard, defence of 108; liberal federalism 115, 116–117; Lippmann Colloquium 95, 98; monetary interest rate and natural interest rate 86–87, 89; as neoliberal 79; Nobel Prize 136, 138, 146, 165; overinvestment as cause of crisis 87–88, 89; post-Keynesian rising influence of 138; post-WWII declining influence of 106, 111; savings as solution to crisis 87, 89; welfare 120

Heckscher, Eli 24

Herodotus 2

Hicks, John 106, 111–112

history of economic thought, as field of research xi–xiv, xvi

Hitler, Adolf 90, 91, 94, 95, 139, 145, 163

Hobbes, Thomas 24, 30

Hobsbawm Eric 39

Hobson, J.A. 86

Holy Alliance 39, 55, 63, 163

Holy Roman Empire 7, 22, 23

Hoover, Herbert 84, 89, 90, 92

Hume, David 29, 55

Hundred Years' War 15, 19

idealistic vision of history xv, 160

imperialist Europe: Berlin, Congress of 63; *communitas*/community 76; legitimacy, failure of 163; *libertas*/liberty 76; *opus*/work 76; protectionism 74–75

inconsistent quartet theory 140–141

internationalism: conformable vs. non-conformable interventions 118, 121, 124; Eastern European Union proposed by Mises 124; free movement of goods, persons and capital 118, 121; intervention for adjustment 119–120; protection of competition 119, 120

International Monetary Fund (IMF) 109, 110, 111, 152

interventionist etatism 72–73, 75, 77n7, 122, 163

IS-LM model 106, 111–112, 129, 137

Italy 74, 83; 1929 crisis, neoclassical response to 93; Bretton Woods, acceptance of 109–110; EMU and 144–145; Fascist corporate economy 88; Institute for Industrial Reconstruction 93; unification of 162

Jesus 4
Jevons, William Stanley 64, 65
John XXII 12
Joseph II 32
justice *see* Byzantine economic thought;
   scholastic economic thought
Justinian 6, 12
just price 10–11, 13–14
just profit 13

Kabasilas, Nicholas 13
Kaczyński, Jarosław 154
Keynes, John Maynard: aggregate demand
   96–98, 102, 107; avarice vs. sloth 108;
   as Bretton Woods protagonist 107–108;
   Cambridge School training 65; central
   banks, blames for 1929 crisis 86; death
   of 111; domestic price stability as goal
   82, 89; as focus of historical research
   xii; gold standard and fixed exchange
   rates condemned by 82, 102, 107;
   inherent instability of economic system
   85; International Clearing Union 108;
   investment volatility 86; as neoliberal
   79; New Liberalism, founder of 95; Paris
   Order, critique of 79, 81–82; poverty in
   abundance 96, 108; quantitative theory of
   money and 26; on Ricardo and Malthus
   40; stimulating investment as solution
   to crisis 86, 89; uncertainty 88, 96, 98;
   underemployment equilibrium 95–96,
   97–98, 108; underinvestment as cause of
   crisis 86, 89; wartime compulsory savings
   97
Keynesianism: "bastard" Keynesianism 112;
   IS-LM as compromise with 106,
   111–112; post-stagflation decline of 137,
   138, 147, 165; post-WWII rise of 111,
   112, 132
Kissinger, Henry 22, 33, 35n4, 56
Kundera, Milan 139

labour, value and dignity of 5–6, 7, 8, 11–12
Laiou, Angeliki L. 8, 13–14
Lausanne School 65, 67
League of Nations 80, 103n8, 123, 125
League of the Three Emperors 64
Le Goff, Jacques xiii, xiv, 2, 15, 17
Lehman Brothers 150, 151
Leo III 7
Leopold, Peter 32
liberal nation-states, rise of: agriculture and
   industry, conflicting interests of 57–58;
   Banking School vs. Currency School

58–59; classical economics, influence of
   56, 59, 60; *communitas*/community 61;
   corporations and communes, decline of
   61; English "peaceful circumvention"
   path to 56–57; free trade, spread of 57,
   58; French revolutionary path to 56–57;
   gold standard, spread of 57; *libertas* 60;
   market as coordinating mechanism for
   common good 60–61; *opus* 61; various
   European forms of 59; Vienna system,
   demise of 55–56; workers' associations,
   prohibition of 61
limited partnerships 15
Lippmann Colloquium 95, 98
List, Friedrich 72–73, 77n7, 123
Lloyd George, David 78
Locke, John 30
Lombard Leagues 7
Lopez, Robert S. 15
Lorenzetti, Ambrogio 12, 19, 166
Louis XIV 19, 26–27
Louis XVI 32, 37, 38, 56
Louis the Bavarian 12
Luther, Hans 91
Luther, Martin 21, 23, 24
Luzzatto, Gino 57, 58

MacDonald, Ramsay 92
Malthus, Thomas 37, 40, 72
Malynes, Gerard de 25, 26
Manuel I Komnenos 8
Maria Theresa 32
Marshall, Alfred 52, 65; consumer surplus
   70; cyclical instability of capitalism
   70; economies of scale 71; partial
   equilibrium 70; period analysis 70;
   predictable value 68; price elasticity of
   demand 70; price elasticity of supply 71;
   producer surplus 71; synthesis of classical
   tradition and marginalism 69–70, 71
Marshall, George 126
Marshall Plan 106, 126, 127, 132, 164
Marsilius of Padua 12
Marx, Karl xiv, 55, 64, 72
Marxism–Leninism 106, 112, 113, 132, 138,
   163, 164
Masaryk, Tomáš 75
materialistic vision of history xiv, 160
May, Theresa 154
McNeill, William xvii n1
Meade, James 131–132
medieval Europe: Byzantine economic
   thought 9, 12–14, 161; as Carolingian
   phenomenon 1, 17; as commonwealth

of Christian nations 16, 17, 21, 161, 166; *communitas*/community 5, 7, 9–10, 11, 12, 14, 15, 16, 17, 20–21, 161, 166; early Roman Catholic contribution to 5–6; Eastern consolidation of power 6, 8, 21, 161; fall of Constantinople 16, 17; as Greek invention 2–4; as late medieval phenomenon 1–2; *libertas*/freedom 3–5, 7, 8, 9, 14, 16, 17, 21, 161, 166; *opus*/ work 5–6, 7, 8, 14, 16, 17, 21, 161, 166; scholastic economic thought 9–12, 161; as unity in diversity 16, 17, 21, 23, 62, 161, 166; Western disarticulation of power 6–8, 21, 161
melting-pot society x, 160
Menger, Carl 64, 65, 67, 68–69, 71, 78
mercantilism: bilateral vs. multilateral trading systems 26; bullionism 26; criticised by classical economists 25, 29–30, 34, 60, 122, 162; dirigiste state 26, 28, 34; England as model of 27; France as model of 26–27; internal vs. international trade 25; practical background of mercantilists 24; profit upon alienation 25; quantitative theory of money 26; restoration England, revival in 39; revolutionary nationalist revival of 36; separation of economics 28; trade balance as main focus of 25–26, 28; trade as zero-sum game 25, 28, 41, 161
Metternich, Klemens von 39, 56
Mill, John Stuart 37, 40, 52; free trade regime 55; gold standard 55; modern liberalism, initiator of 55; as orthodox heretic 52, 55; partial protectionist measures 55; redistribution to poorer classes 54, 55; revision of comparative advantage theory 53–54; separation of production and distribution of wealth 52–53, 55; stationary state as positive scenario 54, 55; wage fund theory 54
Mises, Ludwig von: Austrian School member 65; comparative vs. absolute advantage 120, 121; complete economic freedom, advocacy of 82, 121, 124; critic of Bismarckian etatism 73, 75, 123; Eastern European Union, proposal for 124, 133n6; on ethnic and linguistic minorities in Europe 75, 78, 82, 122, 123, 162; European internationalism, advocacy of 118, 124; Keynes and 84–85; Lippmann Colloquium 95, 98, 99; on

monopolies 99; post-WWII declining influence of 106; spontaneous market adjustment 119
Misselden, Edward 25, 26
Mitrany, David 114, 125–126, 128
Modigliani, Franco 112
monetarism 26, 136–137, 138, 165
Monnet, Jean 128
Montaigne, Michel de 25, 38
Montesquieu 30, 32, 33, 133
Mont Pèlerin Society 100, 111, 136
Morrison, Cécile 8, 13–14
Müller, Hermann 90
Mun, Thomas 25, 26
Mundell, Robert 151
municipalities, emergence of 15
Mussolini, Benito 100

Napoleon III 56
Napoleon Bonaparte 7, 36, 38–39
nationalism: consolidation of nation-states in Western Europe 28, 122; emergence of nation-states 15; French Revolution and 36, 37, 38, 60; interwar nationalism and economic sovereignty 102, 164; militant nationalism in Eastern Europe 122, 162; national sovereignty, rise of 36, 37, 59–60; nineteenth-century uprisings 39; Protestant nationalism 22; resurgent neo-mercantilism and 37, 39; suppressed by Congress of Vienna 39
Naumann, Friedrich 75
Necker, Jacques 32
neoclassical economics: Austrian School 65, 67, 69; Cambridge School 65, 68, 69; classical free trade principles, continuation of 66, 74–75; classical tradition, Marshall's synthesis with 69–70; consumer vs. capital goods 68; Crusoe metaphor 65–66, 67; economic equilibrium, conditions of 66, 67, 70; failure to influence policy 76; interest 69; labour theory of value abandoned by 55; Lausanne School 65, 67; marginal factor productivity 67, 69; marginal utility 66–67, 69; methodological individualism 66, 67; ophelimity 67; predictable value 68; price elasticity of demand 70; price elasticity of supply 71; producer surplus 71; *see also* Jevons, William Stanley; Marshall, Alfred; Menger, Carl; Walras, Léon
neofunctionalism 126, 130–131
neo-Keynesianism 112, 137

neoliberalism: balance of savings and investment as fundamental macroeconomic question 85; free movement of goods, persons and capital 82, 118, 123, 124; Hayekian business cycle 86–88, 89; limitations exposed by Great Recession 158–159, 165; rebirth in 1970s 138, 165; Röpke's Keynesian–Hayekian synthesis 88; sovereignty of the market 87, 89, 99, 102; state's role in defending competition 98–99; *see also* Hayek, Friedrich von; Keynes, John Maynard; Röpke, Wilhelm
Neumann, Franz 77n7, 101
Neumann, Klaus 101
Nicholas II 7
Nixon, Richard 132

oil shock (1973) 127, 132, 137–138, 164
Olivi, Peter 11
ordoliberalism: corporatism, differences from 101; German origin of 79; Lippmann Colloquium 95, 98; as model for post-Keynesian Europe 138, 147; post-WWII influence of 106, 130, 165
Organisation Européenne de Coopération Economique 126
Ostrogorsky, George 6
Otto I 7
Ottoman Empire 16, 28, 63

Padoa-Schioppa, Tommaso 140, 142, 152
Pantaleoni, Maffeo 76n6
Pareto, Vilfredo 65, 67
Paris Order 78–79; British and German unsustainable trade deficits 83–84; *communitas*/community 103; disintegration of 92, 94, 102; ethnic and linguistic minorities, problem of 82, 102; free trade, return to 80, 163; gold standard, return to 80, 102, 163; Great Depression 84; Keynes's critique of 81–82; *libertas*/freedom 102–103; Mises's critique of 82; *opus*/work 103; self-determination of peoples 80, 123, 163; US expansion of money supply 83–84
Paris Peace Conference 78, 79–80, 102, 163
Patinkin, Don 112
Paul, Saint 5, 23
Peel, Sir Robert 58, 59
Phillips curve 137
physiocracy: agriculture as sole source of net product 31, 33, 42; criticised by classical economists 60; eliminating

export restrictions, privileges and monopolies 31–32; embraced by enlightened absolutist monarchs 34, 162; growth vs. spending restraint 30; high rent as premise of economic development 31; *laissez faire* 32; natural order 30, 32, 34; productive, sterile and landowning classes 31; single income tax 32
Piccolomini, Enea Silvio 16
Pirenne, Henri 6
Pitt, William, the Younger 57
Pius XII 117
Plato 13
Plethon, George Gemistos 13
political history of Europe, as field of research xvi
political trilemma 149, 152–158, 165, 166–167
Prague Spring 128
Protestant Reformation 16, 19, 20, 21–22, 161
Prussia 33, 38, 39, 55–56, 63, 122, 133n6, 140
Psalidopoulos, Michalis xiii

Quadruple Alliance 39, 63
Quesnay, François 30, 32, 33

Reagan, Ronald 138
"realistic" vision of history xv, 160
republic of letters, Europe as 32–34
Ricardo, David: comparative advantage, theory of 49–51, 52, 57, 73, 120–121; on Corn Laws 72; domestic vs. international markets 49; as dominant influence in Britain 40; fiscal policy 51–52; as focus of historical research xii; free trade 51; gold standard 51, 59; immobility of factors of production 49–50, 52, 74, 82; monetary policy 51; as orthodox Classical School 37; price-species-flow mechanism 55; as producer of economic culture xi; pure labour theory of value 48–49; stagnation 51; welfare policy 52
Richelieu, Cardinal 23, 35n4, 39
Robbins, Lionel 114, 115–116
Robinson, Joan 112
Rodrik, Dani 152, 153–154, 156, 157
Roman Empire: economic crisis, third-century 5; Greece, conquest of 4; *libertas* 4; *see also* Byzantine Empire
Romania 127–128
Roosevelt, Franklin D. 92–93, 119, 126

Röpke, Wilhelm: Brauns Kommission
90–91; competition, protection of 119,
120; conformable vs. non-conformable
intervention 118, 124; European
internationalism, advocacy of 118;
GATT–Bretton Woods system, support
for 131; intervention for adjustment
119–120; Lippmann Colloquium 98;
neoliberal affinities 119; on New Deal
118–119; as ordoliberal 79, 131, 138;
synthesis of Keynes and Hayek 85, 88, 89
Rossi, Ernesto 114–115
Rothbard, Murray 92
Rousseau, Jean-Jacques xiii, 30, 32–33, 60
Russia: 1812 invasion 39; Bolshevik
Revolution 74; Entente Cordiale 74;
Holy Alliance 39, 55, 63; League of the
Three Emperors 64; as liberal nation-
state 162; protectionism (1881) 74;
Reassurance Treaty with Germany 64,
74; socialism in one country 79–80;
Soviet nationalisation of agriculture and
forced industrialisation 113, 127
Russo-Turkish War 63
Rüstow, Alexander 95, 98–99

Savona, Paolo 144
Say, Jean-Baptiste 37, 40; law of outlets 47,
96; production as creation of utility 47;
productive triad of nature, capital and
labour 47; utility of final goods 47
Schacht, Hjalmar 83, 102
Schmoller, Gustav von 73
scholastic economic thought 9–12
Schuman, Robert 128–129, 156
Schumpeter, Joseph 63
second industrial revolution 63
Sedan, Battle of 56, 63
Senior, William Nassau 57
September 11 attacks 149
Seven Years' War 29, 30
Sismondi, Jean Charles Léonard de 37, 40
Smith, Adam: absolute advantage 45–46;
benevolence 46; capital as wage fund
41, 42–43, 45; circular theory of prices
46; currency stability 41; deregulation
45; division of labour 41–42, 45–46;
exchange value of goods 43–44; as focus
of historical research xi, xii; as founder
of modern economics 37, 40; free trade
regime 41; government, role of 45;
invisible hand of market forces 44–45,
46, 162; labour productivity 40–42,
46; mercantilism, criticism of 25, 45;
productive labour 42–45; self-interest
44–45, 46; trade as positive-sum game
41–42; wages, profits and rent 45; wealth,
definition of 40
social contract theory 24, 30
socialism 72, 101; see also Eastern
Europe; interventionist etatism; Marx,
Karl; Marxism–Leninism; Workers'
Internationals
Spinelli, Altiero 114–115
Spiroto, Ugo 100
stagflation 137
Stigler, George 49
Streeck, Wolfgang 154
Switzerland 120, 124, 131, 155

Thatcher, Margaret 138
Thirty Years' War 22–23, 39
Thornton, W. T. 54
Tito, Josip Broz 113, 127
Tooze, Adam 148
Triple Alliance 64
Turgot, Anne Robert Jacques 19, 32, 36, 57
Turroni, Bresciani 59, 110

United States: 1929 crisis, reflationary
response to 89–90, 92–93; American
Revolution 36, 37, 162; antitrust law
130; Dawes Plan 83; expansionary
policy post 9/11 149–150; as federal
union 155; Glass–Steagall Act 150; gold
standard suspended by Roosevelt 92–93;
Great Recession bailout and stimulus
151; New Deal 88, 92, 119; New York
Stock Exchange collapse (1929) 79, 84;
protectionism 89, 94; scarce currency
clause 108–109; September 11 attacks
149; Sherman Act 74; Smooth–Hawley
Act 89; subprime mortgages 150;
Tenessee Valley Authority 126; war on
terror 150; see also Marshall Plan
usury 10, 11, 13

Ventotene Manifesto 114–115, 116
Verein für Sozialpolitik 64, 65
Versailles, Treaty of 80
Vienna, Congress of 36, 39, 55–56, 62,
163
Viner, Jacon 131
Vito, Francesco 110, 117
Viviani, Carlo 144
Vlastares, Matthew 13
Voltaire 33, 38, 60
von Papen, Franz 93

Wagner, Adolph 73, 77n7
Walras, Léon 64, 65, 67
Washington Consensus 138, 152
Weber, Max xv
Western schism of Christianity 16
Westphalia, Treaties of 23, 28, 33, 34, 39,
    62, 164
White, Harry Dexter 107
Wieser, Friedrich von 65
Wight, Martin 155

Wilhelm II 62, 74
Wilson, Woodrow 78, 80, 106, 123, 163
Workers' Internationals 64, 72
World Bank 109, 110, 111
world history x, xv, xvii n1, 160

Yalta Conference 106, 113, 127
Yugoslavia 113, 127

Zollverein 73

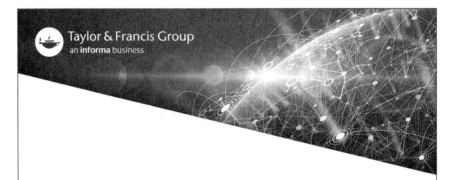

Printed in the United States
by Baker & Taylor Publisher Services